the
Unofficial
Guide® to
Real Estate
Investing

Second Edition

Spencer Strauss
and Martin Stone

D1534286

WILEY

Wiley Publishing, Inc.

Spencer Strauss dedicates this book to Marty Stone for his friendship and never-ending support and to his late father Marty Strauss: "Dad, today I am a fountain pen."

Martin Stone dedicates this book to his wife Lori for her love and encouragement and to his longtime teacher, mentor, and friend Jack Buckingham.

Acknowledgments

We would like to thank all the fantastic people at Wiley Publishing, Inc., who made this book possible: most notably Kathy Nebenhaus, Keith Covington, Suzanne Snyder, and the remarkable Roxane Cerda. Thank you all for your commitment to this book and making our job easy.

We also would like to acknowledge the staff at Hungry Minds who worked so hard on the first edition, including, Matthew X. Kiernan, Randy Ladenheim-Gil, Jessica Faust, Jennifer Perillo, Brice Gosnell, Faunette Johnston, Georgette Blau, William Bronchick, Warren Ladenheim, Ed Stevens, and Amy Lepore.

Finally, we owe a debt of gratitude to the following people, without whom we wouldn't have been able to write this book: Steven D. Strauss, Lori Stone, Sheree Bykofsky, Blake Mitchell, Chris Stone, Sandi Strauss, Larry Strauss, Maria Strauss, Jillian Lewis, Kirk and Leslie Melton, Aaron Cook, Adam Cook, Hans Harder, Ben Walton, Jay Treat, Shelly Stone, James Waedekin, Ned Mansour, Jim Frings, Marianne Choy, Michael B. Moynahan, Kerry and Mia Daveline, Glenn Bozarth and Seymour Fagan. Thanks to all of you for your support.

Contents

Spencer Strauss makes his living as an associate real estate broker working side by side with his writing partner, Martin Stone. In that capacity, Spencer has bought, sold, traded, and managed countless buildings and has helped scores of investors get their start in real estate. Besides *the Unofficial Guide to Real Estate Investing*, Spencer also co-authored *Secure Your Financial Future Investing in Real Estate* (Dearborn Trade Publishing, 2003). He has been featured on television on KABC's *Eyewitness News*, as well as on radio stations KFI, KLAC, and KABC, all in Southern California. Additionally, Spencer's analysis has been featured in *USA Today*, the *New York Post*, the *Chicago Tribune*, the *Long Beach Press Telegram*, and the *Los Angeles Times*. For a free audio cassette on real estate investing, you can contact him via e-mail at spence@spencerstrauss.com.

Martin Stone has been a successful real estate broker and investor for over 30 years. A graduate of USC with a degree in finance, Marty has built more than 50 multifamily apartment buildings, commercial properties, and single-family homes throughout his career. He has also managed more than 1,000 units and written and lectured extensively about all areas related to real property. Marty is the owner/broker of Buckingham Real Estate Investments and Richmond Financial Services in El Segundo, California. Besides this book, he coauthored *Secure Your Financial Future Investing in Real Estate* (Dearborn Trade Publishing, 2003). Feel free to contact Marty by e-mail at gr8profit@aol.com, or visit the office Web site at www.buckinghaminvestments.com.

Whether you are a novice real estate investor or a seasoned pro, *the Unofficial Guide to Real Estate Investing,* Second Edition, is a guide that will help you prosper faster and easier. Notice that we didn't say "fast and easy." This is because anyone who promises that they will help you get rich fast and easy by investing in real estate isn't telling you the truth. Real estate by nature is not a get-rich-quick investment. Rather, it's a long-term proposition — a proposition, however, that can pay off beyond your wildest expectations if you're willing to put in the time.

So from the get-go, here is our promise to you: If you make the effort to read and understand this book, we will impart to you a money-making methodology that works, period. A baker uses a bread recipe to create the same loaf time and again. In fact, if you think about it, that's probably why money is called "dough." You too need a good money-making recipe to create your dough. Now you have found it. In this book we will share the same recipe that countless people through the ages have used to create their dough. Follow the recipe, and you too will get the same result.

Since the first edition of *the Unofficial Guide to Real Estate Investing* was published in January 2000, the real estate market in America has risen sure and steady. In that time, countless Americans who have taken a risk and invested in property have sown the seeds of an abundant tomorrow for themselves and their families. What's more, they have done it in a world and an economy that has been anything but certain. As anyone who has been paying attention to the news over the past few years readily knows, what many of us thought was safe and secure — for ourselves, our families, and our futures — is now anything but.

For survival in this new world, a new way of thinking has taken hold. Americans have realized that when it comes to the safety of our nest eggs, the only person any of us can really rely on is ourselves. It is no secret to anyone that the global economy has seen its share of turmoil over the past several years. It appears as though we have corrected our own course, and now with the twenty-first century upon us, the rest of the world looks like it will follow suit. This economic downturn taught us a lot, specifically about the problems that come with rapid growth, business overhead, the effects of inflation, and a host of other basic business principles that somehow got lost over the years. To right our ship, we were forced to rethink our way of doing business.

Looking back at the early 1990s, one of the industries that suffered mightily was real estate. We could devote the next 375 pages to a discussion of whether the economy caused the problems in the industry or vice versa. Instead, we choose to believe that the real estate industry fell prey to the same excesses as the rest of the economy. That is, when the tough times hit, owners who weren't invested based on sound economic principles simply couldn't stay afloat, causing a domino effect. In a short span of time, a lot of real estate owners became statistics, just as a host of other business owners did.

Since the market began turning the corner in the middle '90s, we have experienced some of the longest growth in America's history. In fact, many experts are referring to this as a "golden era." Federal Reserve Chairman Alan Greenspan was quoted as saying, "I don't recall as good an underlying base for the long-term outlook . . . in the last two or three decades." Part of the reason for our country's success is that we have cut the fat and gone back to the basic principles of running our country like a profitable business. Energetic entrepreneurs who still believe in the American dream are opening up shop again all over the country. These new businesses are lean and mean and are ones in which everyone pulls his or her own weight.

As we have recently learned, many of the young entrepreneurs that have come out of the golden era have a great ability to attract capital to their ideas. But, even great ideas sometimes fail to produce a profit. The collapse of WorldCom, other high tech ventures, and the dotcom bubble in general, all point to the necessity to invest in proven investment vehicles. Thankfully, real estate investing has proven itself as a winner year after year after year.

In fact, as long as anyone can remember, experts have agreed that investing in real estate is the best and safest bet you can make. Today, the market has grown to like all the attention it's getting. A recent article in *USA Today* said, "Not since the 1960s has the housing market been so uniformly strong across the USA." The article added that "the market is largely devoid of extremes," and "today's hot markets can be found in all regions of the country." In January 2003, existing single-family home sales climbed more than 3 percent over 2002, which had set the previous record. David Lereah, the chief economist for the National Association of Realtors,® gave credit to lower interest rates and the fact that, "real estate has become the safe haven for investment." As long as this investment is looked upon as a long-term wealth builder and not a fly-by-night get-rich scheme, investors will make out great.

To that end, the goal of this guide is to highlight the legitimate business side of real estate. Because real estate is a cyclical commodity, it's possible to get caught investing with your pants down — just as a host of other get-rich-quick hopefuls have done through the years. In contrast, our belief is that if you approach real estate as a business and use sound business principles in running and investing in it, the probability of failure is minimal.

Here you will learn the differences between legitimate real estate investing and speculative ventures. The profits generated by speculating on foreclosures and zero-money-down deals seem to get the most press, but we feel this kind of investing should be undertaken only after you have gained some good hands-on experience. Even a beginner, however, can combine the sound principles of compound interest and leverage and generate exceptional returns over the long run without taking any undue risk at all.

Here's a quick illustration of the goldmine that's available if you're willing to be patient: A modest 2 percent growth rate in value translates to a 20 percent return on a property purchased with just a 10 percent down payment. That's right, a 20 percent return. When it comes to work, most of us slave away for 25 or 30 years to receive a small retirement package and a token gift at the finish line. Conversely, if you were to invest $30,000 and were able to maintain a 20 percent return for that same period of time, due to the combination of compound interest and leverage, your initial investment would be worth well over two million dollars — two million dollars!

You see, real estate is a rare investment vehicle. For starters, it can provide you with a place to live while it's working as an investment. What's more, this investment offers several kinds of return including cash flow, equity growth from loan payoffs, equity growth from appreciation, and great tax benefits. How does $250,000 of tax-free profit sound? Probably pretty good. Well, a new twist in the tax laws allows homeowners that exact benefit. (We promise to tell you more about it in Chapter 7, "Subdividing Your Options.")

How about what value appreciation can do for you? Rone Tempest wrote an article for the *Los Angeles Times* about urban renewal in Beijing. There, the Chinese were being forced to raze the old buildings because land prices had escalated to a whopping $6,000 per square meter. That translates to more than $24 million per acre. The question then is, if it can happen in Beijing, why not here? You may not live to see those kinds of prices, but you can still make a fortune by simply taking advantage of the modest value appreciation that takes place in your own area. We'll show you how.

We'll also devote some of our writing to a few key economic principles that affect real estate investing. This might seem like a foreign language lesson as you try to understand how this can impact your need to buy your first modest three- or four-unit building. That's understandable, but come back to these principles after a few years of ownership. Chances are they'll mean more to you then. Understanding how real estate fits into the overall picture of the economy will help your profits multiply in the long run.

A large portion of this guide is dedicated to teaching you some of the hard-earned lessons from our years of experience in this business. In Part VI, "Property Management Essentials," we have outlined many property-management techniques that will allow you to start your career head and shoulders above most of your competition. These principles should help you get your career off on the right foot and should give you the foundation to ask the important questions of the professionals you seek out for assistance.

Above all, our most important message will be to make a plan and then to simply work your plan to achieve your goals. Planning is a common principle for every successful business, but it is sorely lacking when it comes to real estate. You don't have to be Donald Trump or Ted Turner to need a plan. A plan simply gives you the opportunity to catch up to (and eventually pass) them.

For many of you, retirement investments in real estate might be the salvation of your retirement. The recent debacles of company pension plans like those of Enron and WorldCom only prove the point that it's time for you to take charge of your own future. If you don't, it's possible that you will helplessly watch your 401(k) account, company pension plan, and Social Security dwindle until they offer you little to help you survive in your later years. To that end, we implore you to make your real estate investments the centerpiece of your retirement plan.

Finally, beyond reading this guide, we encourage you to continue to educate yourself about this business. A separate book could be written about every section in this guide. Some are listed in Appendix C, "Recommended Reading List." Find and read them with a keen eye. Never stop your search for knowledge. We know that if you learn the business of real estate, believe in your abilities, enjoy the adventure, and take a risk every now and then, real estate investing is the best and safest field for you to make phenomenal profits.

Now, go grab a yellow highlighter pen and start reading.

Spencer Strauss   Martin Stone

Special Features

Every book in the Unofficial Guide series offers the following four special sidebars that are devised to help you get things done cheaply, efficiently, and smartly.

1. **Moneysaver:** Tips and shortcuts that will help you save money.

2. **Watch Out!:** Cautions and warnings to help you avoid common pitfalls.

3. **Bright Idea:** Smart or innovative ways to do something; in many cases, the ideas listed here will help you save time or hassle.

4. **Quote:** Anecdotes from real people who are willing to share their experiences and insights.

We also recognize your need to have quick information at your fingertips, and have provided the following comprehensive sections at the back of the book:

1. **Glossary:** Definitions of complicated terminology and jargon.

2. **Resource Guide:** Lists of relevant agencies, associations, institutions, Web sites, and so on.

3. **Recommended Reading List:** Suggested titles that can help you get more in-depth information on related topics.

4. **Important Documents:** "Official" pieces of information you need to refer to, such as government forms.

5. **Important Statistics:** Facts and numbers presented at-a-glance for easy reference.

6. **Index**

Understanding Real Estate As an Investment

PART I

Planting the Seed

Congratulations! Today your life has changed. By buying and reading this book, you have taken the first step toward making your dreams come true. As any successful real estate investor knows, buying, owning, trading, and selling investment properties are the surest and smartest ways to prosper. It doesn't matter what your long-term goal is; whether it be to finance your children's education, save for retirement, or eventually quit your day job, investing in real estate offers a realistic, tried-and-true way of getting ahead—way ahead.

It is also a good use of your time. In fact, one of our goals in this book, aside from showing you how to use real estate to change your life, is to respect your time. The novice, uninformed investor can make mistakes that cost time and money. By educating yourself from the onset, chances are good that you'll be able to avoid many pitfalls. Our plan is to cut years off your learning curve by sharing the things we have learned the hard way. This way you will prosper quicker, and with less effort.

But we won't promise that it will be easy or effortless. You are not going to be led to believe that buying and flipping distressed properties or placing tiny classified ads in the newspaper is going to make you rich. No, what we are offering here is the chance to learn the same proven methods of success that all prudent real estate investors use to get ahead. Let there be no doubt; it takes work. But it is a system that works. Think of it like a recipe. A chef uses the same recipe time and again to get the same result. Well, here, we want to teach you a real-world, money-making recipe. Learn it and reap the rewards of a more abundant future.

A new world order

Now that we are well into the 2000s, we are living in an era of rapid change. In fact, our world is changing at a faster pace than ever before in human history. This kind of comment surely has been made before, but most of us don't stop to consider the impact these changes might have on us. Think about Mr. Spock from *Star Trek*; he would envy our cell phones. He could only use his communicator to talk to others; we, on the other hand, can talk on our cell phones, see the face of the person we are talking to, and even use our cell phone to check our e-mail.

What about the computer? Back in the early 1970s, it used punch cards, and the computer itself took up an entire room that needed to be air-conditioned. Today, a computer with umpteen times the capacity of that 1970's machine weighs less than two pounds and can easily fit into a small briefcase. Sadly, due to the effectiveness that computers bring to the working world, most of the lower-level jobs of the 1970s are gone. Today, in some companies, the lunch-box worker has been left out in the cold, and computers handle the lion's share of the work. These changes should be an eye-opener for everybody.

In order to preserve our futures, many of us have stood stubbornly firm in the belief that the best way to eliminate risk is to put in a lifetime of service at a good job. Our idea has been to get in at 8:00 a.m., work diligently without complaint until 5:00 p.m., and then do it again tomorrow. In fact, our hope was that we could do this week after week and year after year, ultimately punching the same clock for the next 30 or 40 years.

During our parents' day, this strategy worked. You decided on a career, got an education, and then found a company to call home until your retirement. It was a job. It became part of your social life, and your years of loyal service were rewarded at the finish line with a gold watch and a satisfactory retirement package. Not anymore. With rapid change, the old ways are gone—in fact, long gone. How many engineers have lost their good, high-paying jobs when changes in technology over the last 20 years made their expertise outdated? We recently spoke to a woman with 25 years in the computer industry who couldn't find work. Her experience in DOS was a language that few industries still use.

> ❝By investing in some small apartment buildings, my wife was eventually able to quit her job. She now manages our properties from the house and is able to be a full-time mom for our new baby girl.❞
>
> —Kirk M., investor

It's now survival of the fittest

Today, lean and mean is the way companies survive. Unfortunately, these new rules apply to you now, too. You will need to be financially smarter than workers who came before you. This is because the job security they enjoyed isn't available anymore. What's more, with the stock market tumble that occurred in the early 2000s, too many of us have seen our retirement slip further and further away. The same goes for inappropriately named Social Security; these days, it is anything but secure.

So, with the lifetime career a thing of the past, capital investments less certain than ever, and the government unable to make up the difference, the burden is now squarely on you to create a financial foundation that can carry you for the rest of your life.

It is a new world order, indeed.

Trading time for dollars

In a capitalistic society such as ours, the big rewards are given to those who take the chances—the entrepreneurs. They have the vision, they take the risks, and, consequently, they get the big benefits. The problem for the average person is that, rather than being a risk taker, most of us have gotten into the habit of putting in eight hours a day working for someone else. At the end of the week, we look forward to cashing our paycheck and then doing it all over again. After enough years of this routine, we've programmed ourselves to believe that trading our time for a paycheck is the way to get rich.

Consider your boss, the guy who owns the company for which you work. He's not hurting for money, is he? He knows something that you are just figuring out. That is, working for someone else doesn't work. It certainly doesn't make you rich. Being the employee just makes you the employee. Being the boss can make you rich. In fact, the erroneous idea that you can create real wealth by trading time for dollars is the biggest barrier you can have to achieving it.

Instead, it's time for you to get brainwashed—the kind of brainwash that cleanses you of your beliefs about what it takes to get ahead. Here is the first step: Tap into the mindset you had when you went to school, the concept of investing your time for knowledge, not trading it for dollars.

Think back to your school days. Aside from the fun of hanging out with your friends, school was tough. You always were tight for money, never ate right, and endured many a sleepless night getting term papers done on time. No one paid you a salary to go

Watch Out!

Don't walk out on your job tomorrow because you've decided to invest in real estate today. Creating wealth from real estate is a long-term proposition. In the beginning, it is something you should work at in addition to your day job; that is, until you're so successful in real estate investing that you don't have to.

to class. You just worked at it and received one lone letter grade at a time for your efforts. After a while, the grades added up. In time you got a degree, and that degree got you the job that pays your salary. In school, you didn't trade your time for dollars; you invested it for knowledge. As you can see, the concept worked.

Given that you chose this book and are reading it, odds are you recognize that you're ready for a brainwash of your own. That's good. It is now time to go back to school—time to invest your effort and mental energies into learning the entrepreneurial skills necessary to take back control of your financial house. It's going to require taking some chances. Odds are that some of your loved ones will burst your bubble and tell you why it can't be done. But it can. The difference this time is that it will be with the wisdom of having lived and struggled in the adult world. You now know there is no free lunch. Moreover, you see that punching the time clock day in and day out is not the winning proposition you had hoped for.

This endeavor is about taking back control of your destiny: new cars, nice homes, vacations, security, less stress, more fun, and more time—they all are attainable and within reach.

Investing versus speculating

Once you have mentally graduated from the ranks of a wage earner, one who previously traded time for dollars, it becomes imperative that you understand the difference between the concepts of speculating and investing. The differences are critical, especially when it comes to the security of your hard-earned investment dollar.

Moneysaver

Be wary of late-night TV infomercials that tell you how you can make millions by speculating on distressed real estate. There may be money to be made there, but it is best left for later in your real estate career, after you have had some hands-on experience. Think. Distressed real estate is property someone else has abandoned after losing his or her money.

Speculate: To enter into a transaction or venture in which the profits are conjectural or subject to chance; to buy or sell with the hope of profiting through fluctuations in price.

Speculating seems to be a natural human characteristic. Think about the raffle tickets we used to sell as fund-raisers. The prize offered for the winner usually was pretty enticing: a new car, some money, or perhaps a Hawaiian vacation. Because the tickets were for a good cause (charity, schoolbooks, or another such cause), this began a mindset that speculating is an acceptable way of getting a return.

As we get older, speculation becomes a way of life. On a small scale, who hasn't participated in a football or Academy Awards pool at the office? By participating, we are hoping to make a profit; but in reality, the outcome is completely out of our control.

Because we so willingly speculate with our money, most states have caught on and have lured us to spend our money on their games of chance. Not surprisingly, a vast majority of people in our country spend dollar after dollar on lottery tickets each week hoping to get lucky someday.

Now, consider Las Vegas. Las Vegas was founded as the first legitimate American location for legalized speculation. Most of the nation has caught on to this, too. Whether it be horse racing, organized bingo, blackjack, or slot machines, if you want to play, it's pretty easy to find someone in America willing to take your bet.

How does investing differ? Let's see:

Invest: To commit money or capital in business to earn a financial return. The outlay of money for income or profit.

When it comes to our finances, investing doesn't come naturally. It seems as though we understand investing when it comes to investing our time for education or investing our labors to do work around the house. Investing our money, however, needs to be learned.

Understanding the difference between speculating and investing is simple once you analyze dictionary definitions. The key word in the definition of speculation is "hopes." The key word in the definition of invest is "earn." As you can see, these two concepts are at the opposite ends of the money spectrum. When something is based on hope, it implies that someone or something else is in control of the outcome. When it is based on earning, it requires action on your part to attain success.

Our number-one goal is to teach you how to invest your money in real estate so that you can create something tangible for yourself. The game is not about speculating on buildings with nothing down, buying and repairing run-down fixer-uppers, or flipping foreclosures because to succeed in those ventures often requires hope and luck. No, here we are going to show you the actions needed to reach your dreams through investing—actions like buying fair-market-valued properties and working them like a business for the long haul.

 Bright Idea

Start a savings account into which a small percentage of your paycheck gets deposited automatically. In time, you can painlessly accumulate some extra money to help pay for a down payment on your first investment in income property.

When it comes to succeeding in real estate, investing, action, and earning are the keys to winning. Speculation, on the other hand, relies on luck and hope. As far as we are concerned, rolling the dice is best left for weekends in Las Vegas or Atlantic City.

Taking a chance

Getting started always is the toughest part when taking on anything new. Investing is no different. Perhaps you will breathe easier if you look at people who have a lot of money. In fact, if you look at people who are really, really rich, you quickly will see that real estate is one common denominator many of them share. People such as Donald Trump, Dr. Jerry Buss, Marvin Davis, Donald Sterling, and Merv Griffin all owe their fortunes to this commodity. Of course, some of them started out with a large pot to begin with, but many of them didn't. Most important is to recognize that the principles they used to grow their real estate empires are exactly the same ones we are teaching here.

The beauty of real estate is that a small investor will earn the exact same percentage return that any large investor will earn. In many cases, you might even earn more. There aren't that many grandiose trophy properties available, and even fewer buyers out there who could pull the trigger on them. What's more, the chances of someone like Donald Trump making a mistake when he sells a property and leaving some profit on the table for the next buyer is remote, at best.

So, how do these wealthy people keep making so much money in real estate? The answer is they keep buying it. They know it's the best place to invest, even if they have to pay top dollar. Check the records; Marvin Davis bought Fox Plaza in Los Angeles twice. He paid a good price both times but still made a great profit each time. He knows the secret of making money in real estate; you buy it.

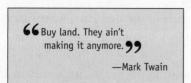

66 Buy land. They ain't making it anymore. **99**

—Mark Twain

Most people get their start in real estate investing by purchasing their first home. Others who really understand the long-term benefits of real estate start out living in a small set of units that they own. This lowers the cost of living while giving them valuable experience in managing a property. In a few years, the savings and other benefits enable them to move into a single-family home while retaining the units as a pure investment. Others get their start by providing housing for a relative in need or a child away at college. After this need has passed, the equity is transferred into a regular rental investment. In short, the reason for the purchase is to provide a very basic human need—housing—but the result is the start of a new and profitable career.

One great advantage of an investment in real estate is that it allows you as much or as little control as you desire. You can choose to be an active manager of your property, or you can subcontract all the day-to-day operations to a management company. By using a management company, you avoid the daily hassles of being a landlord but still maintain control of your asset. If you have other types of investments, such as stock in a corporation, you know that the destiny of your capital is in the hands of someone else. These corporate managers or "experts" may do a good job, but if things go wrong, you can't jump in to help run the company like you can with a real estate investment. The bottom line here is that you are the CEO of your business, and you decide who does what, when, and for how much.

The roots of lending

Most people don't realize that the minute they earn some extra money and put it in the bank, they become an investor. A savings account is the simplest investment you can make. To most of us, making a deposit into our savings account is nothing more than putting money away for a rainy day. In reality, the small amounts of cash deposited by millions of people form the foundation for most lending in our country.

In the classic film *It's a Wonderful Life,* Jimmy Stewart plays a young man who takes over the family building-and-loan business. At their inception, building and loans, now called savings and loans, were started by the little people of a community as a safer place to put their extra money when their mattress just would not suffice anymore. When they were fortunate enough to do a little better financially, they went to the building and loan and borrowed enough money to buy or build a first home. Until that point, they were forced to rent a place to live from someone else.

From simple beginnings, as seen in the movie, savings and loans have grown in huge proportions. Nonetheless, they still are based on the simple economic concept of small investors banding their money together and then having that institution lending the money to others to purchase property—lending it to people like you.

Bankers know that real estate is one of the safest products to loan against. To begin with, they are aware of all the basic economic facts previously mentioned. Second, unlike a car loan, you can't drive their asset away if you quit making payments. For this reason, they can get their security back fairly quickly if something goes wrong. Finally, lenders do an appraisal and check your credit to ensure that you and the property are qualified for the loan they are making. The message here should be clear; if bankers are confident that their loans are safe (for you and them), shouldn't you help them out and use their money to buy some properties?

 Moneysaver

Real estate loans usually get the lowest interest rate, the longest repayment term, and the lowest down payment requirements of any bank loan. This is because bankers are convinced that these loans have the lowest risk of loss to the bank.

Great government subsidies

They say America is a great country in which to live, a true land of opportunity. One of the reasons we have it so good is that we all have an uncle that watches over us. His name is Uncle Sam. Many live in fear of him because they think he is always looking over their shoulder, but these people aren't seeing the whole picture. To the real estate investor, Uncle Sam is our best friend and our staunchest supporter.

When we're just starting out, Uncle Sam gives us quite a hand. First, he loans us the money (at great terms) to buy our first property. He then tells the guy who collects the taxes on the money we earn (the IRS) to give us as many breaks as he can. Finally, in areas where it's tough for some people to pay the fair market rent, Uncle Sam pays it for them (HUD subsidies). What a guy!

Even if you're young, energetic, and ambitious, the fact remains—you still need cash to get started investing. If money is tight and all seems lost, the federal government has two excellent programs geared toward helping the beginning investor get started. These programs are administered through the Federal Housing Administration (FHA) and the Veterans Administration (VA). We will discuss all the specifics of the FHA and the VA in Chapter 5, "Borrowing Big Bucks," but knowing some of the basic details at this point will give you the encouragement you need now.

The FHA is a government loan-insurance program that is open to any citizen who can meet some basic qualifying guidelines. These guidelines are very generous and give most of us the opportunity to buy our first property. And by *first property*, we mean residential real estate, which means anything from one to four units. The most important advantage of this program is that it only requires a minimum down payment of 3 percent of the purchase price. So, for the purchase of a $200,000 piece of property, you need only $6,000 down to get started. There usually are some other costs associated with a purchase, but the

FHA requires that the seller assist you in paying most of them. In the case of the purchase of small units, the transfer of the rents and security deposits at closing can lower your actual out-of-pocket cost even more.

> 66 By using an FHA loan, I bought my first home and made an investment at the same time. I bought a four-unit apartment building. It has a three-bedroom owner's unit that I use for my family, and it also has three attached rental units. The income from those units pays for almost all of my mortgage payment. Yee-ha! 99
>
> —Brad S., investor

The second program the government provides is Veterans Administration loans. The VA guarantees loans to people who have served in the military. Because home ownership is one of the most important tenets of our society, there is no better way to reward someone who has served their country than to help them buy their first home. An eligible veteran can purchase a qualified property with no down payment and, in most cases, with no other out-of-pocket costs. What a country!

Contrary to popular belief, Uncle Sam is also on your side when it comes to keeping your taxes owed to a minimum. Once you are a property owner, the government steps in every year with some extra help in making your new business work through various tax breaks and incentives offered by the IRS. Most of these benefits are mirrored by the states in our country that have a state income tax.

As a property owner, you now will be filing a Schedule C with your regular tax returns, wherein you will be reporting all income and expenses from your real estate business. The money you spend to run the property will be a deduction from the rental income you receive in determining your taxable

Moneysaver

The IRS offers extra benefits to people who own historical properties. Rather than a normal depreciation deduction, the IRS gives these property owners tax credits against any money due come tax time.

profit. This then is taxable, just as any other earnings are. Any legitimate expense of running your property can be a deduction including the money you spend to upgrade the property to increase its value. Major expenses need to be deducted over several years, but they still can help decrease your taxable profit.

The most important tax incentive Uncle Sam provides is the ability to sell a property and trade all your equity into another property while deferring the taxes due on any profit you have made. This is called an IRS 1031 tax-deferred exchange. The number 1031 refers to the code section that contains all the rules governing such an exchange. We will tackle 1031 exchanges in earnest in Chapter 10, "Planning for the Tax Man." For now know that because you can defer the taxes owed, you can have more equity available to trade in for bigger and better buildings in the future. The end result will be a better chance at a higher return. The beauty is that, under the current code, an IRS 1031 exchange can be done over and over again for as long as you choose to grow your nest egg through real estate.

Here is an illustration of how a 1031 exchange may pencil out: Let's assume you just sold a duplex that you have owned for several years. You are getting back your $20,000 initial down payment and a net profit of $30,000. Assuming you are in the 30 percent tax bracket and are going to buy another property with 10 percent down, the following table shows the difference in the property you can purchase:

	Tax Paid	Tax Deferred
Down payment	$20,000	$20,000
Profit	$30,000	$30,000
Tax	$9,000	$0
Equity for purchase	$41,000	$50,000
New property value	$410,000	$500,000

It is important to note that you are not escaping the payment of your tax due; you are just postponing the payment to some time in the future. In a sense, Uncle Sam now becomes your partner in the next property you purchase. This is because you are investing his money (the taxes owed) along with your own. If you do a good job with it, you actually will be increasing his investment, too.

Leveraged compound interest

The biggest little secret of them all is leveraged compound interest. Albert Einstein, when asked what the most powerful force on Earth was, answered without hesitation, "Compound interest!" Ben Franklin defined the term as "the stone that will turn lead into gold." You all know about compound interest because it is the concept the banks and savings and loans talk about when they tell you how your money will grow when you leave it with them. You leave the interest in the bank along with your original investment. In a short period of time, the interest earned on the interest of your original investment makes your return multiply significantly.

We will go over the compound interest formula in great detail in Chapter 9, "Building an Investment Plan," but we want you to get a glimpse now of the reason this works so well with leveraged real estate. The truth is that the return you get on real estate if you pay for your purchase using all cash (without getting a loan) isn't much higher than you get on most other types of investments. With real estate, however, you usually don't pay using all cash. Instead, you use leverage to buy properties. That is, you put down a small down payment on the property, usually 10–20 percent, and you then finance the balance.

The great mathematician Archimedes said, "Give me a lever long enough and a fulcrum on which to place it, and I shall move the world." As investors, we don't want to use a lever to move the world; we just want to use it to buy as much of it as we can. The ability to finance 80–90 percent of your real estate business is the rule, not the exception.

On the other hand, most commodities in which you can invest require that you pay all cash to purchase them. At best, you can obtain some financing that usually requires a substantial down payment and exceptional credit. Take the stock market, for example; unless you are buying on margin, you are required to pay all cash for the shares you want to purchase. This is true whether you're buying stocks, bonds, or mutual funds. This also is true for most investments in coins, stamps, art, and commodities. If you want to own it, you'll be paying for it with your own hard-earned money.

The ability to use leverage with real estate significantly increases the percentage of profit you can make, but more importantly, it allows you to purchase a significantly larger investment than you normally would have been able to. If you have $9,000 to invest, for example, you could buy 9,000 worth of stocks, bonds, coins, or art. With $9,000 to invest in real estate, however, you could purchase a four-unit FHA apartment building worth $300,000. You'd achieve this because $9,000 is 3 percent of

 Watch Out!

Leverage is a wonderful way to multiply the profit on the dollars you invest. Remember, however, that because leverage increases your potential profit, it will also increase your risk because you are obligated to pay back the entire debt on the borrowed money. You can do it, but it will require running your real estate business in a professional way.

$300,000. And 3 percent is all an FHA loan requires you to put down. The structure of this kind of deal could look like this:

Property	Four-unit apartment building
Property price	$300,000
Down payment (3% of price)	$9,000
FHA loan	$291,000

By buying a property with a low down payment and financing the balance, you thereby significantly increase the percentage return on your money invested. To illustrate how this works, let's say you have $100,000 to invest, and you decide to use the entire $100,000 to buy a small two- or three-unit apartment building outright. Your cash flow might look like this:

Property price	$100,000 investment
Gross income	$14,000
–Expenses	–$4,000
Net cash flow	$10,000

Your profit as a percentage of your investment would be calculated using the following formula:

$$\frac{\text{Net income}}{\text{Investment}} = \%\ \text{return}$$

Therefore, your profit would be

$$\frac{\$10,000}{\$100,000} = 10\%\ \text{return}$$

Ten percent on your money isn't bad, especially if you're used to the return you get from your savings account—but now let's use leverage. For the purposes of this example, let's say you put 10 percent down and borrow 90 percent of the purchase price. The loan on the property at 7 percent interest costs you $598 per month. Your cash flow on the building is now:

Gross income	$14,000
Expenses	−$4,000
Loan payment	−$7,176
Net cash flow	$2,824

(Obviously, you will need to adjust these numbers, or any others you see in this book, to meet the interest rate you get.)

Compared to buying the property outright, you see that your cash flow drops from $10,000 to $2,824. At first glance, this doesn't seem so good—that is, until you see what it means in terms of a percentage return on your investment. Because your down payment is only $10,000 (rather than $100,000), the return now looks like this using the formula you just learned:

$$\frac{\text{Net income}}{\text{Investment}} = \% \text{ return}$$

Or:

$$\frac{\$2,824}{\$10,000} = 28.2\% \text{ return}$$

You see, that's what leverage does for you. In this scenario, it would give you a 28.2 percent return on your money. If you buy 10 of these properties with your same $100,000, your annual cash flow would be $28,200. As you will learn later, when you put the power of leverage together with Ben Franklin's "stone that will turn lead into gold," compound interest, you can—and will—make phenomenal returns.

Just the facts

- The old "work 40 years and retire" system no longer applies to the average person.
- To create wealth, you must rid yourself of the belief that trading time for dollars is the way to go.

- Because an investing mentality is not inherent in human behavior, it is a skill you will have to learn in order to get ahead.

- When it comes to investing in real estate, Uncle Sam is your best ally.

- The opportunity to use leverage to buy property is the greatest advantage real estate has over all other investments.

GET THE SCOOP ON...
The profit you see in the beginning ▪ What to
expect in the middle years ▪ Retirement realities
▪ Why a systematic approach is critical ▪
Research—the key to success

The Process and the Plan

In Chapter 1 we covered some of the basic reasons why an investment in real estate can work for you. Now we will explain what you can expect over the entire span of your investment career.

As you are learning, real estate is a long-term investment. With the liquidity of stocks, bonds, or mutual funds, you can get in and out very quickly. Real estate investing, however, requires you to invest with a different mindset. That is, you need to be committed to invest for the long haul. To that end, your goal can't be to buy a property and then hope to flip it and turn a windfall profit overnight. This is because real estate, by nature, doesn't lend itself to making a quick buck. However, by making a long-term commitment you'll come to see that this investment has longevity. In fact, levelheaded real estate investing is destined to pay great returns over the entire course of a lifetime.

What's unique about this investment is that the profits you'll earn through the years are distinctly

Chapter 2

different; a feature you can't find in other investments. You'll note that these different types of profits all build on each other. You retain your short-term profits into your middle years, and you carry both of these profits into your retirement.

We'll begin this chapter by talking about the earnings you can look forward to in the short term.

Short-term profits

You can expect to earn two types of profits in the short term: cash flow and tax benefits. Either one of these by itself can give you just as good a return as most other investments. Taken together, the return they offer usually is far superior to any other investment you might choose.

Cash flow

Cash flow is probably the most sought-after return from any investment. Simply stated, cash flow is the monthly or annual cash return you receive from your investment. Take your savings account, for instance. When you deposit your excess earnings in your account, the bank pays you interest on your money; this interest is your cash flow from that investment. Generally speaking, the greater the cash flow you desire from any investment, the greater the effort and sometimes the greater the risk you will need to take to obtain your goal.

With real estate, it's important to understand that cash flow is a direct function of how much you put down on a property. If you bought a property without the aid of a loan, for example, your cash flow would be substantial. This is because all the

---

 Moneysaver

Negative cash flow exists when your payments are greater than your income. It may sound simple, but one way to avoid negative cash flow is to make sure your rents are at least at market rate. Some investors get too friendly with their tenants. In turn, the investors' big hearts keep them from charging the market rents for their properties that they truly deserve.

money you take in from rent, less operating expenses, would be yours to keep. Conversely, if you buy a property with a minimal down payment and take out a loan to cover the balance, your cash flow will be adjusted accordingly. This is because paying back the loan reduces your cash flow.

To calculate cash flow, use the following formula:

Gross income

−Operating expenses

−Loan payments
_____

Net cash flow

Cash flow doesn't mean much unless you relate it to the amount of money you have invested. Most investors like to talk about the cash-on-cash return they get on their money. Your percentage cash-on-cash return is calculated as follows:

$$\frac{\text{Net cash flow}}{\text{Cash investment}} = \% \text{ Cash-on-cash return}$$

With an investment in real estate, you can structure your financing to obtain the cash flow you desire. Smart investors have the most financing on their properties when they begin their investment careers and have the least when they retire. This is intelligent because when you're working full time, a good goal is to have your steady paycheck cover your current standard of living. That way, your investments can do the job they are supposed to do. Once you retire, however, and aren't getting paid on a regular basis, you will have a greater need for steady monthly income. Reducing the amount of your mortgage by the time you retire is the best way to achieve this result.

Tax benefits

The second short-term benefit in real estate investing relates to taxes. You should view the tax benefits you receive from property ownership as frosting on the cake. With real estate, you can receive a nice cash-on-cash return from your property at the end

Moneysaver

Ordinary and reasonable expenses connected to real estate are deductible as investment expenses including interest, utilities, insurance, property taxes, maintenance, supplies, legal fees, and more.

of the year. This is because you are allowed to deduct your losses from operating expenses on your federal taxes. Most states that have state income taxes also offer a state tax benefit.

The theory behind the tax deduction for operating expenses is rooted in the costs most companies incur to replace expensive equipment needed to produce durable goods. Because machines wear out or become obsolete in just a few years, the IRS allows companies to take a deduction against profits to replace equipment. The business is allowed to deduct the cost of the machine over its useful life so that it can be replaced when it wears out. With real estate, you can produce a positive cash flow and still have a loss as far as the IRS is concerned.

We'll be reviewing ongoing and capital expenses in detail in Chapters 14 and 15, but we want you to understand the benefits to the real estate investor now. As a real estate investor, you will have an opportunity to take a deduction against earnings for an expense that probably will never occur. That is, you will never have to replace your building because it wore out. In truth, real estate never wears out. Structures that sit on land do, but the dirt itself does not.

Note that this depreciation deduction, especially in the early years of ownership, usually shelters all cash-flow profits. In addition, there usually are enough extra write-offs to offset taxes on some of your earnings from your regular job.

Middle-years payoffs

The middle years of ownership should keep you both busy and happy. You'll be busy because you will have the responsibility of running your real estate business each day. You'll be happy because you will be making money. Lots of it.

During the middle years, you can expect to spend most of your time on three phases of operation:

1. Running the day-to-day operation of your properties like a business.

2. Utilizing the equity in the properties like a savings account to provide for some of the finer things in life.

3. Fine-tuning your investment plan to make sure you reach your stated goals according to your set timetable.

The day-to-day operations

You'll recognize that you are in the middle years of ownership when certain clues pop up time and again. For one thing, you'll find yourself skipping over the front-page and sports sections of your newspaper to get to the real estate ads. Perusing that section of the paper, you'll become a bloodhound for rental rates, upcoming vacancies, and any other kinds of information that could impact your business. Additionally, in these years, you'll discover that your Home Depot or Orchard Supply credit card

> 66 We worked hard on our properties, and after five years, we were able to refinance. Because of the appreciation that took place in that time period, we were able to pull out enough money to help build ourselves a brand new home. 99
>
> —Jim S., 54

bill is consistently larger than your Macy's or Nordstrom's bill. Finally, when you travel to your favorite vacation spots, you'll always be checking out rental rates and the price of small units. Your master plan will be to buy a vacation home there and let tenants pay the mortgage when you're not on holiday.

At this point, you have arrived. You're in business for yourself, and you're enjoying the challenges and the profits. This is when all the things you learn in this book will be the most meaningful to you. You will see this business as just that—a business. The profit plans you have designed will become as important as your paycheck is at your day job. Going to your property won't seem like a chore; instead, it'll feel like an opportunity to check on your investment. Did the gardener do his job? Does anything need to be painted or fixed? Are the tenants happy? Can I charge more rent?

You'll start taking trips around the neighborhood to see what the competition looks like. Yes, you will now see all the other buildings in your neighborhood as competition. How do they look? What are they charging for rent? Which ones always seem to stay full and why? Just as grocery stores and department stores compete for customers, you'll begin to compete for tenants with the other building owners in your neighborhood.

The first few days of the month will now have a new meaning for you; they will be the days you collect your rents and pay your bills. The first challenge will be getting all the rents in on the first of the month. Even in the best areas, it takes work to get your tenants trained to pay on time. After collecting rent, you'll have to pay out a lot of it to cover bills. This will become a game to you, and you will constantly be asking yourself, "How can I keep the most for myself?" At your day job, your boss asks you to increase revenue and to do what you can to cut down on expenses. You do it there because it is your job; now you'll do it because the money you save is yours to keep.

Utilizing your equity

As your real estate holdings move into the middle years, the cash flow and equity grow. This is because, by this time, you will have raised your rents and found ways to curtail expenses. Now is the time when you can use your property as you would use a savings account—to buy things you couldn't afford on your salary alone. These middle-years items should be the kind of things that will give you the extra incentive to work that much harder at this second career.

Watch Out!

Avoid the idea of buying a property for your child to live in while he or she is away at college. Prices in college towns usually are pretty high, and kids are known to transfer schools or drop out all together. What's worse, college-age tenants tend to trash your units.

Providing an education for their children is one of the first things many people do with the money they make from real estate. Indeed, education comes with a large price tag. A recent study predicts that the cost of a public college education in the year 2018 will be more than $70,000, and the cost of a private university education will be more than $180,000. These are staggering numbers, especially when you multiply them by the number of children you have.

There are, however, some more pleasurable things you can look forward to doing with your money. The equity in your properties can be tapped to help provide for that larger home in the better neighborhood where you have always wanted to live. You also might choose to invest some of the money you're making into a vacation home in the mountains or the desert. Instead of sitting vacant while not in use, it becomes another holding in your investment portfolio. You earn income from renting it when you're not vacationing there.

A vacation home offers an interesting mix of benefits. You might be able to take depreciation, but if not, then you may be able to deduct expenses as a second home. The best news is that you can probably use the 1031 tax-deferred exchange to shelter your profit. We'll tackle this subject in detail in Chapter 7, "Subdividing Your Options."

Finally, let's talk about all the other luxuries you would like if you had a few extra thousand dollars at your disposal. How about a couple of jet skis like your neighbor has? What about a trip to Hawaii or Europe with the family? In short, your properties should provide you with the funds to pay for all those "if only I had the extra money" things about which most people only dream.

Of course, new water toys and vacations sound great, but do you want to know how it is realistically possible? Here's how: Your real estate is going to produce some income through cash flow, and it will also provide you with a nice cushion come tax time. But, in truth, your nest egg will grow to truly astounding heights due to two other areas of return. They are

1. Appreciation in value (inflation + demand)

2. By paying down your mortgage

Let's first talk about value appreciation. Inflation has always been a part of our economy. In the past, you weren't happy during high inflation because the cost of everything you needed to live seemed to correspondingly grow. Now, however, higher inflation will be your best friend. This is because not only will the value of your property increase because of inflation, but you also can increase your monthly income by raising rents during inflationary times.

Additionally, your equity will increase as you pay off your mortgage. In the beginning, principal reduction will only constitute a small portion of the pie. But as the years go on it becomes a significant part of equity growth. It takes longer to see the big dollars add up from this component of return, but every dollar paid off increases your net worth correspondingly.

This increased equity also gives you borrowing power at the bank. Your banker should gladly loan you money based on the appreciation that has taken place on your property as well as the increased value you have created by paying down

 Moneysaver

Be sure to contact your existing lender when it's time to refinance. Many times, you can save on loan fees, escrow fees, and other costs by using the same lender the second time around. They want your business, so don't be afraid to try and negotiate their fees down.

your loans. Any new loan you get will first be used to pay off your old loan. Then, if there is money left over, you can do with it what you choose.

One of the greatest advantages of refinancing is that the funds you pull out are not taxable. Conversely, if you sell stock and realize a profit, you will have to pay the tax. But when it comes to refinancing real estate, because you are borrowing your profit, there is no tax to pay. This is because you are obligated, at some point, to pay the loan back. The good news is that you will be doing that with tenant income. If you have increased your rents to keep up with the market, these increased rents usually will pay any increase in your payments because of the higher loan you now have.

Tweaking your plan

You will use the middle years to fine-tune your knowledge of any and all real estate investment opportunities. The more you get involved, the more you will want to know about real estate and the business of owning it. This should lead you to seminars, books, lectures, tapes, and discussions with other investors.

Through the years, you probably will be following in your mind various types of properties you might consider buying. There are single-family homes, small units, commercial buildings, and developable land that you might try your hand at. Additionally, you might consider buying distressed properties. Situations such as fixer-uppers, mismanaged properties, bank repossessions, use conversions, and development deals all provide opportunities to make more money (see Chapters 7 and 8)—that is, after you gain the proper knowledge and experience from taking a more traditional route to wealth-building through real estate first.

At some point, you will make a decision whether real estate will remain a secondary career to you or whether you will quit working for someone else and hire yourself to manage your real estate holdings full time. Whatever your choice may be, you will find that the middle years of property ownership will provide you with plenty of flexibility. In Chapter 10, "Planning for the Tax Man," you will see that there are some great tax advantages to being directly involved in your real estate ventures. The IRS calls this being "in the business" of real estate.

The retirement years

As you make your decisions about your future in real estate, you'll also be setting the stage for your retirement. For some people, real estate will be one part of a diverse retirement portfolio, a true passive investment. Many investors choose to purchase only one property in their careers and to manage the financing so that it is paid off by the time they retire. This isn't such a bad idea. By the time they retire there is no mortgage to worry about, which will provide plenty of positive cash flow.

Other investors purchase many properties in their careers and decide that they just want to call it quits. For them, a perfect life would be fishing in the mornings and golfing in the afternoon. If that is their goal, their properties can be sold, they can settle up with Uncle Sam, and then bank the remaining cash. From that point forward, they can fish and golf to their heart's content.

Another option is to sell the properties and become the banker by carrying notes against the property. This strategy will be discussed in detail later in this book, but in short, carrying notes against your properties offers two distinct advantages over an outright sale:

1. You don't pay your taxes until you receive your profit. This means you can carry interest-only notes and defer any taxes due for the entire term of your contract. As you can see, by utilizing this technique you can earn interest on all your equity including the money you eventually will give to the IRS for taxes.

2. You will find out that you will earn a greater interest rate on your money by being the banker than by letting the banks pay you interest. Remember, early on we learned

that the banks pay you interest when you give them your money, and then they lend it to others to buy property. By carrying the financing yourself, you cut out the middle-man (the bank) and keep the profit all for yourself.

Many people find that their real estate holdings make a great part-time retirement business. Managing the properties is just enough to keep them busy, but doesn't require a daily 9 to 5 commitment. For others, real estate might grow into a family business, with the kids learning at a young age the lessons you had to learn while working two jobs.

A last option is to relinquish all the operations of your business to a property management company. At this point, your new job will be to supervise your management company rather than your properties. The management company will have all the duties of running the properties and paying the bills. They will then send you a check each month for your profit. Even better, they can easily deposit your funds to the bank of your choice, and you can draw on them from anywhere in the world.

A systematic approach to investing

Now that you understand the kinds of profits you can expect, you need a plan for attaining the biggest return. What we intro-duce to you now is a *systematic plan* for investing in real estate that works—period. We don't make that claim idly. We know that the plan works because we have *seen it work* for years for our-selves and for our clients. You need not reinvent the wheel. Instead, learn the plan here, and then implement it for yourself. The wheel will then roll for you too.

This approach to investing has five phases. They are

1. **Learn** about real estate as an investment vehicle.

2. **Research** the market in your local area.

3. **Plan** how to invest your money.

4. **Invest** your funds according to your plan.

5. **Manage** your investment to meet your plan's goals.

Let's touch on each of these phases one at a time.

Learning about real estate as an investment vehicle

For starters, recognize that the education you are putting yourself through now isn't meant to be a course called "Real Estate 101" that goes in one ear and out the other. Instead, you must think of this kind of learning as if it were a continuing-education class—one that you chose and will be involved with for the rest of your investment career. Just as you educated yourself for your day job, we want you to educate yourself for this investment career. You go to work each day and trade your time for dollars. In your real estate career, you will be letting your investments do most of the work, but you need to be the brains behind the operation.

We know that this learning phase can be the most difficult step for lots of people. This is because learning anything new requires lots of personal effort and time. The truth is, not many of us have the time to brush our teeth in the mornings, let alone the time to learn all about a new business venture. As a partial cure, what about spending your morning commute listening to books on tape about real estate and investing? You can literally turn your daily drive into a classroom by listening to educational tapes instead of more sports talk or a Top-40 station. It would be a trade-off, but one that could get you that much closer to catching the golden goose.

The truth is, if you want to take this game seriously, there are literally thousands of books, tapes, newspaper articles, magazine articles, classes, and seminars available to help you get educated. Even better news is that most of the books, articles, and tapes will probably be available free at your local library. Your only job will be to seek them out.

Watch Out!

Make sure to do some stringent checking before you pay big money to attend some of the "get rich quick" real estate seminars offered. Be especially wary of the ones that are free; often they are designed to just get you in the door so that they can sell you some expensive books, tapes, or additional training.

To supplement your independent study, there are plenty of colleges and adult-education schools that offer courses on everything from basic accounting to property management to buying and selling every kind of real estate you can imagine. What's great is that these classes usually don't cost much, especially at the community-college level. The biggest advantage is that people who have hands-on knowledge of the subject matter usually teach the classes. In addition, if you have an apartment owners association nearby (see Appendix B), it might offer property-management seminars where you can learn management skills and the latest rules and regulations for your local area.

Finally, many authors and lecturers offer weekend seminars covering a range of real estate–related subjects. Often held only in larger cities, these courses can be a great source of information.

The lesson here is to take this road seriously. By turning yourself into an expert, you will shave years off your learning curve. The end result will be more money in your pocket—way more.

Researching the market in your local area

While you are learning about real estate in general and real estate investing specifically, you need to begin educating yourself about the actual market for property in your area. Our book, and most others, can only provide a broad overview of real estate investing. Markets can change drastically within a few miles, let alone across the entire country. Therefore, it's critical to truly understand your own market and how it performs before you start buying.

Begin by finding a real estate agent who is willing to help long before you are ready to buy. Don't worry; you won't have to pay him anything because he will earn a commission paid by the seller only if, and when, you purchase a property. Your goal at this stage is to get a basic understanding of the pricing of properties in the area where you expect to buy. You won't be calculating returns or looking for something to actually buy at this point. Your goal is simply to get a basic understanding of what properties sell for. If you can answer the question "What would a duplex cost in my neighborhood?" or "What is the price per unit for a fourplex?," you're well on your way to a solid foundation. If, when asked those questions, you said, "I need to know whether the units are one or two bedrooms and how many bathrooms they each have," you probably have an excellent handle on value.

While you are researching value, it also is important to become familiar with rental rates in your market area. Working with an agent, you'll be able to see what current properties rent for, but this is only part of the picture because all of those rents are based on units that have rented at some time in the past. You also will want to find out what owners are asking for units currently on the market.

Keep in mind that many small-property owners don't do a very good job of keeping up on rental rates. In fact, it's not unusual for some owners to rent a vacancy at the last rate they were getting without verifying the true current market rate. Your goal will be to discover what the trend is. Are rental rates in the area going up or down over a period of time? Is the area stable, improving, or declining?

Once you have a current understanding of property values, you'll want to research the historical value in your area. Again, the help of a good real estate agent will be invaluable because most have access to this information through their local Board of Realtors. If you can find an agent who specializes in investment property, he may have the data you want readily available for the asking.

You will want to look for the same information about properties in the past as you got for the properties on the market today. Information about rental rates also will be helpful because you want to see the trends for increase over the years. The further back you can get information, the better. You then will be able to see how trends in real estate values in your area compare to the trends in our economy in general.

The accompanying chart shows the historical trends of real estate values in the city of El Segundo, California. This chart uses a mathematical calculation called linear regression analysis to determine the change in the values from the first year to the last. This is the kind of historical data that would be helpful for your own market. At the very least, the most important facts you want are the trends in values for as many years as you can get. Knowing this percentage increase is important when doing forward projections for an investment plan. Although past history is no guarantee of the future, it often is a prologue and therefore is a better way to make an estimate than picking one out of thin air. In Chapter 6, "Real Estate, the Economy, and Your Target Market," we'll illustrate a specific technique that you can use to estimate value appreciation for yourself.

Once you have a handle on the present and the past, it's time to start worrying about the future. This is when you have to go back to school for a review of some basic economic principals. When doing this kind of study, you will learn that lots of outside factors can impact your real estate business. Therefore, in order to protect your bottom line, you will have to have the skill necessary to recognize changes in the economy that can affect you both positively and negatively.

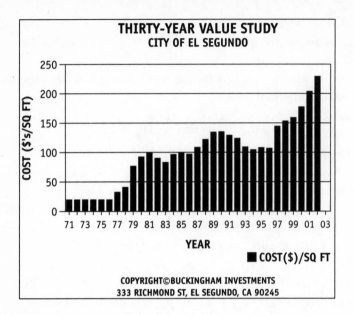

You should be reading the business section of the paper with a new perspective. Finding out about future business expansion, for example, will mean that there will be more people to rent your units. Likewise, a new shopping mall in your area should bring both more revenue to the city and more employees who need a place to live close to work. Increased inflation means higher prices for goods and services and, best of all, higher rents for you.

In addition to the newspaper, you also should look for other publications that will give you insight into changes in your local economy. Most chambers of commerce have information about what is happening in the local economy. Some banks and savings and loans have research departments that compile this kind of information. Finally, most cities have departments designed for the sole purpose of attracting new businesses. These city departments can be a good source of information about the existing state of your local economy and what they project for the future.

Remember, the goal of all this research is to keep you tuned in to what's going on out there. This way, you can take advantage of any positive changes in the economy and can make provisions to protect your investments if you see that negative changes are on the way.

Planning how to invest your money

Now that you have accumulated the knowledge to invest and you understand the product, it is time to put a plan together. The foundation of the plan will be your goals. For many years, we have observed investors and—with very few exceptions—the most successful all had very well-defined goals. There is nothing unique about this observation. Hundreds, if not thousands, of authors, scholars, teachers, and so on have, over the centuries, touted the need for goal orientation as a key to success. It's amazing how many of us have a job that requires us to make plans at work for our performance and the performance of the department we head up, but we don't ever do the same for our own lives. Until now, most of us have really been missing the boat.

Chapter 9, "Building an Investment Plan," will teach you how to put your investment plan together. Nonetheless, it is important at this point to start thinking about some specific things you want to accomplish through investing in real estate. It's not enough just to say that you want to find some "good deals," or that you want to get rich. These concepts don't have anything personal to hang on to. Instead, getting specific is the key. A new house overlooking the park in five years or $75,000 set aside for Sydney and Mara's college education are specific goals that have meaning.

 Moneysaver

By properly defining your goals, you will avoid paying extra for a property to satisfy an unfounded emotional need. We always say to buy the ugly property for less; spruce it up with flowers, paint, and awnings; and then manage it into profitability.

Finally, have you ever heard an interview with someone who just won the lottery? The reporter invariably asks, "What are you going to do with the money?" The answer usually is a list of things like a new house, a car, trips, and doing something nice for a relative or friend. It's not the money; it's what you can do with the money that keeps people buying the tickets. The right set of personal goals will give you the incentive to work your new business, and in a few years, you'll have the payoffs just like you'd won the lottery yourself.

Investing your funds according to your plan

The last step in our plan is where you make your move. This is when you get to put that knowledge and research to work by investing and buying a piece of rental property. Know that this is where the real work starts because it's not just a mental game now—it's the real McCoy.

When you've finally decided that it's time to buy something, this can be as exciting as your first kiss, and as scary. At this point, take a deep breath and review all you've learned and researched. The first investment will be a big step, but you should have a higher level of confidence than most. You have educated yourself about investing, you are knowledgeable about your target market, you have a plan that lays out what you are trying to accomplish, and you know the kind of property you need to get started. As they used to say in the Old West, "Just go ahead and pull the trigger!"

Though you'll surely be excited at this point, you must also be prudent. To that end, we don't recommend trying to hit a

> **❝** It was tough to make the decision to buy that first property. My agent, Eve, suggested that we start with just half the capital we planned to start with. This cushion gave us the courage to make the move on that first one. **❞**
>
> —Victoria P., investor

home run on your first purchase. Many beginning investors make a colossal mistake in the beginning by seeking out bank-owned repossessions or fixer-uppers right out of the gate because they have heard how much money they can make by doing so. Money can be made, but it takes the experience of many years in the business to find success that way. On the other hand, a mistake in buying one of those kinds of buildings from the onset could sour you on real estate investing long before you ever get out of the starting gate. Instead, we recommend that you use your first purchase to apply the sound business skills you are learning here.

By starting smart, you will help ensure your success.

Managing your investment to meet your plan's goals

Once you are trained, the good news is that you will own the property and you can do as much or as little of the work as you like. You are in charge of the building, the rents, and the tenants. Of course, you can subcontract the management of your property if you so choose. This can be very tempting, especially because the cost of management usually is just a small percentage of the gross income collected. We strongly recommend, however, that you don't hire out management on your first few properties. It's important to experience firsthand the duties of running a property yourself. You need to put the knowledge you have learned to the test to see how the real world works.

This hands-on experience will also be invaluable to you later, when you do turn your properties over to a management company. At that point, your job will be to manage the management company. To do this effectively, you need to have had the actual experience doing the job yourself. It's one thing to read about something in a book; it's another thing to actually have gotten your hands dirty down in the trenches.

You'll find that if you are doing your job right as the manager, you'll be constantly revisiting the first four steps of the systematic approach we're laying out here. As you manage, you learn—not from books this time, but from the actual doing of the job. Running a property is really an on-the-job research project. You'll become quite an expert as you handle the day-to-day operations of your property.

Along the way you'll take the time to assess the current market and compare your position with the goals of your plan. At some point you will make the decision as head of this company that it's time to trade up or refinance. Either way, you may realize that the time is ripe to acquire more property and you are going to use your prior properties to help you do it. When this happens, it's back to step 4 all over again as you'll have a new building to manage. The party is just getting started!

Just the facts

- Real estate ownership has three phases of profits—short term profits, middle-years payoffs, and retirement rewards.

- One of the greatest advantages of real estate is the fact that it is a business you can start while you keep your regular job.

- As your property equities grow, you can use them to finance luxuries you never thought you could afford.

- Don't swing for the fences on your first purchase; make it a learning experience.

The Secrets of
Real Estate Investing

PART II

GET THE SCOOP ON...
Determining cash flow ▪ Loan reduction and
how it adds up ▪ Why value appreciation is
the real money maker ▪ The tax benefits of
real estate ownership

Elements of Return

With an investment in real estate, four elements of return will help you reach your goals. These elements are cash flow, equity growth from loan reduction, equity growth from appreciation, and tax benefits. In this chapter, you will learn about each of these elements of return individually, and how to calculate the combined effect of all four to give you an estimated overall return on your investment.

Learning how to do this properly will tell you two things. First, it will show you what kind of profit you can achieve on any potential investment. Once you are able to do an apples-to-apples comparison and have a benchmark on which to consider potential purchases, your decision on which property to actually buy should become easy. Second, by knowing how to calculate return yourself, you can make sure your percentage return always stays high enough to ensure that you reach your investment goals on schedule.

Chapter 3

Watch Out!

Remember that the four elements of return don't arrive at the same time. As a result, many investors fail to pay close enough attention to all of them and end up missing out on earning the highest possible return on their equity.

333 Richmond Street

To help us demonstrate each element of return, we will use an example property that we will come back to time and again. We'll call our example "333 Richmond Street," in honor of the building that has housed our own real estate sales office for the past 30 years. For purposes of this book, the Richmond Street property is a 20-year old, four-unit apartment building that is listed for sale at $225,000. The building is in good condition and it has a unit mix that consists of four two-bedroom/one-bath apartments. The units bring in $550 per month, and the expenses on the building are calculated at 30 percent of the gross income. These details of the example lay out as follows:

Address: 333 Richmond Street, El Segundo, California

Asking price: $225,000

Number of units: 4

Unit mix: 4 units at 2 bedrooms/1 bathroom each

Income: $550 per unit = $2,200 per month = $26,400 per year

Expenses: 30 percent of gross income = $7,920 per year

Square footage: 3,200 square feet

Lot size: 50 × 150 feet

Age: 20 years old

Features:

- Newer carpets and drapes
- Built-in stoves
- Natural stone fireplaces
- Four garages

Cash flow

The first of the four elements of return is cash flow. Simply put, cash flow is the money left over after you pay the bills. To determine cash flow on any property, you need to know three key pieces of information:

1. The annual gross income

2. The annual expenses

3. The total debt payment on your loans

We will use the example property at 333 Richmond Street to illustrate. Let's say we negotiated the asking price of $225,000 down to a purchase price of $220,000. Our down payment was $30,000, and we financed the remaining $190,000 at a 9 percent interest rate. This gave us a monthly loan payment of $1,450 and an annual debt payment of $17,400 ($1,450 × 12 = $17,400). We have four units that rent for $550 each. This gives us an annual income of $26,400 ($550 × 4 × 12 = $26,400). Finally, remember that our annual expenses are $7,920 (30 percent of the gross income). Knowing all this, we can compute our annual cash flow by subtracting the annual operating expenses and annual loan payments from the gross annual income, as follows:

Gross annual income	$26,400
Less annual operating expenses	−$7,920
Less annual loan payments	−$17,400
Annual cash flow	$1,080

 Watch Out!

Many investors think cash flow is the ticket to getting rich. In reality, a high cash flow at the onset of property ownership, more often than not, indicates that the investor isn't taking advantage of as much leverage as he could.

Bright Idea

Don't buy into the mistaken belief that a big cash flow is the most important element of return. While you're young and still able to work, it might be wiser to structure your deals so they will produce a large cash flow only after you retire. That way, you will have cash available when you truly need it.

After we know the cash flow, we then can use it to determine the percentage return on the investment. This is achieved by dividing the cash flow by the down payment, as follows:

$$\frac{\text{Annual cash flow: } \$1,080}{\text{Down payment: } \ \$30,000} = 4\% \text{ return}$$

As you can see, this is a fairly simple process; however, in the real world of buying a property, making sure the components of this calculation are correct often creates confusion. The first thing to decipher is how much money a building really brings in.

The annual gross income

There are three ways to look at the income stream of a building. The first way is by examining the scheduled rent. The scheduled rent is the total of all the agreed-upon-rents in the building, assuming that all the tenants are paying and that there are no vacancies.

The second way to look at the income is by analyzing potential rent. Potential rent is the income you feel you could earn based on the rents other property owners are receiving in your market area. Alternatively, potential rents are those you feel you could earn provided that your building had more attractive amenities, and you could charge more than the competition.

The third way to analyze the income of a building is by evaluating the collected rent. The collected rent is the actual amount of money the current owner took in over a given period of time. It reflects the market, but more than that, it reflects the current owner's ability to manage in that market. You may do

Moneysaver

Make sure you get into the habit of inquiring about available units in your area. By knowing what the competition is charging for rent, you can avoid underestimating the market when it comes time to market your own vacancies.

better, or you may do worse. Collected rent is impacted by the vacancy factor and credit losses incurred from tenants who did not pay.

The annual expenses

The second thing you must do in order to calculate a building's cash flow is to determine the building's true expenses. As the owner of residential income property, you will encounter the following three types of expenses:

1. Fixed expenses
2. Variable expenses
3. Planned capital expenses

Fixed expenses are the regular recurring costs encountered in holding a property. These expenses include items such as property taxes, insurance, and city business-license fees. They are called *fixed expenses* because the amount you pay does not fluctuate, or if it does, it usually is only a nominal change one time per year.

Variable expenses do fluctuate. They are all the other costs you might incur while managing your rental property. The biggest variable expenses you will encounter will be utility payments, necessary repairs, general maintenance, and vacancies in your building.

Planned capital expenses are major items that have a useful life of more than one year. These are items such as a new roof or exterior paint. According to the IRS, these expenses must be capitalized for tax purposes. This means you must write the expense off over a period of years. To account for these types of expenses in your cash flow, you need to include a reserve of a certain percentage of the income based on the condition of the property. We will cover this in greater detail in Chapter 14, "Managing the Expenses."

The management of all these expenses will play a major role in how much cash flow your property produces. Reviewing the former owner's records before you buy can give you insight into how the property might perform, but this information also can be misleading. The seller might be a great manager who has been able to keep expenses under control, or he might be an awful manager who can't control a thing. Therefore, it is important for you to do your homework on the types and cost of normal expenses for your area. Your ability as property manager to use the information you gain from your research will determine whether or not your property outperforms that of your competition.

The debt payment on your loans

The final component of the cash flow equation is the payment on your loan or loans. Recognize that there is always a direct correlation between the amount of your down payment (your *equity*) and your cash flow. It stands to reason that if you pay for a property without getting any loans at all, your cash flow will naturally be significantly larger than if you have loan payment obligations. Conversely, if you buy property with leverage (by means of a loan), your cash flow will be much less, but your percentage return will be much higher.

 Watch Out!

You cannot build an investment plan for your area based on expectations from other areas of the country. Your own market will dictate the amount of cash flow you can expect based on typical down payment amounts and financing.

Equity growth from loan reduction

The second way your equity will grow is through loan reduction. When you first close escrow on a piece of property, your initial equity is your down payment. Know that this equity will change over the years as you make monthly payments on your mortgage. The principal portion of your payment decreases your loan balance, which increases your equity. At first, the lion's share of your mortgage payments will go toward paying off interest, but don't fret. As the years go by, principal reduction accelerates considerably and becomes a significant cause of equity growth.

For the purposes of the following calculation, assume that the loan payoff is a constant amount. Note that you will be able to get the exact payoff at the end of each year when your lender sends you the 1099 form that you use to file your tax return. Recall that on the Richmond Street example, we put $30,000 down and financed the balance of the purchase. Our loan on the property was for $190,000, payable at $1,450 per month. That payment included principal reduction and interest at 9 percent per year. The total payments on the loan for the year are $17,400 (12 × $1,450 = $17,400). Roughly speaking, the interest paid to the bank would be 9 percent of $190,000, or $17,100 (.09 × $190,000 = $17,100). The calculation looks like this:

Total loan payments:	$17,400
Less interest paid:	−$17,100
Principal reduction:	$300

 Bright Idea

As your cash flow improves, you might choose to pay off some extra principal each month on your mortgage. This way, you will get your loan paid off early, and you will have that much more cash flow available for retirement.

Watch Out!

A common mistake many investors make is to calculate their return after many years of ownership by using the original down payment in the calculation. You must remember that, with a pay-down on your loans, your true equity will be much larger than your original down payment.

As you can see, the difference between the $17,400 loan payment and the $17,100 interest is $300. This $300 is the approximate principal reduction the first year. To find out your percentage return on your investment due solely to reduction of the principal balance of your loan, divide that reduction by your down payment as follows:

$$\frac{\text{Principal reduction: } \$300}{\text{Down payment: } \$30{,}000} = 1\% \text{ return}$$

Don't let this modest 1 percent return the first year scare you. As mentioned previously, principal begins to pay off at a much faster clip in future years of ownership, and your percentage return dramatically increases.

Equity growth from appreciation

The third, and most significant, way you are going to earn money in real estate is through value appreciation. Value appreciation results from two factors:

1. Inflation
2. Demand

Inflationary appreciation

Inflationary appreciation sounds just like what it is—the increase in a property's value due to inflation. This is the same phenomenon you see in supermarket prices. Even when the number of items you purchase at the store stays the same, the prices nonetheless continue to go up every year. This appreciation rate is related to the general inflationary rate of our overall economy. When the country's inflation rate is up, the appreciation rate of property is usually also up.

Two components make up the value of any piece of property: the structure itself and the land. Although land never wears out, structures do. Inflation affects the cost of both of these items, but this component of appreciation can be stagnant when it comes to the structure. This is because the structure is deteriorating (as 2×4s do over time) at the same time the property as a whole may be appreciating. A number of factors combine to give a structure a limited useful life. They include

1. Wear and tear from usage

2. Wear and tear from the elements

3. Changes in building advances

The factor that makes the biggest difference in inflationary appreciation is the value of the land itself. Except in rare cases, usually caused by toxic waste problems, land increases in value over time. Therefore, the value of the land as compared to the value of the structure itself has a great impact on the increase in value from inflation. This is called the land-to-improvement ratio.

The land-to-improvement ratio can shift dramatically depending on what area of the country or what area of a city you are in. In many metropolitan areas, for example, the land value can be as much as 90 percent of the value of the entire property. In smaller, more rural areas, these numbers can be entirely reversed: The structure might represent 90 percent of the value and the land a mere 10 percent.

To see how this can affect the increase in value, we will look at the example of 333 Richmond Street as if it were in both areas. We will assume that the inflation rate is 3 percent and that there is no inflation increase for the structure because of the offsetting depreciation.

In the smaller community, let's say the value of the land is $22,000 ($220,000 purchase price × 10 percent land value = $22,000). This gives us a return from inflation on the land of

$660 ($22,000 × 3 percent inflation rate = $660). In the metro-politan area, we'll assume the value of the land is $198,000 ($220,000 purchase price × 90 percent land value = $198,000). This puts the inflation return at $5,940 ($198,000 × 3 percent inflation rate = $5,940). Again, because we put down $30,000 to purchase the property, we can illustrate the appreciation return from inflation as follows:

	Small Areas	Metropolitan Areas
Appreciation	$660	$5,940
Down payment	$30,000	$30,000
Return	2.2%	19.8%

Demand appreciation

Demand is the second reason your property will make you money because of value appreciation. Demand appreciation is related to four different economic principles. They are

- Scarcity
- Transferability
- Utility
- Demand

The combined effect of these four economic components pushes property values up at a greater rate in some areas while pushing values down in others. Let's look at each component one at a time.

 Moneysaver

Densely populated metropolitan areas usually have the greatest appreciation from demand. This is due to the lack of land available for new construction.

The *scarcity principle* can best be seen when comparing a metropolitan area to a rural one. In the metropolitan area, there is very little undeveloped land available. In many cases, an existing older structure must first be demolished before a new building can be constructed. Therefore, developers first have to find someone willing to sell. When they do, they'll be paying for both the land and the structure that sits on it. Naturally, this increases the cost of any property under those circumstances. Rural areas, on the other hand, tend to have large amounts of vacant land. This greater availability of land makes it a lot easier to find willing sellers and lower prices.

Transferability refers to the ease of buying and selling a commodity. As you know, investment vehicles such as stocks and bonds are fairly liquid; that is, you can transfer them from one owner to another pretty quickly. Real estate, on the other hand, can't be transferred as fast. This fact usually is related to the number of potential buyers and the ability—or lack thereof—to find adequate financing. There might be many buyers and hundreds of lenders for the duplex you are trying to sell, but how many buyers and lenders might there be for the purchase of the Empire State Building? Not too many.

Utility refers to the usability of the property. The value of a property is directly related to its highest and best use. A commercial lot close to a railroad-loading yard, for example, could be a valuable location for a manufacturing plant. Rule of thumb: The greater the utility value, the greater the value of the property.

Demand is the last economic principle that drives prices. Demand correlates to the upward desirability of the property. This is the same phenomenon that affects the price of tickets to major sporting events, music concerts, or top Broadway shows. Think about the scalpers that roam the parking lots of these events. The reason they are able to get top dollar for their tickets is because the demand for the product is so great. For example, scalped tickets to see a long-running Broadway show or the seventh game of the NBA Finals would certainly be pretty pricey. If scalpers were selling tickets to see a high-school production of *Grease*, however, the tickets wouldn't cost nearly as much.

Demand can increase or decrease due to general trends in the economy. Many investors move from one investment vehicle to another based on the investment's ability to produce a profit. When stocks are hot, their money is there. When bond yields go up, they sell the stocks for bonds. When real estate is moving, they start buying. This sends the message to small investors that it is time to buy. This increased demand for a limited supply causes the appreciation rate to increase.

We can illustrate demand appreciation with our example property. Remember that we bought 333 Richmond Street for $220,000; we put down $30,000, and it brings in an annual income of $26,400. The investor purchasing this property is paying 8.33 times the gross income for the property ($220,000 ÷ $26,400 = 8.33)—see "The Gross Rent Multiplier" section in Chapter 4, "Appraising Like an Appraiser." Let's say the demand for the property increases. If so, and investors will now pay 9 times the gross income, the value would now be $237,600 ($26,400 × 9 = $237,600). Note that this is a $17,600 increase in the value of the property with no increase in rental income whatsoever ($237,600 − $220,000 = $17,600).

There is another way that demand can affect the value of your property. You see, investment real estate prices are directly related to the net income the property produces. An increased income stream should produce an increased value, even in a

---

 Bright Idea

Most local newspapers publish statistics about increases in property prices in the Consumer Price Index. Make sure you check these statistics often because they are a good indicator of appreciation.

Watch Out!

Each component of return can vary greatly by geographical area. One location might offer a high cash flow but a lower return from value appreciation. Another might offer good appreciation but minimal tax benefits. Furthermore, these components can vary not only from state to state but from neighborhood to neighborhood.

market where there is no increase in demand from investors. In this case, the demand would come from the tenants' willingness to pay more rent for your property. This usually happens because of an increased number of tenants in an area with a limited supply of places to rent.

Here's how an increased income affects the Richmond Street example. Let's say we raised the rents from $550 a unit to $600 a unit, and therefore increased the gross income from $26,400 to $28,800 a year. If investors were still willing to pay 8.33 times the annual income of the property, Richmond would now be worth $239,904 ($28,800 × 8.33 = $239,904). This is an increase in value of $19,904 ($239,904 – $220,000 = $19,904).

Now that you understand the impact of both inflation and demand, we will do a value appreciation illustration with the example property. Let's assume that the 333 Richmond Street fourplex appreciates at a total of 5 percent per year from all the components that affect value. This means an additional $11,000 in profit the first year from appreciation ($220,000 × .05 = $11,000). Remember, we put down $30,000 to purchase the property, so we can compute the appreciation return as follows:

$$\frac{\text{Appreciation} \quad \$11,000}{\text{Down payment} \quad \$30,000} = 36.6\% \text{ return}$$

As you can see, 333 Richmond Street earned a return of 36.6 percent the first year, due to value appreciation alone. Not too bad considering the appreciation rate used for this example was only a modest 5 percent.

Tax shelter benefits

The final return on your investment from real estate is tax shelter benefits. These are the paper losses you can deduct from the taxable income you receive from the property.

As the owner of an investment property, the IRS gives you an annual depreciation allowance to deduct against your income. The theory is that this deduction will be saved up and will be used to replace the structure at the end of its useful life. This is a necessary deduction in most businesses because equipment wears out quickly. Because most property owners rarely keep their buildings long enough for them to wear out, however, the tax savings from the deduction are a profit you can keep.

Determining depreciation via your tax bill

There are a couple of methods you can use to determine your annual depreciation allowance. The first is to use your property tax bill as your guide. This bill is broken down into two components:

1. The assessed value of the improvements (the structures on the land)
2. The total assessed value of the entire property

Don't be alarmed if the actual dollar amount shown on the tax bill does not agree with what you are paying for the property; it is the ratio we are looking for. You will use these numbers to get the percentage you need to determine the value of the improvements. To do this, use the following calculation:

$$\frac{\text{Assessed improvement value}}{\text{Total assessed value}} = \% \text{ value of improvements}$$

 Watch Out!

Be sure to do your homework on your depreciation. As your income increases, you will need the write-off.

The percentage you get from this calculation will be used to determine the amount of improvements as follows:

% value of improvements × price = depreciable improvements

The good news is that the IRS rarely challenges this method of determining depreciation because if they did, they would be challenging the county tax assessor (another government entity), which probably wouldn't bode too well. The bad news, however, is that the ratio from your tax bill is not always accurate. If this were the case, your deduction could be unfairly limited. Thankfully, the IRS also allows alternate methods of determining your depreciation allowance.

Determining depreciation via your appraisal

A second way to determine the percentage of depreciable improvements is to use the appraisal that was done when you purchased your property. In the section of the appraisal that covers the reproduction cost method, you should find the appraiser's opinion of value for both the land (the dirt) and the improvements (the structures). The appraiser will estimate the cost to build the improvements as of the date of the appraisal. This is called the *reproduction cost.* An allowance is then made for any depreciation, and the remainder is the appraiser's value of the improvements. Assuming the appraiser is licensed or otherwise qualified in your state, this should be a good estimate to use. Just use the same formula as follows:

$$\frac{\text{Estimated value of improvements}}{\text{Appraised value}} = \% \text{ value of improvements}$$

Like before, the percentage you get from this calculation will be used to determine the amount of depreciable improvements. To do this, use the same calculation:

% value of improvements × price = depreciable improvements

Note that the depreciation schedule you pick when you put your real estate investment "in service" stays with you until you

Moneysaver

When you get a loan from a lender, make sure you get a written copy of the appraisal. You will need it when it comes time to calculate your annual depreciation allowance.

have used up the entire write-off. Therefore, it pays to find an acceptable method that gives you the best deduction. Thankfully, you don't have to establish your depreciation schedule until you file your tax return. There is usually enough time, therefore, between the closing and the filing deadline for you to determine which method to use. Regardless, you should discuss all the alternatives at your disposal with your accountant or tax professional.

Modified Accelerated Cost Recovery System

The second step in determining your percentage return from tax benefits involves utilizing a tax-code change from 1986. At that time, the IRS established the Modified Accelerated Cost Recovery System (MACRS). This code established the recovery period, or useful life, of assets to be depreciated. Like much of the tax code, these periods usually bear no relationship to reality with regard to the useful life of an asset. In the case of improved property (land with structures on it), there are two classes and two recovery periods to know about:

Type of Property	Recovery Period (Useful Life)
Residential	27.5 years
Nonresidential	39 years

When using the MACRS method, remember that it does not matter what the true age of your property is. For residential, you use 27.5 years. For nonresidential, you use 39 years.

To arrive at the annual expense, you simply divide the value of the depreciable improvements by the recovery period, and this gives you the deduction as follows:

$$\frac{\text{Value of depreciable improvements}}{\text{Recovery period (useful life)}} = \text{Annual depreciation allowance}$$

Now let's take a look at the calculation using the Richmond Street example. Remember that this is a two-step process. First find the value of the improvements and then divide by the correct recovery period. In this example, we are paying $220,000 for the Richmond Street property and have decided to use the tax bill to do the calculation. The tax bill shows the land assessed at $20,000, the improvements assessed at $35,000, and the total assessed value of the property at $55,000. We then would calculate the depreciation allowance as follows:

$$\frac{\$35,000 \text{ (improvements)}}{\$55,000 \text{ (total assessed value)}} = 63.6\% \text{ improvements}$$

$$\$220,000 \text{ price} \times .63.6\% \text{ improvements} = \$139,920 \text{ depreciable improvements}$$

In order to make things simple, we'll round up the depreciable improvements to an even $140,000. Therefore, we can determine our annual depreciatioin allowance as follows:

$$\frac{\$140,000 \text{ (depreciable improvements)}}{27.5 \text{ (years)}} = \$5,090 \text{ annual depreciation allowance}$$

Now that we know how much of a depreciation allowance we can get, let's go back to our example to determine our overall

---

 Bright Idea

Many inexpensive software programs will allow you to keep accurate records and file your tax returns electronically. If you can use one of these systems, it could save you a lot of aggravation come tax time.

tax shelter savings. We will assume that you are an active investor and that you are in the 28 percent federal tax bracket. To calculate tax savings, we first need to shelter the taxable profit from our property. As you will recall, we have a taxable cash flow of $1,080 and a taxable equity growth from loan reduction of $300 per year. We calculate the carryover loss as follows:

Depreciation allowance	$5,090
Less cash flow	−$1,080
Less equity growth	−$300
Tax benefit	$3,710

The tax savings is calculated by multiplying the tax bracket by the shelter benefit as follows:

.28 × $3,710 = $1,039 tax savings

Many states have a state income tax. Their rules usually are similar to the federal rules when it comes to deductions and depreciation. If you live in a state with a tax, you will receive additional savings, and you can use this same formula to estimate them.

Calculating the return

Congratulations, you've made it this far through a tough, but critical chapter in your education. Now, let's look at our total first year return on our investment combining all four elements of return. To recap, we have a cash flow of $1,080, equity growth from loan reduction of $300, equity growth from appreciation of $11,000, and tax savings benefits of $1,039. Our total tax-deferred return on investment is

Cash flow return	$1,080
Equity growth (loan reduction)	$300
Equity growth (appreciation)	$11,000
Tax savings	+$1,039
Total return on investment	$13,419

We can then compute the total percentage return on the investment by dividing the first year return by the down payment as follows:

$$\frac{\text{Total return: } \$13,419}{\text{Down payment: } \$30,000} = 44.7\% \text{ return}$$

At 44.7 percent for the first year, we're off to a pretty good start with the Richmond Street fourplex. A good growth-oriented strategy might be to keep the building running well until our return drops below, say, 20 or 25 percent. At that time, we could refinance and start earning a higher percentage return again. Or, if the building was giving us problems for one reason or another, we could sell and trade up via an IRS 1031 exchange (see Chapter 10, "Planning for the Tax Man").

Use the accompanying Property Analysis Work Sheet to calculate the components of return on any property you are considering. All you need is a forefinger and a calculator. If math gives you a headache, though, there are many computer-generated systems for calculating return that will be just as easy. One example is Turbo Tax, which does a great job with depreciation. Some are proprietary systems written by the firms that own them, and many are just modified spreadsheet systems. If you have access to one of these systems, it will save time, but having an automated system is not necessary.

PROPERTY ANALYSIS WORK SHEET

Address: _____

_____

1. Value of Property _____

2. Loans on Property _____

3. Equity in Property _____

4. Gross Income _____ Mo. × 12 = _____

5. Expenses _____ Mo. × 12 = _____

6. Loan Payments _____ Mo. × 12 = _____

7. Interest (_____ Loan Amt. × _____ %)= _____

8. Loan Payoff (Line 6 − Line 7) = _____

9. Cash Flow (Line 4 − Line 5 − Line 6) = _____

10. Depreciation Deduction _____

11. Tax Shelter (Line 10 − Line 9 − Line 8) = _____

12. Tax Savings (Tax Bracket _____% × Line 11) = _____

13. Building Profit (Line 8 + Line 9 + Line 12) = _____

14. Basic Return (Line 13 ÷ Line 3) = _____ %

RETURN ON EQUITY

15. Cash Flow (Line 9) _____

16. Loan Payoff (Line 8) = _____

17. Tax Savings (Line 12) = _____

18. Appreciation _____% × Line 1 _____

19. Total Investment (Lines 15 + 16 + 17 + 18) _____

20. Return on Equity (Line 19 ÷ Line 3) = _____ %

Just the facts

- Cash flow is calculated by deducting the mortgage payments and other operating expenses from the rent you collect.

- A key element of return is the reduction in your loan balance paid from rental income.

- Your property might increase in value just because of the effect of inflation.

- An increase in demand from investors to buy properties in your area can increase the value of your building.

- The Modified Accelerated Cost Recovery System allows you to write-off a residential property in 27.5 years and a nonresidential property in 39 years.

Appraising Like an Appraiser

Chapter 4

F or people just getting started in investing, picking that first property can be a nerve-racking experience. Of course, the goal is to make your decision based purely on financial parameters, but that becomes pretty hard to do, especially on the first purchase. Usually, your emotions will kick into gear and try to dictate what you should buy. Many first-time investors indignantly declare, "I'm not going to buy anything that I wouldn't live in myself." If you recognize yourself in this statement, however, know that your emotions have taken over and you're on the verge of investing with your heart rather than your head. What's worse is that you may be leaving some good opportunities behind for the next guy to discover.

Don't fret; it's easy to figure out why emotions come into play—you're scared of losing your money. In fact, fear of losing money is as much a motivator (if not radically more so) as is the promise of gain from investing it. To illustrate, let's say you were invited to a meeting at 10 p.m. tonight to learn about an opportunity that could make you $1,000 on a $10,000 investment. After a bit of thought, you might decide to spend that hour watching TV instead. If you got a call, though, and were told you would lose $1,000 if you didn't go to that 10 p.m. meeting, what do you think you'd do? Exactly.

There is no shame in being a little scared. Buying a piece of property is a big deal. In fact, the purchase of an investment property will probably be the largest dollar investment you make in your lifetime. For this reason alone, you have a right to be nervous. But it doesn't have to be that way.

When investing in anything, there are concrete steps you can take to minimize risk. The first, and most prudent way to quiet your mind, is to thoroughly educate yourself about the commodity in which you are investing. In this chapter, your education continues with a lesson on appraising value. Here we will teach you how to appraise like an appraiser. The goal is to make you completely self-sufficient when it comes to valuing real estate. In fact, the fear of ever paying too much for a property should soon become a nonissue.

Methods of valuing property

From an investment standpoint, the two most important aspects of property are its value as an asset and its return on your invested capital. Your goal is to invest your money and obtain an annual return on that invested capital until you sell or otherwise dispose of the property. Naturally, at the time of sale, you will

Moneysaver

If you are in the market for a property with an investment of $30,000 down, don't consider buying that "great deal" you just found that requires $50,000 down. Even if you have the money, stick to your game plan and you will sleep better at night.

expect to recover your original investment as well as some equity growth and appreciation. Learning how to buy at "fair market value" will ensure that you will be able to recover your original investment along with the other profit you expect.

Unfortunately, unlike buying a used car, there is no Blue Book for establishing the value of used property. In addition, individual properties always have unique components that can affect their value. The question then becomes, how do you as an investor determine what is fair market value for a used piece of real estate? It's tricky, but doable. Let's begin by looking at the definition of fair market value itself:

Fair market value: The price a willing buyer will pay a willing seller for a property that has been on the market for a reasonable period of time.

As you can see, there are a number of variables to this equation, two of which are completely subjective in that they have to do with the motivation level of the buyer and the seller. The truth is that it is nearly impossible for you or even a professional appraiser to look at the information on a closed escrow and know the motivation of the principal parties. At best, you can get a feeling for the market from looking at the trends you see from comparable sales that have recently closed.

Like many things in life, appraising can be described as more of an art than a science. Nonetheless, whether you are a professional appraiser or a novice real estate investor, there are a number of acceptable appraisal techniques that you can learn for establishing value estimates. The three commonly accepted appraisal methods are

1. Comparative market analysis

2. Reproduction cost approach

3. Capitalization of income approach

Let's review each of these appraisal techniques one at a time and see if we can get our arms around this subject.

Bright Idea

Your real estate agent is a great source of information about the seller. Pick her brain to find out the seller's motivation for selling. Once you know what it is, you might just be able to offer exactly what the seller is looking for.

Comparative market analysis approach

Comparative market analysis is the easiest method for the average investor to use when estimating value. In essence, it is the same technique most of us use when making any big purchase. Simply put, before you make a deal on, say, a car or some new furniture, you should check with several other vendors to get an idea of what they each are charging for the same item. The same premise holds true here. When doing a comparative market analysis for real estate, you need to compare and contrast the major features that affect the value of property between the subject building and some comparables. The major features to consider are

- Price of the most recent sale
- Date of the most recent sale
- Square footage of living area
- Number of units
- Mix of bedrooms and bathrooms in each unit
- Lot size
- Age of building
- Income-producing capability (current rents vs. market rents)
- Overall condition of building and lot
- Expense factors (master-metered utilities vs. tenant pays)
- Parking (garages vs. carport, or none)
- Extras (views, fireplaces, multiple baths, patios, or decks)
- Proximity to subject property

Watch Out!

Comparative analysis can be tricky in areas such as beachfront communities, resorts, or high population areas. In these areas, the properties are not usually "like properties." This will throw off sales prices and make the accuracy of your analysis suspect.

The goal is to find recent sales in the same, or a similar, neighborhood in which these features are as close to being the same as possible. Because time has an effect on value, the sales should be within the last six months or so, with the greatest weight given to the most current sales. This method of appraisal is not difficult and, with a little practice, can be used by anyone.

We will show you an illustration of the comparative analysis method using our example property at 333 Richmond Street. Remember that this property is a 20-year-old, four-unit apartment building. It is on a 50 × 150 lot. The units are unfurnished and in good condition with new carpets and drapes. They all have built-in appliances and even have fireplaces. The neighborhood is good in terms of the condition of all the surrounding properties and their maintenance. The current owner is asking $225,000 for this property. After checking with local brokers and appraisers, you have been able to locate three sales that appear to be comparable to this property.

- **Property A:** This property is identical with respect to the building and looks like it might even have been built by the same contractor. However, it is on a larger lot, 75 × 150, with nicer landscaping. This property sold two months ago for $270,000.

- **Property B:** This property does not have the same floor plan, but it is the same age, size, and condition as your property. The units lack fireplaces, and they have open parking instead of garages. This building closed escrow three months ago for $200,000.

- **Property C:** This property is another just like yours in every way except it sold a year ago for $215,000. We shouldn't use this sale because it was so long ago, but it is the only other comparable property we can find.

See the chart on the next page for a recap of the facts we have on the properties.

There are enough variations that we will have to make some adjustments to come up with an estimate of value. This is when the comparative market analysis method becomes a bit more difficult to use, especially for the first-time investor. The adjustments take the experience of watching enough sales in the market area to be able to estimate the financial impact of the differences. Have heart, though; with a little practice, you will be able to do it, too.

For the purposes of comparing the subject property at 333 Richmond Street to Property A, an adjustment will have to be made in the price of Property A because it is on a much larger lot. To do the adjustment, the value of lots in the area needs to be determined. This can be achieved by contacting local builders and real estate professionals, and asking how much lots are selling for in the area. For our example, we will assume that we did that kind of investigation and discovered that 50×150 foot lots zoned for apartment buildings sell for approximately $100,000. The lot on which Property A sits is 1½ times larger than the lot the Richmond Street building is on. Therefore, it would have a value of 1½ times the value of the Richmond lot, or $150,000 ($100,000 × 1½ = $150,000). From this, we can conclude that Property A is worth $50,000 more than the Richmond property because of the additional land. For the purposes of estimating the value of the subject property on 333 Richmond Street, we will decrease the value of Property A by $50,000.

Item	Subject Property: 333 Richmond Street	Prop A	Prop B	Prop C
Price	$225,000	$270,000	$200,000	$215,000
Footage	Same	Same	Same	Same
Condition	Same	Same	Same	Same
Location	Same	Same	Same	Same
Lot Size	50 × 150	75 × 150	50 × 150	50 × 150
Features	Fireplace	Fireplace	None	Fireplace
Garages	4	4	None	4
Sale Date	Unsold	3 Months	2 Months	1 Year

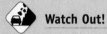

Watch Out!

Investors should not blindly trust any appraisal offered by the seller as justification of value. Although such an appraisal might be accurate, smart investors should do their own homework as well.

Property B also needs to be adjusted because, unlike 333 Richmond Street, Property B doesn't have fireplaces or garages. These items can be estimated by researching the cost of these components with local builders. For our example, we have determined that the cost of installing a fireplace is $1,000. This makes the loss in value of our four missing fireplaces $4,000 ($1,000 × 4 = $4,000). We have also determined that the cost of building a garage in this area is $30 per square foot. The four missing garages would have been 600 square feet, so the total cost to build them would be $18,000 ($30 × 600 = $18,000). To compare the sale price of Property B to the subject property on Richmond Street, we would have to add the value of the missing items, or $22,000 ($4,000 for fireplaces + $18,000 for garages = $22,000).

The adjustment to Property C is tougher because a year has gone by since it sold. Appraisers do not like to use comparables that are this old because so many things can happen in that time span to affect the value of property. Because we cannot find another sale, however, we will use this one. To be able to use it, we need to know how much property has appreciated in the last year. For our example, we have determined the appreciation rate over the last year to be 5 percent. This means that Property C would have increased $10,750 over the last year ($215,000 × .05 = $10,750). To do our comparison, we would have to add the $10,750 to the sale price of Property C.

Let's do a recap of the adjustments:

Item	333 Richmond Street	Prop A	Prop B	Prop C
Price	$225,000	$270,000	$200,000	$215,000
Adjust	0	$–50,000	+$22,000	+$10,750
Value	?	$220,000	$222,000	$225,750

The last step in doing a comparative market analysis is to make an estimate of value for the subject property. This will be based on the adjusted prices of the comparables. Appraisers usually take an average value of the comps. Therefore, if we averaged the three values of those properties, the indicated value is $222,583 ($220,000 + 222,000 + 225,750 ÷ 3 = $222,583). Rounded off it would be $222,500.

Because of its relative ease, comparative market analysis is the appraisal technique of choice for many investors. But it isn't the only method of determining value. Let's move on and learn how to do the reproduction cost approach.

Reproduction cost approach

The reproduction cost approach to appraising is the "what would it cost to build it today?" method. Basically, you establish value by pretending to buy a lot at today's value and then constructing a "used" building to match the existing building. This method requires a good knowledge of the market for land and an even better knowledge of construction and the current costs of building. Because we can't build a "used" building, we then need to depreciate it based on the fact that it is not new. This requires significant skill and experience. Nonetheless, let's give it a try.

The first step is to determine the value of the lot. To do this, you need to contact brokers and builders in the area to find out what they are paying for similar lots. If there aren't enough lots of the exact size of the subject property, some adjustments will have to be made. You would then use the same comparative analysis method we just used. It would be easier to do, however, because you would only be making an adjustment based on the price per square foot differences.

Next you will take a survey of the building to determine the square footage of the living areas and the square footage of the garages and other utility areas. These footage costs are based on the type of construction, the size of the building, the quality of construction, and the part of the country in which the property is located. Builders or bankers might be able to give you a general idea of the cost for your local area.

For the purpose of our example, we will assume that the cost to build a standard wood frame and stucco two-story building is $60 per square foot and that the cost to build the garages is $30 per square foot. Now let's return to our example on Richmond Street and estimate the value using the reproduction cost method.

The first item to value will be the land. In our example, our lot is 50 × 150, or 7,500 square feet. We previously determined in the comparative analysis method that the land is worth $100,000. This works out to $13.33 per square foot ($100,000 ÷ 7,500 = $13.33).

Now we need to determine the value of the structures on the property and all the other amenities such as landscaping, walkways, and driveways. Each of the four units in our example building is 800 square feet and includes two bedrooms, one

 Bright Idea

Building cost tables should be available at your library. These tables provide the current cost per square foot for building the living areas, the garages, and all the other components you might find in a property.

bathroom, a kitchen, and a living room. There are four garages of approximately 150 square feet each. This gives us a living area of 3,200 square feet (800 × 4 = 3,200) and a garage area of 600 square feet (150 × 4 = 600). In addition, we have determined that the other amenities (driveway, landscaping, etc.) would cost approximately $15,000. The following chart shows the total cost to build our building in today's market:

Item	Square Feet	Cost	Total
Building	3,200	$60 sq. ft.	$192,000
Garages	600	$30 sq. ft.	$18,000
Amenities	N/A	N/A	$15,000
Total			$225,000

We have a problem, though. The building and the garage are not brand new; they were built 20 years ago. Our task is to determine the amount of value that has been used up, or depreciated. For this example, we will use a method based on the estimated useful life of a property. For apartment buildings of average quality with wood frame and stucco construction, a useful life of 40 years is commonly accepted.

The Richmond Street property is already 20 years old, so using a 40-year useful life, we see that this building has lost half its useful life and, therefore, half the value of these improvements. Because the new value of the building is $210,000 ($192,000 building + $18,000 garages = $210,000), the remaining value of these improvements is $105,000 ($210,000 ÷ 2 = $105,000) given that the property has lost half its useful life. An appraiser would call this the depreciated value of the improvements. Note that we did not take depreciation into account on the amenities because they are usually items that do not depreciate.

Watch Out!

One drawback to the cost approach is that builders' costs can vary greatly depending on the number of units produced and the individual builder's profit margin. You might have to make market comparisons of builders' costs in the same way that sellers' prices are compared.

We can now finish our estimate of value using the reproduction cost method as follows:

Cost of lot	$100,000
Cost of amenities	$20,000
Depreciated value of buildings	+$105,000
Total	$225,000

Capitalization of income approach

A third accepted method of appraising value is called the capitalization of income approach. This technique sets value based on the building's profitability. This is the "what would I make on my money if I paid all cash?" appraisal method. This is probably the most difficult of the methods to use properly, but it is the preferred method when valuing income property.

The concept of a capitalization rate is well known to most of us but under a pseudonym. We recognize capitalization rates as interest rates. When you think of putting your money in a bank, the first question you ask is, "What interest rate will I get?" In truth, what you are asking for is the capitalization rate on that bank account.

Before we move on to understanding the capitalization rate in real estate, let's look at the formula for calculating the interest rate from a simple savings account and then expand it to the form we need to use for real estate appraising. Let's assume you have $10,000 in your savings account, and at the end of the year, you earned $500 in interest. The following formula will show your profit percentage:

$$\frac{\text{Interest earned}}{\text{Amount invested}} = \text{Percentage profit}$$

Or:

$$\frac{\$500}{\$10,000} = 5\%$$

Translated to the language of appraising, this becomes

$$\frac{\text{Net income}}{\text{Price}} = \text{Capitalization rate}$$

When dealing with real estate and other investments that have various expenses associated with their operation, we need to expand the equation to the following:

$$\frac{\text{Gross income} - \text{Operating expenses}}{\text{Capitalization rate}} = \text{Price}$$

Simplified, this becomes

$$\frac{\text{Net income}}{\text{Capitalization rate}} = \text{Price}$$

Keep in mind that when appraising property we are not trying to find out the profit; we are trying to estimate its value. In the case of investment property, what better way to estimate the value than by using its ability to produce a profit as a guideline? This ability to produce a profit is expressed as the interest rate you earn on your investment. Once we know the interest rate we should be getting on our money when we buy a property, we can use it to project a value.

Therefore, to estimate the value of a property using this method, you need to know a few things, including

1. The gross scheduled income

2. The operating expenses

3. The capitalization rate investors expect in the area where the property is located

Watch Out!

A higher cap rate means you can make a greater return on your money. But, be careful, properties like these usually require more intensive management than ones with a lower cap rate. It's an okay trade-off if you are up to the job; just be aware of what you are getting yourself into before you do it.

We will review each of these items as well as some of the things for which you need to watch out.

The gross scheduled income

The gross scheduled income (GSI) is the total amount of rental income collected in the year plus any other income such as laundry income or garage rentals. One problem that arises here is how to handle the income from a building in which the current owner has under-rented some or all of the units. This is very common with smaller units because most absentee investors seem to get happy with a certain level of profit and then don't want to rock the boat by changing things.

This problem is a common source of debate between appraisers, bankers, and investors that we won't attempt to solve here. In practice, appraisers will sometimes make an allowance for market rents, bankers won't use the market rents when calculating their loan amounts, and investors look for under-rented properties with lower sales prices.

The operating expenses

The next component you need to know is the annual expenses on the property including property taxes, insurance, utilities, gardening, management fees, repair cost, vacancies, and so on. You do not include interest expense because the capitalization of income approach presupposes that you paid all cash. We are sure you can appreciate the difficulty in getting a clear picture of what a potential property's true expenses might be. One owner might do all the management and maintenance himself; another might hire a management company that subcontracts all the work to the most expensive contractors in the area. One owner has low rents and has not had a tenant move in five years; the owner next door is charging market rents and has had some tenants move out. The units have higher rents, but the owner lost some revenue and has had all the fix-up expenses of getting the unit ready to rent.

What this dictates for appraisers is a method of estimating expenses based on the type of property being appraised and the area of the country in which it is located. Take the following two examples, for instance:

- A small four-unit building with no amenities will have far less expense as a percentage of the income than a large, full-security building with swimming pools, tennis courts, elevators, and extensive landscaping.

- The cost of heating a building in Southern California will be far less than the cost of heating a building in Minnesota.

You see, factors like these translate into higher operating costs and higher repair costs when the units break down. To attempt to equalize these differences, appraisers use tables of expenses based on a percentage of the gross. The following chart is typical for property in Southern California. Remember, expenses will vary by area, so make sure you check with your local experts.

 Bright Idea

Many lenders have several approved appraisers at their disposal. When it comes to appraising your purchase, encourage your lender to chose the appraiser with the most experience appraising income property. That way, you can ensure that you'll get the most accurate result.

Number of Units	Expenses
2–4	20%–25%
5–15	25%–35%
16 and up	30%–45%

The range gives appraisers a way to make an allowance for variations in the expenses associated with operating the building and the amenities it has.

The capitalization rate

The last item necessary for this appraisal technique is the capitalization rate based on what kind of return investors expect to get in that market area. This rate not only will vary in different parts of the country, but it also can vary in different parts of a city, even in buildings within a few blocks of each other.

In addition, different kinds of properties (residential, commercial, and industrial) will have a different expected cap rate, even in the same location. Remember, the capitalization rate is the measure of the profitability of an investment. Different types of properties have different risks and, therefore, a different expectation of profit for taking that risk.

Now let's return to the example at 333 Richmond Street and see how this method is used. We determined that the total rental income for the property is $26,400 ($550 per unit × 4 units × 12 months). A rental survey of the area shows that this rent is in line with the market. The expenses are reported at $7,920 for the year. This is 30 percent of the gross income

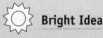

Bright Idea

You probably can obtain the cap rate you need to use from a local investment real estate agent or appraiser. Be sure to ask the person to show you how he or she arrived at the rate provided. It is important that this figure be accurate because most investors give considerable weight to this method of estimating value.

($7,920 ÷ $26,400 = .3). We contacted several local appraisers, and they told us that the expected capitalization rate was 8.4 percent. Remember that a capitalization rate can be expressed as a percentage (8.4 percent) or as a decimal (.084). Be sure to clarify this when someone tells you the rate. If the person gives you the rate as a percentage, you will need to convert it to a decimal before you do your calculation.

Putting this all together, we would calculate the value estimate with the following steps. The first step is to determine the net income:

Gross annual income	$26,400
Less operating expenses	−$7,920
Net income	$18,480

The formula to find value is

$$\frac{\text{Net income}}{\text{Capitalization rate}} = \text{Price}$$

To complete our calculation, substitute the following information into the equation:

$$\frac{\$18,480}{.084} = \$220,000$$

A summary of value

The question you might be asking now is, "Which method of appraisal should we rely on to determine the value for our four-unit example on Richmond Street?" You will learn that in the real world of appraising, it is not always practical or prudent to rely equally on the values obtained using each method. Depending on the type of property being appraised, one of the methods usually gets the most weight in the final value. With single-family homes, for example, the comparative method works best because in most areas there seem to be plenty of similar houses. For that reason, it is easy to find enough current sales to come up with an estimate of value.

On the other hand, the reproduction cost method carries the most weight for specialized properties and for new construction. For a special property such as a church building, this method constitutes the only practical way to estimate a value. This method also works fine for new construction because the land probably was just purchased, and the cost of the structure is easy to determine because there is no depreciation to estimate.

Finally, for all types of investment property, the capitalization of income method carries the greatest weight. You should use the reproduction cost method and the comparative analysis method to check the value arrived at by capitalizing the net income.

In this instance, we will do what many appraisers do, and take an average of the three methods previously illustrated to determine the value of the fourplex at 333 Richmond Street, as follows:

Comparative analysis value	$222,500
Reproduction cost value	$225,000
Capitalization value	+$220,000
Total	$667,500

$$\frac{\$667,500}{3} = \$222,500 \text{ average value}$$

With a value of $222,500, we can see that the list price of $225,000 was right on the mark.

The gross rent multiplier

Now that you are aware of the three classic methods of appraising real estate, here's another way to value property. Real estate isn't much different from any other industry where people "in the business" have developed a quick and easy way to get things done when time is of the essence. In real estate we use a number called the gross rent multiplier to value property when this is the case. This is similar to the use of the PE, or price earnings ratio, in valuing stocks. It presupposes that there is a number, the gross rent multiplier, that you can multiply by the gross income of a property to estimate its value.

Let's look at our example to see how to arrive at the gross rent multiplier:

$$\frac{\text{Price of property}}{\text{Gross income}} = \text{Gross rent multiplier}$$

For our example on Richmond Street, the calculation is:

$$\frac{\$220,000}{\$26,400} = 8.33 \times \text{gross}$$

For estimating value, the equation is changed as follows:

Gross income × Gross rent multiplier = Value of the property

The following chart shows the effect of several gross rent multipliers on the value of our example:

Gross Income	Gross Rent Multiplier	Value of Property
$26,400	× 8.0	= $211,200
$26,400	× 8.5	= $224,400
$26,400	× 9.0	= $237,600

As you can see, it's easy to see how a small difference in the gross rent multiplier can make a big difference in the value of a property.

Although helpful in a pinch, or when you are first comparing properties, there are times when a gross rent multiplier analysis will fail to tell you anything valuable at all. Inaccuracies in a gross rent multiplier analysis are usually due to one of three factors:

1. **The owner of the property has kept the rents well below market value.** In such an instance, the gross rent multiplier will not be an accurate appraisal technique.

2. **The property's expenses are too high.** The gross rent multiplier does not take into account the expenses of the property. Some properties have far higher expenses than others, which would affect the net income to the owner. The most typical reason for high expenses is that the utilities are paid for by the owner rather than the tenants. If you were to pay the same price for a master-metered building with high expenses as for one with normal expenses where the tenants pay their utilities, you would end up with a substandard return.

> 66 For me, the gross rent multiplier is the quickest and easiest way to value property. I've always been bad at math and numbers, but even I was able to learn how to use this simple method of appraisal. 99
>
> —Sandra B., Investor

3. **The property consists of furnished units or units that have all the utilities included in the rent.** These kinds of units usually rent for substantially more than unfurnished rentals. If you were to apply the same gross rent multiplier to this type of property, you would be paying a premium for the right to pay someone else's utilities or to own used furniture.

It is important to remember that the gross rent multiplier is a rule of thumb that should be used only when you fully understand all the financial details of the area in which you are looking and the property you are considering. It does, however, provide a quick way to rank properties when you are first looking around. You then can review the income and expense figures and determine which property will give you the better net return on your investment.

Finding hidden value

When an appraisal is ordered on a piece of property, the person making the appraisal will want to know the purpose for the appraisal. For instance, the valuation for a loan will be different than the valuation to settle an estate. Likewise, the valuation of a lot with a home might be less than the valuation of the lot alone if it had the potential to build something more valuable on it such as an apartment building. These variations point to the importance of understanding appraising as a tool for finding hidden value in property.

Knowledge of appraisal methods can be very helpful when it comes time to negotiate the purchase of a property. Most sellers list their property at the price they want, which may or may not be related to its true value when compared to current sales. If you present your offer at a lower price without facts to back it up, the seller might take it personally and dig in his heels when considering your lower offer. If you come in with an offer based on recognized appraisal techniques, however, you have a much better chance of obtaining the property at the lower price.

Let's make a small change in our example on Richmond Street and see how lower-than-market rents will affect its value. Instead of an annual income of $26,400, which is $550 per month per unit, let's assume the owner has not kept the rents up to market. In this example, we'll say the rents are $495, $510, $500, and $525, for a monthly total of $2,030. Multiplying $2,030 by 12 months gives us an income of $24,360. Remember, our

---

 Moneysaver

By fully understanding the techniques of appraising, you can learn to use the appraisal as a tool to drive down the price you pay. At the same time, you can use it as a tool to dig up some hidden profit.

annual expenses are $7,920, and the capitalization rate we are using is 8.4 percent. In preparing our offer, we include an attachment with the comparable sales information and an estimate of value based on the capitalization of income method. The valuation now looks like this:

Gross annual income	$24,360
Less operating expenses	−$7,920
Net income	$16,440

Remember, once you have the net income, the formula to estimate value is

$$\frac{\text{Net income}}{\text{Capitalization rate}} = \text{Price}$$

Or, substituting in our values, we get

$$\frac{\$16,440}{.084} = \$195,714 \text{ offered price}$$

Our estimate using the three classic appraisal methods indicated a value of $222,500, so anything you can save below that price will be an extra profit for you. Of course, there is no guarantee the seller will take the lower offer, but if your agent presents a convincing story about your desire to purchase at a fair price based on your diligent analytical work, you might very well prevail.

Now let's use an appraisal to find some additional hidden profit based on potential rent. You have done all your research on the market area and have found that the market rent for these units is $575 per month and that garages add a premium of $15 per month. This gives the building the potential gross of $28,320. The value estimate now is

Gross annual income	$28,320
Less operating expenses	−$7,920
Net income	$20,400

Let's work the valuation formula again:

$$\frac{\text{Net income}}{\text{Capitalization rate}} = \text{Price}$$

Or, substituting in our values, we get

$$\frac{\$20,400}{.084} = \$242,857$$

With this information in your possession, you could even pay the full asking price of $222,500 and still have found some hidden profit because of your knowledge of the market. It will take some effort and time to get the rents up to market, but once you do, the profit is there for the picking.

Highest and best use

An important concept to understand in real estate is "highest and best use." Have you ever driven through a commercial area with office buildings and retail stores only to see an old single-family home that looks like someone still lives there? If that home comes up for sale, should it be appraised as a single-family residence or as a commercial lot? The answer is probably as a commercial lot because this is now the "highest and best use" of the property.

Understanding that developed property can have more than one use often will yield a hidden profit. The following are some situations that would warrant valuing a property for its highest and best use rather than its current use:

- A house or small units is on a commercial or industrial lot.
- A house or small units is on a large lot zoned for multi-units in an area with many new buildings.
- A parcel map of the property shows that the building sits on two separate lots.
- A four-unit property consists of two side-by-side duplexes on two separate lots according to the parcel map.

- The apartments in the building currently have one bedroom, but the bedroom is very large and could be made into two simply by adding one wall and a door for much greater rent.

- A small house is on a multi-unit zoned parcel where extra units can be added.

- A vacant commercial building can be converted to loft apartments or live/work lofts.

In all of these cases, the property can be valued in more than one way. The highest and best use for the property might not be its current use. Remember, property not being utilized at its highest and best use will have less value than other, comparable properties based on this standard. The highest and best use might not always be obvious, as in the case of the building that sits on two lots. In that case, the land value of the two lots might be significantly higher than the value of the building alone.

The lesson here is that real estate is a multidimensional asset. If you fail to look at all its facets, you might fail to realize the full potential of your investment. Finding the hidden value in a property does not mean you have to immediately realize it by making a sale. This hidden profit should give you extra confidence in the security of your investment.

In addition, you now have two chances to make more profit in the future. In the example of the building on two lots, the building and its income stream probably will be worth more as the market increases. In addition, the land will be worth more for development purposes, and that value might increase faster than the building value.

Just the facts

- Knowing the fair market value of any property under consideration will help to ensure your success as a real estate investor.

- Comparative analysis is an easy and effective method of appraisal that even the most novice investor can do.

- The reproduction cost approach is the most difficult method for the nonprofessional to use when trying to estimate value.

- Capitalization rates tell you how much you will make on your investment if you paid all cash for it.

- The gross rent multiplier is just a rule of thumb, but it will give you a great head start on your analysis.

GET THE SCOOP ON...
Great government lending programs to help you
get started ▪ The qualifying criteria used by conventional lenders ▪ The facts behind fixed- and
adjustable-rate loans ▪ Why the "neg-am"
adjustable could be your ticket to wealth ▪
Finding and negotiating private-party loans

Borrowing Big Bucks

For the Average Joe or Jane, plunking down all cash for a piece of property is simply beyond what is reasonably possible. Besides the whopping negative number it would create in most of our checkbooks, it would actually defeat the best part of real estate investing. That is, it would eliminate leverage from the equation. As a result, to buy real estate we must find outside sources willing to finance our investments.

In theory, this sounds great. But, of course, finding someone to loan you hundreds of thousands of dollars probably sounds like an overwhelming prospect. In fact, you probably have some burning questions that need answers: "Can you qualify?," "How much will you have to borrow?," "Where will you find a lender?," "Should you go with a fixed or variable rate?," and so on. But fear not; in this chapter we'll break down all the intricacies of borrowing big bucks. Here, we will explain how real estate is

Chapter 5

financed, tell you about the three major sources of money, and give you inside tips on how to make sure the loan you find is all it's cracked up to be.

Show me the money

As you start shopping for a loan, you'll find that the costs of borrowing money vary widely. Conventional lenders might charge for one thing while the federal government or private parties might charge for others. You'll discover that the two greatest factors affecting your borrowing costs will be first, who makes the loan, and second, what type of loan it is. The following table covers most of the more common fees that different lenders charge:

	Government Loans	Conventional Loans	Private Loans
Good-faith deposit	X	X	
Loan fee—points	X	X	
Appraisal fee	X	X	
Credit report	X	X	X
Tax service	X	X	
Document recording fee	X	X	
Loan processing		X	X
Drawing documents	X	X	
Funding fee	X		
Prepaid interest	X	X	
Mortgage insurance	X	X	
UCC filing	X	X	X
Flood certification	X	X	

	Government Loans	Conventional Loans	Private Loans
Loan escrow	X	X	X
Alta title insurance	X	X	
Setup fee	X	X	
Warehouse fee	X	X	

Thankfully, the government has taken all of the guesswork out of determining which fees apply when borrowing money for real estate. The governing federal law is the Real Estate Settlement Procedures Act (RESPA). RESPA requires that all lenders, except private parties, give the borrower an estimate of all their lending fees.

Along with the RESPA estimate, the lender must also disclose the annual percentage rate (APR) on your loan. The APR will take into account all the fees paid on the loan up front to give you a true picture of the annual interest rate you will be paying

The biggest expense of your loan is the loan fee, or "points." Each point represents 1 percent of the loan amount. For example, one point on a $150,000 loan would be $1,500 ($150,000 × .01 = $1,500). This large cash expense is a sore point for most investors. But like anyone who is in business, lenders are there to make a profit; and in the case of lending money, charging the borrower points up front is one of the ways in which they do it.

You will sometimes see advertisements for no-point and no-fee loans. Obtaining a loan like this can be an okay trade-off if

 Moneysaver

Don't hesitate to negotiate on points and other lending fees with your chosen lender. They are never set in stone.

Moneysaver

Depending on market conditions, some lenders offer incentives for borrowers to pay points up front. If you plan on owning your property for a long time, paying some points to obtain a loan will probably pencil out better in the long run. Conversely, if you'll be flipping the property soon, low or no-point loans might make better sense.

you need that kind of help to buy, but be keenly aware that the lender will certainly make his money somewhere along the line. We caution you here because the truth is that the only way any institution can give away loans for "free" is by charging you a higher-than-par interest rate. A "par" rate, in lending terms, is the best rate on any given day charging normal closing fees and points.

Keep in mind that you only have to pay for points and loan fees once, but if you get help paying your points on the front-end you will be stuck paying the higher interest rate for the entire life of the loan. The trade-off is yours to analyze.

Locating a lender

When it comes to financing smaller residential real estate, there are three primary sources to find money. They are

1. The federal government
2. Local savings and loans and banks
3. Private parties

Let's see what the federal government offers first.

The Federal Housing Administration (FHA)

The best source for government-supported financing for anything up to four units is through the Federal Housing Administration (FHA). The FHA doesn't actually provide the funds for the mortgages; rather, it insures home mortgage loans made by private industry lenders such as mortgage bankers, savings and loans, and banks. This insurance is necessary because

FHA loans are made with low down payments and have favorable interest rates and terms compared to the conventional lending market.

FHA loans are designed for people just starting out. To that end, they offer the investor fantastic leverage with a minimum requirement of just 3 percent down, while the remaining 97 percent is financed by a lender. As you can see, by just having to come up with 3 percent, most anyone could afford to purchase a small set of owner-occupied units via an FHA loan and be well on the way to achieving their goals in real estate.

The following chart shows the maximum loan amounts available for FHA loans in three areas of Southern California at the time of publication. Make sure you check with your mortgage broker in order to determine the maximum allowable limits in your area.

Number of Units	Orange County	Los Angeles	San Diego
1	$261,609	$237,500	$261,609
2	$334,863	$267,500	$334,054
3	$404,724	$325,000	$404,724
4	$502,990	$379,842	$468,300

Be aware that one stringent requirement of obtaining FHA financing is that the borrower must live in the property as his or her primary residence, usually for a minimum of one year. Therefore, it's essential that you do actually move into your units, at least initially. It's not unheard of for lenders to follow up on their borrowers, and it would be a disaster to have them call your loan due because they discovered you never actually moved into your property, as promised.

If you do opt for an owner-occupied, 3-percent-down FHA loan, the good news is that the two- to four-unit market usually has the largest selection of properties available. This gives you a great probability of finding a property with a unit that will make

Moneysaver

FHA deals are great for the beginning investor. Because you will be living in the property, you can roll up your sleeves and make upgrades that no doubt will improve its value. When it comes time to sell or refinance, you will have created some sweat equity for yourself.

a nice home for you and your family and a nice rental for some tenants. Of course, the American dream is to own your own home. If you can be patient, however, consider having your first purchase be a set of FHA units. By tapping into your equity in just a few years, you can move up to a single-family residence and can own a nice piece of income property to boot.

Another advantage of the FHA program is that it uses FHA-approved appraisers to value the properties. During the appraisal process, an additional goal of the appraiser will be to make sure there are no major problems with the building and that all the basic safety measures have been met. If a property fails to meet these FHA standard guidelines, the seller must either comply with the appraiser's request to fix the problems, or, in essence, lose the deal. Nine times out of ten, sellers comply. By the time you move in, all major repair work will have been fixed and your purchase will sparkle like new.

VA loans

At the end of World War II, congress approved the Serviceman's Readjustment Act of 1944. The common term for this program is the GI Bill of Rights. The purpose of the Act was to give war veterans a new start and to ease their expenses in civilian life by providing them with medical benefits, bonuses, and—best of all—low-interest real estate loans.

VA loans work much the same as FHA loans in a couple of ways. First, VA loans are not made directly by the Department of Veterans Affairs but, rather, are guaranteed by it. Secondly, VA loans are designed for owner/occupant purchasers only. There is, however, one significant difference between the two programs. That is, VA loans for qualified veterans can be for 100 percent of the purchase price. This means the veteran doesn't have to come up with any money whatsoever for a down payment.

Besides not having to come up with any money for a down payment, the other important things to know about VA loans are

- Favorable rates and terms are available for eligible veterans.

- Loan amounts generally do not exceed $240,000.

- Eligible properties include single-family homes, including VA-approved condominiums and townhouses.

- VA loans are secured by the Department of Veterans Affairs.

- There are no monthly mortgage insurance premiums to pay.

- Limitations exist on buyer's closing costs.

- You have the right to prepay the loan without penalty.

- The VA performs personal loan servicing and offers financial counseling to help veterans avoid losing their homes during temporary financial difficulties.

Today, more than 29 million American veterans and service personnel are eligible for VA financing. Even though many veterans have already used their loan benefits, it may be possible for them to buy homes or units again with VA financing using remaining or restored loan entitlements.

First-time-buyer programs

Many communities offer first-time-buyer loan programs intended to help people purchase their first homes with little money out-of-pocket. Like FHA and VA loans, these kinds of programs usually require the borrower to be an owner/occupant for a minimum period of time. Remember too, that residential real estate is categorized as anything from one to four units, which broadens the type of investment you can get started with. Make sure to check with your local city hall to see if there are any programs like this that might work for you.

The conventional route

Conventional loans are the cornerstone of the majority of lending that takes place on residential real estate. These loans are offered by banks, savings and loans, and mortgage companies and most are packaged using the Federal National Mortgage Association, commonly called Fannie Mae, or the Federal Home Loan Mortgage Corporation, nicknamed Freddie Mac. These are quasi-public organizations with the benefit of government sponsorship. All conventional loans fall into one of two categories:

1. Residential loans for one to four units
2. Commercial loans for five units and up

There are significant differences between these two categories including the number of lenders willing to provide loans for them, qualification criteria, and terms. Let's look at residential loans first.

Residential loans: One to four units

Residential loans come in almost unlimited shapes and sizes. Call any major lender or mortgage broker in your area and ask for a list of their loan programs; you'll be amazed at the options that exist. Here, we'll attempt to simplify the list so that you can zero in and sift through the sea of options from the get-go.

The standard conventional loan is for 80 percent of the appraised value of the property. This means the borrower will have to put down 20 percent of the purchase price in cash. They can either pay the 20 percent themselves, or, in some cases, structure a deal with a seller whereby he finances a portion of it for them in a second loan. A common scenario has a buyer paying 10 percent, a seller financing 10 percent in a second loan, and a lender lending 80 percent (10% + 10% + 80% = 100%). Note that some lenders will allow you to get a second loan and some will not, so be sure to check and see if this is an available option when doing your loan shopping. If so, the extra effort of finding a seller willing to carry some paper might be well worth it.

Sometimes you can find residential one-to-four-unit loans advertised that offer financing for 90–95 percent of the value of the property. Like FHA and VA loans, most of these programs are designed for owner/occupied properties only. If your plan is to buy units to live in, however, putting less money down and keeping more in your pocket is a great option and one you should consider.

For any financing where you put less than 20 percent down, you will normally be required to pay for private mortgage insurance (PMI). PMI is insurance that will guarantee the lender not to lose part of or the entire loan in the event of a foreclosure. With PMI the lender passes on the cost of the insurance to the borrower by increasing the interest rate. This increase can be ¼ to ½ percent higher, and the PMI can add another ¼ to ½ percent on top of that. Although it sounds expensive, the benefit of more leverage and less out-of-pocket money might make a loan that requires PMI advantageous.

Qualifying for conventional loans

Qualifying for conventional residential loans depends primarily on one criteria, your personal credit worthiness (and thereby, your ability to pay the loan back). Lenders discover this information in two ways. One way is by the use of your FICO score. FICO is a rating system based on a standardized ranking by the three major credit agencies as calculated by the Fair Isaac Credit Organization. The formula they use is not disclosed by the

 Moneysaver

Keep track of how much equity you have in your properties. When your equity exceeds 20 percent, you should be able to negotiate an immediate end to your PMI obligations.

credit bureaus, per decisions made by the U.S. Congress. Simply put, the higher your FICO score, the better risk you are, and the higher the likelihood is that you will get favorable rates and terms for real estate loans.

Some known FICO parameters are as follows:

- The number of bank card trade lines
- The worst level of delinquency on an installment loan
- The number of months in the file
- The number of months since the most recent bank card opening
- The number of months since the most recent derogatory public record
- The delinquency on accounts
- The number of accounts with balances
- The length of revolving credit accounts
- The date of inquiries
- The number of retail accounts

The other method of rating credit is based on a ratio system, consisting of a top and bottom ratio. The top ratio is calculated by dividing the monthly principal, interest, taxes, and insurance payments on your purchase by your total monthly income. The bottom ratio adds all your debt payments to the payment on the property and divides this by your total monthly income. This number takes into account how much debt you have, how much credit you have available on credit cards, late payments, delinquencies, judgments, bankruptcies, and so on.

Most lenders also talk about credit and their loan programs based on a ranking system of A, B, C, or D credit. The following is a summary of the criteria they use to determine your credit grade:

- **A credit:** Very few or no credit problems within the last two years. One or two 30-day late payments. A few small collections, and no more than one 30-day late payment on your mortgage, if you have one.

- **B credit:** A few late payments within the last 18 months. Up to four 30-day late payments or up to two 60-day late payments are allowed on revolving and installment debt, and one 90-day late is allowed.

- **C credit:** Many 30-to-60-day late payments in the last two years as well as late mortgage payments in the 60-to-90-day range. Bankruptcies or foreclosures that have been settled in the last 12 months are also part of this category.

- **D credit:** Open collections, charge-offs, notice of defaults, and so on, as well as several missed payments, or bankruptcies and/or foreclosures.

A conventional lender also will do an appraisal on the property that will figure into the decision on whether or not to lend. Though your lender will certainly be committed to making sure you are not overpaying for the property, make no mistake, their appraisal of you is what is most important when lending on one to four units. In the end, this is what will determine how much and what kind of a loan you qualify for.

Though it sounds like a tough nut to crack, if you have less than perfect credit (like many Americans do), don't let the criteria of the conventional lending market frighten you. Rather, let it inspire you—inspire you to clean up any derogatory past debt and work to get your credit scores as high as they can be. That way you'll always be able to qualify for the best rate and terms for future real estate purchases.

 Bright Idea

If you have trouble qualifying for a conventional real estate loan, consider going to the hard-money market. When it comes to hard-money lending, rates are higher, but qualifying is easier. In all likelihood you will still be able to achieve your goals by obtaining a property to fit your plan.

Commercial loans: Five units and up

At some point in your investing career, you might start looking at larger properties. Any property with five units or more falls out of the residential loan category and becomes one where you need to obtain a commercial loan. If this is where you're headed, know that at a minimum you will have to put between 25 and 35 percent down on your purchase. Compared to the 0 to 20 percent required down payment on residential loans, this component of commercial lending is often what puts these larger buildings out of reach for most beginning investors.

> 66 The best advice I can give a potential borrower is to be an informed consumer when it comes to their credit report and credit history. Be aware of your potential problems, and have adequate answers available for the questions that will most certainly be asked by the underwriter. 99
>
> —Larry S., mortgage broker

Unlike with residential loans, qualifying for a commercial loan (five units or more) is primarily based on the ability of the property itself to generate sufficient cash flow to repay the loan. Most lenders want a debt coverage of 1.1–1.25 percent of the monthly debt payments. This means that the property needs to have a net cash flow after expenses and vacancy reserves of 1.1–1.25 times the loan payment. The building should be able to pay all its expenses, pay the mortgage payments, and have some positive cash flow left over for the investor.

Here is what you need to know about commercial loans:

- Lenders require significant down payments, usually between 25 and 35 percent of the purchase price.

- Commercial loans will always be more difficult to obtain than residential one-to-four-unit loans.

- Loan fees and interest rates are generally significantly higher than for properties in the one-to-four-unit range.

- The appraisal will be considerably more extensive and more expensive than for a one-to-four-unit building.

- The lender will want to see specific, up-to-date information about rents and expenses on the building.

- Commercial loans tend to take much longer to process than loans on one to four units.

Another difference between these loans and smaller residential loans is that most commercial loans for five units and up are nonrecourse loans. A nonrecourse loan is one in which the lender is prohibited from getting any compensation from the borrower for a loss if the lender has to foreclose and take the property back. The exact opposite is true for residential loans.

Fixed-rate mortgages

Two types of interest rates are available on any kind of loan you get: fixed rates and adjustable rates. At a gut level, most people think they'd prefer a fixed-rate loan. You know what the rate is today, and you know what it's going to be tomorrow. This predictability is very attractive and, for that reason alone, makes a fixed-rate loan desirable. The problem is that in the one-to-four-unit market, it's hard to get a fixed-rate loan for nonowner-occupied units. If you plan to live in one of the units you buy, that's one thing. If you plan on just having an investment, however, finding a fixed rate on one to four units will be tough.

For argument's sake, let's say you did find a fixed-rate loan on a nonowner-occupied piece of residential real estate. Here is what you can expect: For starters, the loan usually will be at a much higher interest rate than the typical adjustable-rate loan. This is because, in theory, the lender has to retain the loan at the fixed rate for 30 years and thereby take the risk of having the cost of money for him increase without any recourse. This is great in a stable economy, but during periods of inflation, the cost of funds for the lenders can erode any profit margin they might have had.

Besides higher interest rates, a fixed-rate loan will probably have higher initial fees, the loan won't be assumable, and most will have a prepayment penalty for the first 3–5 years. What's more, some loans also require a balloon payment to be made in 7–10 years from origination. "What," you ask, "is a balloon payment?" Here's how it works: Most government and conventional loans on smaller properties are fully amortized. A fully amortized loan is one in which you make 30 years worth of payments, and at the end of that time, your loan is paid off in full. In the case of many fixed-rate loans, payments on the loan would be made as though you were paying off the loan with a 30-year amortization schedule, but at the end of the agreed-upon time, the balloon would be due. This payment would be equal to the balance of the loan at that time.

Though it seems like the odds might be stacked against you, don't let these hurdles sway you from considering a fixed-rate loan. If you can get one, and the terms work for you, then go that route. If not, educate yourself about the second type of available conventional loans—adjustable-rate mortgages.

Adjustable-rate mortgages (ARMs)

A banking lesson would be in order here: When it comes to making real estate loans on smaller properties, savings and loans and banks are the ones that provide most of the money to borrowers. The loans are made for 10–30 years. The money they lend is money they borrow from their customers. The system works because you bring your money in the front door and open a savings account, on which you earn interest. The interest you get is the cost of funds for the bank. The money goes out the back door when your neighbor goes to that very same bank and gets a loan for a new house or some rental units. The difference between the rate your neighbor pays for his home loan and the rate you get on your savings account goes toward the bank's overhead and profit.

The reality, however, is that most people don't put their money in the bank for 10–30 years. Instead, they put it in for a couple of days to a couple of years. What this means is that banks are lending money on real estate for 10–30 years based on their projected cost of funds today. To that end, lenders take a big risk by lending long term on a short-term supply of capital and thereby have to charge higher interest rates for fixed-rate loans. That way, they build in protection for themselves. In the 1970s, the banks learned this lesson the hard way. This is why the adjustable-rate mortgage was invented. Today, with adjustable-rate mortgages as part of the mix, banks win, as do borrowers.

The interest rate of the modern adjustable loan is based on an index plus a margin. It's actually pretty simple. An index is a source from which interest rates are determined. It generally is either treasury bills or treasury bond rates or the cost of money in local federal districts. The most common indexes are

- **COFI:** COFI stands for the Cost of Fund Index. This is the average cost of deposits and borrowing for a savings institution in a given Federal Home Loan Bank District. For example, the 11th District Cost of Funds Index is comprised of California, Arizona, and Nevada.

- **CMT:** CMT is the Constant Maturity Treasury Index. This is the weekly average yield on United States treasury securities adjusted to a constant maturity of one year. For larger fixed-rate apartment and commercial loans, which may have a maturity date of 7 or 10 years, the index used would be based on 7-and-10-year treasury securities.

- **LIBOR:** LIBOR stands for the London Inter-Bank Offered Rate. This is the average of lending rates from a number of major banks based in London, England.

- **CD:** The index based on certificates of deposit (CDs) is a weekly average of the secondary market interest rate on certificates of deposit with a 6-month maturity date.

Now that you are up to speed on the index, here is what a margin is: A margin is a pad that gets added to the index to make up the total interest rate. It's there to cover the lender's overhead, cost, and profit. It can and will vary depending on market conditions and competition.

You can calculate the interest rate on your ARM loan using the following formula:

Current rate of index + Margin of loan = Interest rate

As an example, if the index is 4.92 and the margin is 2.25, the interest rate on your ARM would be 7.17 percent, as follows:

4.92% (Rate) + 2.25% (Margin) = 7.17% interest rate

There are basically two types of adjustable-rate mortgages. There are "no-neg" adjustable loans. No-neg loans are ones that do not allow for any negative amortization. There are also "neg-am" adjustable loans, which are loans that do allow for negative amortization. Negative amortization refers to the possibility of your loan balance increasing, rather than decreasing with some of your payments.

Here's a simple illustration to help explain this concept: Let's say the agreed upon minimum monthly payment on your ARM for a given year is $850, but it would take $900 a month to pay off the loan in 30 years based upon the current interest rate. If that was the case, the difference of $50 a month will be added to your loan balance. That's negative amortization.

In actuality, however, negative amortization is not nearly as bad as it sounds. In fact, the neg-am ARM is the loan that many seasoned investors prefer. The benefits for the investor are twofold: First, by allowing the investor to make just a minimum payment each month of interest only, the neg-am ARM allows the investor to maintain a healthy working cash flow on his properties. Second, by keeping more money in his pocket, a smart investor can buy much more building than he normally could have. In the end, this is the loan that helps more investors reach their goals in real estate on time, or sooner.

Moneysaver

Because they have the least risk for the lender, adjustable loans are probably the most common loans today, especially for smaller investment properties. This allows banks to offer them at the most favorable terms to the borrower.

Nonetheless, there are additional pros and cons to both types of adjustable-rate mortgages. The facts are laid out in detail in the following sections, so you can decide for yourself.

The "no-neg" ARM

As mentioned, the "no-neg" is an adjustable loan with terms that do not allow for any potential negative amortization. In guaranteeing that there will be no negative amortization, the lender builds in protection for potential market interest rate increases. For example, the loan may provide for two interest adjustments each year, one every six months, with a maximum increase or decrease in the interest rate of 1 percent each six-month period and a corresponding increase or decrease adjustment in the payment. For this maximum increase or decrease, the bank will absorb any costs above the 2 percent (1 percent every 6 months) increase per year.

To illustrate, let's look at the potential increase on a $190,000 loan at 7 percent interest with a 30-year payment schedule. We'll assume the interest rates increased 1 percent each adjustment period. The change will look like this:

Interest Increase	Monthly Payment	Amount Going to Interest	Amount Going To Principal
1st 6 Months	$1,264.07	$1,108.33	$155.74
2nd 6 Months 1%	$1,394.15	$1,266.67	$127.48
3rd 6 Months 1%	$1,528.78	$1,425.00	$103.78

The difference between the initial monthly payment of
$1,264.07 and the jump in a year and a half to $1,528.78 per
month is $264.71. As you can imagine, $264.71 is a pretty large
monthly increase to swallow. At first glance, the best solution
might be to offset this increase by simply raising rents.

If you remember, the rents on the Richmond Street example
totaled $2,200 per month. If we wanted to preserve the same
cash flow we had when we began it would take the following
increase in rent every six months:

Second 6-month adjustment

Second payment	$1,394.15
First payment	−$1,264.07
Increase	$130.08

$$\frac{\text{Increase} \quad \$130.08}{\text{Rent} \quad \$2,200} = 5.9\%$$

Third 6-month adjustment

Third payment	$1,528.78
First payment	−$1,394.15
Increase	$134.63

$$\frac{\text{Increase} \quad \$134.63}{\text{Rent} \quad \$2,330.08} = 5.8\%$$

The net result is that you'd have to raise your rents almost
12 percent if you wanted to maintain the cash flow you started
with (5.9% + 5.8% = 11.7%). Even in a good economy, this may
be more than most tenants would tolerate.

You are left with two choices here: Take the no-neg
adjustable loan, and as time goes on accept a lower cash flow, or
begin to think outside the box and consider a second option—
the neg-am adjustable loan.

The "neg-am" ARM

The "neg-am" ARM differs in that the limit is put on how much the required cash payment can increase rather than how much the interest can increase. To protect the cash flow for the borrower/investor, lenders have built in payment caps to neg-am loans, usually set at a maximum of 7.5 percent increase per year. Using our example loan, this means the required loan payment could only go up $94.81 ($1,264.07 × .075 = $94.81) the first year, no matter what happened to the actual interest rate.

To compensate the lenders for the lower required minimum payment, the interest rate may be allowed to adjust every month according to the index to which it is tied. These adjustments usually will start six months after the loan begins. Given these parameters, the payment schedule on the example looks like this:

Interest Increase	Monthly Payment	Amount Going to Interest	Amount Going to Principal
1st 6 months	$1,264.07	$1,108.33	$155.74
2nd 6 months 1%	$1,264.07	$1,266.67	–$2.60
3rd 6 months 1%	$1,358.88	$1,425.00	–$66.12

With the neg-am adjustable loan, there would only be one change in the payment in the 18 months of our example. We showed the interest increasing in the second and third periods, however, so it affected the principal reduction part of the loan payment. Because the principal due was not paid (that is, it actually was negative), the loan amount increased by the amount of the unpaid balance during these periods.

Now let's see how the payment increase compares to the existing rental income. If we want to preserve the cash flow for our building on Richmond Street, we'll need the following increase:

Second payment	$1,358.88
First payment	−$1,264.07
Increase	$94.81

$$\frac{\text{Increase} \quad \$94.81}{\text{Rental income} \quad \$2,200.00} = 4.3\%$$

A 4.3 percent increase amounts to only $23.65 per month on a unit that rents for $550 per month. Now, compare that to the 12 percent increase you would have had to offset with a no-neg ARM. As you can see, the big advantage of the neg-am loan is that the low payment increase enables you to offset it with an affordable rent increase that maintains the cash flow you desire. If everything goes as planned and the cash flow isn't needed, you can always add more money to your payment each month so that no negative amortization takes place.

Because you have multiple payment options with each mortgage payment, many lenders refer to the neg-am adjustable loan as the flexible-payment-plan loan. The idea is as follows: If your building is running well, you can pay the interest due plus the principal due and not go negative at all. If, on the other hand, cash flow is necessary because, say, a water heater went out at your building, you can pay a minimum payment of interest only and keep more cash in your pocket to pay for your expenses. The choice is yours, as the lender allows you to change your mind with every payment.

 Moneysaver

Keep in mind that the portion of your payment that goes to reducing the principal is taxable because it came from tenant income. Therefore, there isn't any real advantage in taking the money out of your bank where it is earning interest and paying down your loan. The cash in the bank is your security. If you keep it in the bank, you can pay the loan down anytime.

> **Bright Idea**
>
> Feel free to mention other loan quotes to lenders. The best approach often is a straightforward statement: "You know, Mel at Excalibur Mortgage offered me the same loan for 1/2 point less. Can you beat that?"

Finally, many people bemoan that neg-am adjustable loans create the possibility that the loan balance can increase rather than decrease. Sadly, many borrowers/investors dismiss adjustable-rate loans outright without ever being truly financially literate on the subject.

In reality, fear of negative amortization is a psychological problem and not a practical one. Why is it that we can finance a brand-new car, knowing full well that the loan will be larger than the car's value the moment we drive it off the lot? And everyone knows that the computer systems we buy today will be behind the times in less than six months, but we continue to buy new computer systems all the time. In truth, we buy new cars and computers because they enhance the quality of our lives. Using adjustable-rate mortgages to purchase the real estate that will improve our lives should be no different.

Most importantly, keep in mind that lending is just a tool to help you reach your dreams. If you can use an ARM to grow your nest egg, go ahead and do it. If, however, you find that it is not in your best interest, find a fixed-rate loan, pay all cash, or invest in the stock market. The choice is yours.

Shopping lenders

Regardless of the type of conventional loan you choose, it's important that you shop around for the best possible rate and terms. As you can see, many variables will affect your costs. Use the following uniform checklist to compare programs effectively:

- Interest rate
- Fixed or adjustable
- Loan-to-value ratio

Watch Out!

It is not just the interest rate you should take into account when shopping for a loan but a combination of all factors on your checklist and how they impact your long-term investment goals.

- Debt coverage percentage
- Points
- Appraisal fee
- Environmental review fee
- Margin
- Index
- Interest rate cap
- Payment cap
- Required impounds
- Prepayment penalty
- Yield maintenance
- Assumability
- Recourse or nonrecourse
- Processing, review, and closing time
- Good-faith deposit
- Other fees

Assumable loans

Assumable loans are loans that are already in place and can be taken over by the person purchasing the property. That is, the buyer can "assume" the existing loan rather than finding new financing and paying all the fees to obtain it. There usually are some small fees charged for assuming a loan, but they can be significantly lower than what it would cost to get a new loan from scratch. Your real estate agent should know whether the properties you are considering have assumable loans.

One advantage of taking over an older, assumable loan is that it often will have better terms than a similar new loan would have today. The major difference usually is in the margin. Remember that the margin is the profit that the bank adds on to the index to get the total interest rate on the loan.

When a loan has been in place for 10 to 15 years, it starts paying off principal at a faster rate. This means that principal, rather than interest, is now a larger percentage of each monthly payment. Because more principal is being paid to the loan, assumable loans allow for a faster buildup of equity. For this reason, many investors getting ready for retirement look for properties with loans like this that they can assume. The idea is that they won't have to add much additional principal to each payment to get these seasoned loans to pay off at about the same time as they retire.

Know that when you assume a loan, you still have to qualify just as the original borrower did. There are some loans, however, especially older FHA loans, that allow you to take the loan over and just start making payments. This is sometimes called taking the loan "subject to." Taking a loan subject to leaves the original borrower on the hook in case you default. They may be hard to find, but are like jewels in the dust when you do.

Private-party financing

The last source of financing is through private parties. These loans often are made by the sellers themselves, and they have several advantages over conventional loans. The first advantage is that you can save a lot of money in lending fees if you borrow privately. This is because most of the costs associated with conventional financing don't apply to private loans. This is a great help when assembling the initial cash required to close a deal.

Good rates

Many times, private loans have interest rates that are lower than the conventional market. If you look at the loan on 333 Richmond Street, which is $190,000, and assume you can save a mere 1 percent on the interest rate through private financing, it adds up to $1,900 per year. The following chart should be an eye-opener, as it demonstrates how a $1,900 per-year savings adds up over the span of 30 years:

Year	Savings
1	$1,900
5	$9,500
10	$19,000
30	$57,000

Low down

The down payment on most transactions is determined by the requirements of the institution making the loan. In the case of private financing, down payments are entirely negotiable. In many instances, sellers who are willing to carry a private-party loan don't want any money for a down payment at all. This is because they are not looking to get cash out of a sale. Instead, they want the monthly income from carrying the paper because any cash they receive is just a tax problem for them. In fact, you will find that many sellers only want enough cash down to pay closing costs.

Terms

In the grand scheme of owning a property, the terms of your financing can be far more important than the price you pay for a building. If you and the seller can agree, anything goes. Not only do many sellers carry the financing at lower interest rates,

 Bright Idea

If money is tight, ask your real estate agent if he would be willing to take his commission in monthly payments. If so, you might be able to close private-party loans with only as much cash as it takes to pay title and escrow fees.

they also can make the payment plans fit your needs. The golden rule says, "He who has the gold, makes the rules." In private-party lending, this couldn't be truer.

It isn't unusual for some sellers to carry financing long term with interest-only payments. This way, they are not using up any of the principal balance of the loan. Remember that any principal the seller receives is taxable as a capital gain. Many times, sellers who truly understand real estate investing would rather loan the money to you and receive interest-only payments than pay Uncle Sam capital gains tax.

In reality, a seller can make your loan payment any amount he wants. We (the authors) have seen many transactions over the years in which the payment schedules were actually lower than interest-only to accommodate the particular needs of a transaction. In most cases, this is because the seller has not kept the rents up with the market but wants a price calculated on rents closer to what they should be. The seller can carry the loan at a graduated payment schedule to give the buyer time to raise the rents.

Due dates

Another major component to consider in a private-party loan is the due date. This also is up for full negotiation. The parties involved can agree for the due date to be in 1 year, 5 years, or 30 years, just like any conventional loan. In addition, it's not unusual for private loans to have partial payoffs at set times. These partial payoffs often coincide with the cash needs of the seller. The seller might have loans he needs to pay off in the future or some special need such as providing a college education for a grandchild. In the case of these partial payoffs, many sellers will allow you to get the funds by refinancing the

> 66 When my agent talked the seller into carrying a straight note for me, it made the difference in being able to buy the property I wanted with a payment I could afford. 99
>
> —Michael B., investor

property and putting their loan in the second position. If you plan well enough ahead, these payoff obligations should be easy to meet.

Straight notes

You might find that some sellers don't need any cash flow at all and are willing to carry a straight note (or notes) with deferred interest. A straight note is a note that has one payment, which is due at the end of the loan. In the period between the start of the note and the due date, the interest accrues and is due at the same time as the principal. Other sellers might only want part of the interest and will allow the unpaid interest to accrue and be paid when the loan is paid off.

All-inclusive loans

An all-inclusive loan is one in which the loan the seller is carrying includes the seller's equity and any other loans the seller had previously put on the property. Sometimes seller-financed loans take this form because the terms of the existing financing don't allow the loan to be transferred, or—in many cases—because of tax reasons associated with the seller's capital gain position.

We'll discuss the problem of mortgage over basis in Chapter 10, "Planning for the Tax Man," but in short, it's a problem created by taking part of your profit out though refinancing. A taxable event occurs when the seller is relieved of the responsibility for the debt. Rather than allowing you to assume a loan that has a mortgage over basis problem, the seller can carry an all-inclusive loan.

Let's assume the $190,000 loan on the Richmond Street example was actually an all-inclusive loan. This might be the actual structure:

Sellers equity	$90,000
First loan	+$100,000
All-inclusive loan	$190,000

In this case, you make a payment to the seller according to your agreed upon contract, the seller makes the payment on the existing first loan, and he keeps the difference. In this scenario, the seller has not been relieved of his responsibility for the repayment of the $100,000 loan, so in many cases, this will not trigger the taxes due.

Land sales contracts

Another type of private lending is the land sale contract, or the contract for deed. In this case, buyers enter into a contract with a seller to purchase a property, but the buyer doesn't acquire the title until sometime in the future. These deals often are structured this way because the underlying financing is favorable to the buyer.

Land sales contracts and contracts for deed are structured in much the same way that cars are financed. That is, the bank keeps the title to the car even though you are the registered owner. When you eventually pay the car off, the bank gives you the legal title. The same premise holds true here.

Buyers need to be careful here. Many loans have acceleration clauses that make the entire loan due and payable if there is a title transfer. Lenders can't accelerate a loan, however, unless they know about the change. Because the title isn't actually transferred, many times, no one is the wiser. Nonetheless, agreeing to these kinds of terms might be a risk, so make sure you do your homework and be careful.

 Watch Out!

When you are using creative financing such as a land sales contract, you always should consult a real estate attorney. That way you can go into a deal with complete peace of mind.

Watch Out!

Some people with money to loan advertise in the newspaper. You've seen the ads, "Money to loan!" You should use extreme caution here. Have your lawyer read the fine print carefully so that you are both well aware of what you are agreeing to.

Hard money loans

One final source for private financing is known as the hard money loan. This is when third parties make loans on real estate as if they were a conventional lender. Most of these loans are made to borrowers, or on properties, that can't get financing in the conventional arena for one reason or another. It might be due to the buyer's poor credit, or it might be that the property is in disrepair, and the buyer is making the purchase as a rehab project. Whatever the reason, know that hard money loans are available for those deals that cannot get financed conventionally.

Be aware that this route will be more expensive than the conventional lending market when it comes to up-front fees and interest rates. These higher costs shouldn't prevent you from investing, though. Rather, it should just keep you on your toes when it comes to keeping your other expenses at a minimum. You see, financing is just a means to an end. If the hard money market is where you need to go to get money to invest so that you can create a fruitful future for yourself and your family, then by all means, go there.

If you do some looking around, you sometimes can find family or friends who would be willing to make you a loan on real estate. In fact, making a real estate loan to you could create a great win-win situation for both parties. For instance, if your friend is currently getting 5 or 6 percent interest in a savings account, you could offer her 10 or 11 percent to loan the money to you instead. In this scenario, everyone walks away happy; you get the money you need, and your friend gets an investment that pays a much higher rate than she can get anywhere else.

And most important

Remember that financing is just a tool used to acquire the property that best fits your investment-plan goals. Don't get caught up in the emotion of the points or the margin being too high and then miss out on an opportunity to acquire a property that is perfect for your plan. Likewise, by carefully investigating the underlying financing of all properties under consideration, you might find one with exceptional assumable financing that makes it a better investment than another property with a lower price.

Just the facts

- The federal government has a number of programs that allow you to get into an investment and a home with a minimal down payment.

- Residential loans for one to four units come in all shapes and sizes.

- Qualifying for a loan on one to four units from a conventional lender rests primarily on your personal credit worthiness.

- A lender's primary concern when lending on five units or more is how the property performs as a business.

- If you choose an adjustable loan, the best way to maintain a steady cash flow is with the neg-am ARM.

- The beauty behind private-party financing is that it allows buyers and sellers to negotiate all the terms of the deal.

Mastering the Market

PART III

Real Estate, the Economy, and Your Target Market

By the time you finish this guide, you hopefully will have all the tools at your disposal to make an educated decision about what, where, when, why, and how to buy real estate. Ultimately, you will choose from a limited number of available buildings in a specific target market. Before you do that, however, it is important for you to understand how those few properties fit into the global market of which we are all a part.

In an effort to accomplish this goal, we need to have a quick lesson in basic economics, specifically how the economy affects real estate. By understanding some basic economic principles and how they can affect you, you can either take action and profit from market swings or, if bad times are ahead, be able to take preventative action and ward them off. From there, we'll talk about economic trends closer to home. This is because regional trends directly affect the market in the area in which you are trying to make a profit. Finally, we'll conclude by teaching you a methodology that you can use to become an expert in your own target market.

The big picture

Most investment strategies are based on a study of past and present trends and benefits. The idea is to examine what has happened in the past to gauge what might happen in the future. In economics class, we learned about business cycles and the fact that real estate is a cyclical industry. That is, it responds to the overall cycles of our economy. When the economy is moving, so is real estate. When things slow down, real estate does, too. Even in a struggling economy, however, the clever individual can make a profit. This is because our product is a basic necessity of life; everyone needs a place to live.

A closer look at the economy as a whole will show you the dominating influence of real estate. It's easy to see how the buying, selling, and renting of property has a general impact on the economy, but this impact goes much further. Take the savings and loan industry, for instance. This industry is built around lending money to finance every aspect of real estate including its purchase and remodeling. Think of the revenue generated from all the goods and services that go into keeping all this real estate functional and looking good. Finally, consider all the money spent on property insurance and construction. As you add up all these dollars, the figure becomes staggering.

> 66 A cellular phone company was looking for locations for cell sites. I gave them the use of my roof, and they've decided to supplement my income for the next 30 years. 99
>
> —Jay T., commercial property owner

Real estate is such a powerful storehouse of economic wealth that we literally have built our local city governments around its value. For starters, real estate is the tax basis for most local governments. The money generated provides funding for fire and police protection, education, health and social services, and most of the other services cities provide. This value enables cities to raise the capital they need to function. In fact, some of the greatest advances in local communities come when civic leaders take over a blighted area through the condemnation process or a redevelopment district. They then can use municipal bonds and various incentives to turn these blighted areas into the crowning jewels of the community.

To make a long story short, real estate is probably the largest single segment of wealth in our nation. It has been estimated that two-thirds of the wealth of our country is composed of land, what's under that land, or what's built on top of that land. We even see the airspace above the land in some highly developed areas being sold as a separate commodity. It is this wealth that attracts investors to real estate.

Regional economic trends

To understand real estate as a vehicle to making a profit, you need to remember that the profit is made when we as consumers get together and utilize that product. Therefore, real estate functions more as a consumer product than as the capital asset it really is. It is a storehouse for wealth on our balance sheet, but we make the maximum profit by recognizing the consumer's needs and desires for it.

Take an apartment in Bakersfield, California, for example. There, a one-bedroom unit might rent for $300 per month. The same size unit in Malibu, California, could rent for $1,900 per month. How can this be if the units are exactly alike? The answer is simple enough—because one location is more desirable than the other. In fact, the value is really set by the people who buy or rent the property. The more they want a scarce product, the higher the price will usually go. It's really like an auction when it comes right down to it. As you know, the real value is in the land. If consumers don't want to be there, however, land can be virtually worthless.

The market for real estate is the process in which we as consumers get together to buy, sell, and rent property. It is this market functioning within the economy in general that establishes value and trends. The following list covers some of the major factors that can impact values:

- The supply and value of money
- Occupancy levels (supply and demand)
- Rental rates and controls
- Employment levels
- Population growth and family formations
- Building activity
- Perceptions of the future
- Government regulations

Let's examine these factors one at a time.

The supply and value of money

We buy real estate for one of two reasons. The first reason is to provide a roof over our heads or to house a business. The second reason is as an investment to make a profit. The supply and cost of money isn't as important in the first case because, when purchasing a home, your foremost concern becomes what kind of lifestyle it provides. Most people's attitude is as long as they can afford it, they will buy it. If it goes up in value, that's great, but their life won't depend on how their home appreciates. The same holds true for a business looking for a location.

As an investor, however, the supply and cost of money does matter. This is because trends in the money market can either make or break your investment. The variables to consider are

- The supply of money to finance investment property
- The cost of borrowing (rates and fees)

- The percentage that can be borrowed (leverage)
- The length of time that the money can be borrowed (term)

These factors will have the greatest impact on your ability to make a profit. This is because an active money market for financing real estate usually goes hand in hand with a market in which you can earn some healthy profits catering to the consumers' desire for that product.

Occupancy levels, rental rates, employment levels, and population growth

The next four areas—occupancy rates, rental rates, employment levels, and population growth—all work together to impact the profitability of most real estate investments. When you see these four indicators on the rise in your area, it is a signal that there will be some opportunities to profit from the increased demand.

Obviously, the best environment in which to invest is one with a steady increase in demand and a shrinking supply of land to satisfy that demand. Manhattan and Hong Kong are perfect examples; there, they demolish fairly new high-rise buildings to build even newer and higher buildings.

We can't all live in or afford to invest in these areas, but we can learn from their example. Growth in an area with a lot of undeveloped land will minimize the increase in value for the existing properties. This is because, as the population increases, developers will build new buildings on the available raw land to satisfy the increased demand. These properties will be brand new and will have the latest styles and amenities. Human nature being what it is, this attracts the buyers who have the money.

 Bright Idea

You can track most of these statistics through your local chamber of commerce or the business development department of your city.

These people usually are new residents brought into the market by new jobs.

We are talking about real growth brought on by new jobs that require an increase in population to fill the positions. In areas where unemployment is higher than the national average, jobs can be created that will have little or no impact on real estate values or rental rates. In these areas, real estate can increase in value, but this usually just reflects the impact of inflation rather than true growth.

Building activity

When there is an increase in building activity, it should have a direct impact on the value of existing properties. The amount of the increase usually depends on the amount of vacant land available. In areas with plenty of land available, builders usually can supply the demand for housing easily.

In areas that are more fully developed, however, it becomes tougher to satisfy the demand for new housing. Old homes need to be demolished to build new ones. Therefore, there is some upward movement in the price of the existing product. This is the cost-push increase, and it is similar to the increase from inflation. The biggest increases come from demand pulling the prices up. The consumers bid up the price because they want the product and supply is limited. This is the same thing that drives up prices at auctions for paintings and other commodities in limited supply.

The one instance in which this growth can be impacted in a negative sense even in a growth environment is when some kind of price control is put into effect. This usually is in the form of rent control. Make no bones about it; rent control can have a disastrous effect on your ability to generate a profit or to sell a property. In truth, it takes a very sophisticated investor to be able to generate a profit in areas with rent control. We're not saying avoid investing in such areas all together. Rather, just make sure you do your homework beforehand so that you know what you will be up against.

Watch Out!

Beware of investing in areas that are governed by rent control. Unless there is some allowance for rental increases when existing tenants move out, these areas prove to be hard ones in which to turn a profit.

Perception of the future

Another factor that can influence value is the perception that people have about the future. This involves emotions and gut feelings based on what has happened in the past. Perceptions are not always accurate, but they usually get lots of play in the press. Once the media gets an idea in its head and begins to publicize it, people tend to fall right in line and agree.

Understanding that popular opinion is not always accurate can be very profitable for smart investors. It's one thing to make a good buy when the economy isn't doing well. It's even better to make that same buy when the economy is improving but when sellers have yet to figure that out. The important thing to understand is that you must not be swayed by public opinion. Look for the facts and then make your decisions accordingly; you can wave to the masses in your rearview mirror.

Government regulations

It's important to be aware of the fact that the regulations local and state governments place on property can have an effect on property value. Fortunately, most of the changes are for the good in the long run. As you explore purchasing your property, be sure to pay attention to any recent or planned changes that may affect your property or the area close by.

Down-zoning is an example of what many cities do to hold down growth in the community. A piece of property that might have been zoned for 8 units 10 or 20 years ago might only be approved for 3 or 4 units today. If you bought your property to build on and this happened, you may suffer a loss for awhile. But, for most income property investors, this won't affect your property's value. Down-zoning encourages the construction of larger units with more amenities, which usually sell at a higher price. In actuality, this pulls values up and the land values just increase that much more.

A growth moratorium is the ultimate form of down-zoning. A government will enact a law that halts residential development. The need for this law is based on overcrowding of schools or a lack of resources, such as water or sewage treatment capabilities, because of too many new people in a community. The government halts development until it can study how to efficiently deal with the population influx. This creates a constraint on the supply of properties and should accelerate price appreciation. Redevelopment usually brings many changes to zoning and usage of property. Over time it can make huge changes in values, but since it requires so much government involvement, the impact on value can take a long time. Be careful if you are in a redevelopment area that isn't completely settled. The uncertainty may scare away future buyers of your property and might make it tougher to get any loans you may need.

It's important to note that laws and rules effecting how property is built are constantly being changed. Many newer properties become "legal non-conforming" just a few years after they are completed. This is because building codes change at such a rapid rate. If that's the case, just think of how many codes that 50-year-old building you are thinking about buying violates. Don't worry. In the vast majority of cases you don't have to concern yourself with these non-conforming issues. Code changes are rarely retroactive, and those that are usually cover critical health and safety related issues. A good example would be the retroactive requirement to have working smoke alarms in all rental units.

Your target market

Regardless of the size of your community, it probably will have some definite neighborhood divisions. As is true in most places, there will be upscale sections, working class sections, and sections that are on "the other side of the tracks." You will need to look at all these areas before you make a final decision about which one offers the best opportunities to make a profit. As you zero in on this section choice, the following checklist will give you some factors to consider:

- Neighborhoods growing or declining
- Criminal activity and trends
- Current supply and demand for housing
- Adverse infrastructure changes
- Positive infrastructure changes
- Economic deterioration of the commercial districts
- Changes in local ordinances that affect real estate

Let's now touch on each of these factors one at a time.

Analyzing the neighborhood

A class in economic geography would show that an evolution takes place in all cities. We learn how they are founded, how cities expand over the years, how they deteriorate, and then how they're rebuilt through the redevelopment process. Even stagnant communities seem to go through these phases, although they might be harder to detect because the changes lack the momentum of the demand push

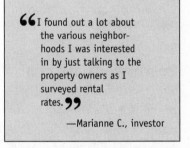

❝I found out a lot about the various neighborhoods I was interested in by just talking to the property owners as I surveyed rental rates.❞

—Marianne C., investor

from new residents. As an investor, what you want to do is make sure you on the correct side of the growth curve.

Criminal activity and trends

Local crime statistics can be a good indicator of what is happening in neighborhoods. Many communities publish crime statistics, and gathering this kind of historical data can be really helpful. Your goal would be to see if you can spot trends rather than to find out about the specific kinds of crimes. Obviously, you will shy away from areas that have severe drug or gang-related problems.

Supply and demand for housing

Local neighborhoods all have their own mix of residential and commercial real estate. There also will be a certain percentage of owner-occupied properties as well as rental properties. Analyzing how much there is of each will dictate what kind of opportunities you will find to profit as an investor. Later in this chapter, we will discuss the actual statistics that help determine which areas offer the best opportunity for you to make money.

Adverse infrastructure changes

The city itself might have a negative impact on some neighborhoods with changes in ordinances or adverse infrastructure changes. We've all heard the story about the small motel that went out of business because the highway was moved. This is the kind of change we're talking about. A trip to city hall will let you know what kind of major capital expenditures are in the works. The most common city projects with adverse effects seem to involve work on streets and highways.

Positive infrastructure changes

You should also be on the lookout for positive infrastructure changes. For example, a new zoo, a federal building, or some other major attraction could improve the neighborhood because of new jobs or other commercial activity that follows. In Denver, for instance, the building of Coors Field in the middle of an empty, drug-ridden war zone resulted in a positive explosion of commercial and residential redevelopment.

Economic deterioration of commercial districts

Most communities have several levels of commercial districts. We'll call them the "A," "B," "C," and "T" districts.

- **The "A" district:** This is the new district with the mall or the freestanding mega-retailers.

- **The "B" district:** This is the area that used to be the "A" area but couldn't keep up because it lacked the space to handle the larger shops.

- **The "C" district:** These areas serve as neighborhood business strips. They have the "mom and pop" shops and all the other smaller offices and retailers. You will see accountants, beauty shops, doctor and dental offices, and all the service businesses such as tune-up centers, tire stores, fast-food restaurants, and computer stores. These kinds of small operations thrive on serving the local community.

- **The "T" district:** "T" districts are commercial or small industrial areas that have deteriorated and are now in transition. Usually they are the old downtown commercial or manufacturing areas and can be easily spotted because they often have many "For Rent" and "Vacancy" signs around. These areas have deteriorated because the economic growth has moved to the suburbs. The transition and rejuvenation happens as developers and young professionals rediscover them. Old office buildings are turned into retail with offices and residences above, and old warehouses become live/work lofts.

Savvy investors can find opportunities in these areas by following the trends where other investors and developers are buying and fixing up formerly deteriorating properties. Many investors see huge potential gains in these transition areas. It's important to understand that these

---

 Watch Out!

Be careful when you see "C" districts deteriorating. This usually is a good sign that the residents who have money to spend are going elsewhere. In addition, it's often the first step before they relocate their residence.

changes can take many years even if the city's powers that be are talking about the changes happening soon. If these kinds of sweeping changes happen to get started just as the economy slows, it can take many years for any significant impact on value to actually occur.

Changes in local ordinances that affect real estate

Most cities have master plans for how they see the city developing. Many times, these master plans can include sweeping changes to certain areas to accomplish the projected needs of the community as a whole. That new "A" business district no doubt was in the planning stages for many years. These kinds of changes can offer an opportunity to make a profit if you learn about them early on.

Learning about city planning in advance also can save you from making costly mistakes. An apartment building on the edge of a redevelopment area, for example, might suffer through years of waiting for the boarded-up buildings and vacant lots to be replaced by the proposed new shopping mall. This is especially true where public funds are involved. Announced projects are often delayed for years. In Brooklyn, a major development project was announced around the rebuilding of a train station. Ten years have passed and private investors have since opened a mall and new housing has been built, but the promised train station remains a weed-strewn empty lot. The result is that private investors have not been able to realize the profits they had hoped for.

 Watch Out!

A trip to city hall and the planning department can give you an update as to what kinds of changes are in the works for your city. But be wary. Projects are often announced, commenced, then stalled indefinitely or even abandoned. Public projects are notorious for delays; private ones may go bankrupt.

Researching local markets

In addition to economic cycles and local trends and changes, it's important to look at historic appreciation in specific areas to help determine your best target market. As noted earlier, real estate is a cyclical commodity. It responds to the ups and downs in the global economy and to things that affect the local economy. There is no guarantee that history will repeat itself, but knowledge of how your local area has responded in the past is a more reliable forecasting tool than pure guesswork. Without something to base future projection on, it's tough to make a long-term plan of where you are going with your investments.

Take a look at the chart on the accompanying page. It shows value appreciation as seen in the greater South Bay area of Los Angeles covering the last 30 plus years. Notice that value is expressed as a price per square foot of living area. We showed the price-per-square-foot chart because the trend in price from this information enables us to calculate the yearly increase in value over the entire period. Note the 7.4 percent average appreciation rate shown at the top of the chart. This is the interest rate used in the compound interest formula (i) to estimate your rate of return over an extended period of time. (See the section on "Determining your general plan" in Chapter 9, "Building an Investment Plan.")

As you can see, the increase in value was not constant over the last 30 plus years. Looking at the chart, if you had done your projecting based on the data from just 1977–1981, you would have gotten pretty excited about investing because the market kept getting better and better. If you only had data for 1991–1996, you might have decided never to invest at all because we were in a downswing. As you can see, the market has started moving upward again. The lesson is to make sure you get plenty of years of data because that is the only way to determine a true appreciation rate for any given area.

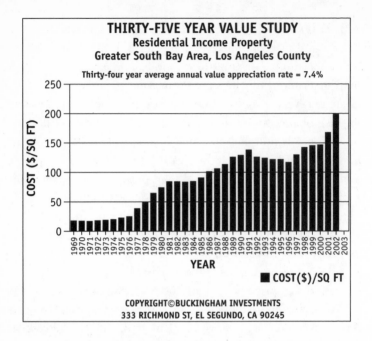

THIRTY-FIVE YEAR VALUE STUDY
Residential Income Property
Greater South Bay Area, Los Angeles County

Thirty-four year average annual value appreciation rate = 7.4%

COPYRIGHT©BUCKINGHAM INVESTMENTS
333 RICHMOND ST, EL SEGUNDO, CA 90245

You might find that it can be pretty difficult to gather this type of information, especially if you're looking for income-producing property alone, rather than at single-family homes. If you are fortunate enough to find an expert agent who specializes in income property in your area, he might have saved the kind of data you need. If not, you will need to do some research on your own to get some sense of the trend in property values. This is vital in projecting the long-term growth of your investments. The following list covers the data you should look for:

Bright Idea

Recruit a local librarian to help you research values in your area. Most libraries have great databases, and the librarians probably would be happy to help.

- **Price per square foot:**

$$\frac{\text{Sale price of the property}}{\text{Square feet of living space}} = \text{\$/sq. ft.}$$

- **Gross rent multiplier:**

$$\frac{\text{Sale price of the property}}{\text{Gross income of the property}} = \text{G.R.M.}$$

- **Price per unit:**

$$\frac{\text{Sale price of the property}}{\text{Number of units in the building}} = \text{\$/unit}$$

- **Rental rate:**

$$\frac{\text{Total rent per month}}{\text{Square feet of living space}} = \text{Rent/sq. ft.}$$

In the event that you are not able to find data for income property sales, you can use sales information for single-family homes to give you some indication of the trends. Many realty offices save sales data to assist in estimating the sales prices for listings and sales they make. If not, it's time to do some detective work. The information is out there; you just have to find it. The following are three good sources that can help you find this information:

1. Tax assessor's records

2. Appraisal services and title companies

3. Newspaper ads

Let's see how these sources can be used to help us gather the information needed.

 Bright Idea

As the use of the Internet increases, more sources are available to track comparable sales (as well as any other data you may require). If you're computer savvy, go online and give it a try.

Tax assessor's records

Your local assessor's office should have records of the property values for many years in the past. The problem with the assessor's data is that the assessed valuation does not always reflect the actual fair market value of the property in the area. Some of these valuations are so old, or are based on original valuations done sometimes 50 or more years ago, that they occupy the realm of fantasy. The truth is that it is impossible for these departments to appraise all properties every year, so the valuations are based on current data combined with any historical data they might already have.

When using the tax assessor's records, it's important to choose a section of property that hasn't changed much for many years. A large tract of homes, for example, would be a good place to start. Then you need to check valuation changes in that area back as many years as you want your study to cover. Once you do this, it should show you a trend in the valuation of property in that area.

Appraisal services and title companies

Most appraisal services and title companies keep large databases for comparable sales of property. By contacting their customer service departments, you might be able to find one that would let you look through files of buildings that have changed hands. Some companies, however, use outside services to gather this kind of information. If they do, ask them who they use and then contact the service yourself. It might cost you something, but in

 Bright Idea

If you are struggling to get someone to help you, contact a title representative that works at one of the local title companies. Tell her that if she helps you gather the data you need now, you'll give her your title business on the building you buy when it comes time for you to make a purchase. For a commissioned employee like a title representative, the idea of having a deal in the bank would probably be pretty attractive.

Bright Idea

It isn't necessary to look at every paper for every month of the year. Ask your agent which months of the year seem to be the most active in your area. This usually is just after school is out because most people don't like to move their kids in the middle of the year.

the long run, having this understanding about the history of value for your target area will be well worth a small expense.

Newspaper ads

A third method of acquiring appreciation data requires spending some time in the archives of your local newspaper or library. As with the research at the assessor's office, you will want to pick a section of your community that hasn't had much physical change for the time period you are researching. The best choice would be a housing tract in which the houses are advertised using the name of the tract. As an example, in Hawthorne, California, the most popular housing tract in the city is called Holly Glen. In Holly Glen, there are only a couple of floor plans in the entire tract, and they each have 3 bedrooms and 1¾ bathrooms.

When you find the ideal tract of homes, it's time to gather and crunch some numbers. Look at the "For Sale" ads in the Saturday and Sunday papers as far back as the year the tract was built. You should be able to get enough sales prices to get a good feeling about the average price in the tract. Because you know the average number of square feet in the homes in this tract, it will be easy to get the average price per square foot for that year. When your research is complete, you will have enough data to do an estimate of the appreciation rate.

We'll assume you have reviewed past newspaper ads and have identified a tract of homes as previously discussed. The following shows how you could lay out your chart.

Year	Price	Change in Dollars	Percentage Change	Average Change
1993	$89,500			
1994	$93,500	$4,000	4.4%	4.40%
1995	$98,500	$5,000	5.3%	4.85%
1996	$97,500	–$1,000	–1.0%	2.90%
1997	$95,000	–$2,500	–2.5%	1.55%
1998	$95,000	0	0	1.24%
1999	$97,500	$2,500	2.6%	1.46%
2000	$101,500	$4,000	4.1%	1.84%
2001	$106,500	$5,000	5.0%	2.24%
2002	$113,000	$6,500	6.1%	2.67%
2003	$119,950	$6,950	6.2%	3.02%

The percentage change can be calculated by dividing the change in dollars by the price the year before. For example, the dollar increase from 1993 to 1994 was $4,000. The percentage change is $4,000 ÷ $89,500 = 4.4 percent.

The average change is calculated by dividing the percentage changes by the number of years of changes. For example, the average change from 1993 to 1995 is 4.4 percent + 5.3 percent ÷ 2 = 4.85 percent. We divide by two because we have owned the property for only two full years, 1993 and 1994. The percentage change shown on the line for 1995 is the value at the start of the year.

While you are researching the house ads in the paper, make sure you also look for ads for small units. You may find some useful information about old rental rates and even unit prices for prior years. Your study might just show the impact on houses, but our experience has shown that most properties in a given economic area appreciate at about the same rate.

Bright Idea

Most new calculators and computers have programs that can do linear regression analysis. If you can learn to use those programs, you will be able to chart appreciation rates quickly and easily.

The "comfort zone"

At a minimum, you now have a reasonable idea of what is happening in your area. It's time to start narrowing down the geographic area and deciding on one or two areas in which you'd feel comfortable investing. Establishing this zone where you feel comfortable will be a combination of the economic cycles of the communities and your personal feelings about the areas.

The best way to pick areas is by doing a comparison of the financial returns of all the areas in which you could buy. Pick a property size, let's say a 4-unit, and find one for sale in each of the areas in which you could invest. Next, calculate the return on investment for each property. Use the same down payment and loan terms so that you get an apples-to-apples comparison.

Invariably, you will be drawn to some areas emotionally but won't be able to afford them. Other areas will have an exceptional return, but you wouldn't feel comfortable in them. In the end, you should find several areas that could work for you, and we'll call these your comfort zones. As you learn about financial planning in Chapter 9, you will use this comfort zone information and the other statistical facts you've accumulated to complete your investment plan.

Just the facts

- A clever investor always can make a profit because housing is a basic necessity of life.
- Understanding the economic principles of supply and demand will help you succeed as a real estate investor.

- Be wary of letting public opinion influence your investment choices.

- To make long-term projections for your investments, you need to chart value appreciation in your target market.

- Finding your comfort zone is the first step in long-term real estate planning.

Chapter 7

Subdividing Your Options

Much of this guide is built around our sample four-unit apartment building. This allows us to demonstrate many of the concepts of real estate investing with an easy-to-understand example. There is more to this game, however, than just four-unit buildings. There's land for development, smaller and larger apartment buildings, condominiums, single-family homes, commercial strip malls, and industrial properties to name just a few.

Yet, many investors develop tunnel vision when they begin making money in real estate. If someone is doing well investing in small apartment buildings, the odds are good that they won't even consider buying homes or commercial centers. Maybe an owner of an office building hasn't had a vacancy in five years. Why should he sink his money into commercial strip malls when he's doing great as it is? The reason is that there are opportunities to make lots of money investing in all kinds of property. To illustrate our point, in this chapter we'll give you a guided tour of the entire market so you can choose the venue that will produce the best return. Let's begin with the foundation of all real estate, land itself.

Land ho!

When you own real estate, it's important to recognize that it's the dirt that holds the real key to the ultimate value of your property. A beautiful house on the beach that goes up in value every year isn't appreciating because the 2×4s that went into building it are worth more annually. It's appreciating because the demand for the location is increasing—the demand for the land. You will learn that the secret to making money on a land investment is being able to recognize an increase in demand and then being able to capitalize on your insight.

Here, we'll focus on three different types of land investments. The classic purchase is raw land that sits in the path of progress. The other two involve buying land in areas that already are developed. Once you know the principles behind these three, you will gain a basic understanding of the opportunities and pitfalls that exist in this market.

Raw land

When thinking about investing money into raw land, you need to consider a number of variables. First off, know that raw land is a capital-intensive investment. What's worse, besides starting with a big bank roll, you will have to be willing to wait a good long time before you see any financial return. Unfortunately, these facts are just the nature of the beast.

 Bright Idea

The county planning office is a good place to start when considering a raw land investment. Ask them to help you plot out the business, industrial, and residential growth of the community over the past 30 years. Your map of the past should give you insight into plans for the future.

Many smart investors try to get ahead of the game by researching growth trends in certain areas and then rolling the dice and hoping their predictions come true. Sometimes they pan out; sometimes they don't. Here's a real-life example:

> In California, the communities surrounding the Los Angeles airport had become so crowded that there was talk of building a new airport 100 miles away in the city of Palmdale. The thought was that this would take the pressure off the Los Angeles basin and would provide millions of affordable acres for new jobs and new homes. In the movie *Field of Dreams* it was said, "If you build it, they will come." In *Field of Dreams* it worked. Kevin Costner had a vision to build a baseball diamond in a cornfield. He built it, and the people came. In Palmdale, however, they never built it, but the investors came anyway. Many sunk their savings into raw land thinking they were going to get rich, but the project fizzled. Will Palmdale ever be the thriving center envisioned? Probably, but not in the lifetime of those who had the dream.

As you can see, investing in raw land is an inherently risky proposition. This is because a land investment

- Often has enormous up-front costs including the cost of the land, sewers, utilities, roads, plans, permits, engineering, and so on
- Is extremely difficult to get financed
- Pays you no income at the beginning
- Might be highly taxed
- Usually is very slow to rise in value
- Might come with legal barriers to hurdle
- Is highly speculative
- Is subject to the whims of local politicians

This isn't to say, however, that you can't make money here, because you can. If you are in an area of rapid growth, have the money to risk, and see raw land as a potential winner, you should

- Do an in-depth analysis of growth trends, the speed of growth, and the direction of growth
- Determine which uses grow fastest in your area: commercial, residential, or industrial properties
- Attend planning meetings
- Obtain utility expansion plans
- Review historic examples of similar growth

Once this analysis is completed, you should have a pretty strong idea about whether raw land is an area of real estate where you want to sink your money.

In-fill opportunities

An "in-fill" project is another type of land investment. It involves buying a vacant lot surrounded by existing buildings of one type or another. The idea is to buy the lot, build something useful on it, and then sell it off for a profit. Compared to a raw land investment, these projects have considerably less risk for the investor because these opportunities are found in areas that already are developed.

In many cases, an owner has held a vacant lot next to his home or business for as long as he can remember. His original idea was to keep it just in case he needed it in order to expand. Now he is getting ready to retire and he realizes that he really doesn't need the property at all and, therefore, he decides to sell. This is where you come in.

Remember that, when buying this kind of lot, you need to do the same kind of research you would do if you were buying raw land. Check with the city and utility companies to see what can be built on the site. It would be disastrous to buy a lot with the intent and resources to build a small apartment building only to find out it is zoned for a parking lot only.

One important issue that comes up when doing an in-fill deal is determining whether there are any pollutants in the soil. As the developer of vacant land, this concern is now your problem. Think back to all the old gas stations and "mom-and-pop" manufacturing sites that may have closed near your property's location. If one of those types of businesses was located on your lot, and if it left any pollutants behind, which is very common, you are the one who is legally required to clean it up. Most cities require developers to do extensive environmental testing. These tests always are expensive, and if any problems are found, the cost of removal can be staggering.

As real estate investors ourselves, we developed many apartment and commercial projects in the late 1980s. One time, while doing the foundation excavation for an apartment building, we found concrete and asphalt mixed in with the soil that filled the rear of the lot. The city could care less that the problem wasn't toxic. They still forced us to excavate the entire rear portion of the lot, remove the concrete and asphalt, and then recompact the soil. This was because the dirt wasn't natural. Instead, it was fill-dirt and was not compacted properly. The concern was that it would cause settling problems after the foundation was built. Because the integrity of the entire structure rests on the foundation, the process had to be observed and regulated by an expensive licensed soils engineer. This unexpected problem cost us all the money we had in reserve and then some.

Redevelopment opportunities

The last type of land investment we'll touch on is called a redevelopment opportunity. This is when a piece of property is worth more for the value of the land itself than for the value of the land plus the existing structure that sits on it. In this situation, you are not looking for vacant land to build on as you did with the in-fill project. Instead, you are looking for a bargain property that should (and will) be torn down eventually. Like an

Moneysaver

Find an architect who is willing work for a percentage of the profit when your project is completedHe'll get paid on the back end, and you will save cash on the front end.

in-fill, however, once you have an empty dirt lot, the goal is to build something useful on it and then sell it off for a profit.

When doing a project like this, the rewards for the developer can be hefty. As an example, let's say you found an older two-bedroom house on a 50 × 150 R-3 (multi-unit) lot. The house can be had for $60,000, and after checking, you determine that R-3 land in that area is going for $10 per square foot. Here is how a redevelopment deal could yield a profit even before you build on it:

Value of land (50 × 150 × $10 per sq. ft.)	$75,000
Cost of the house	−$60,000
Potential profit before building	$15,000

One great thing about redevelopment deals is that the structure sitting on the lot might already be producing income when you purchase it. This is especially helpful if the market for land isn't too strong when you initially find the property. You still can take advantage of the opportunity by buying the lot and then renting out the structure until the market improves. This way, you avoid the high cost of holding undeveloped land while you wait for the appreciation. In addition, you could begin the development process with the city and be able to have a turn-key project to do on your own or to sell to a builder when the time is right.

Condominiums

For many people, condos provide a pretty nice home. They're affordable, often have great floor plans, and include amenities like pools, gyms, and saunas that that are just too expensive to obtain in a single-family home. But, truth be told, as far as a real estate investment goes, you can do better putting your money in other places.

Here's why: The trouble with condos is that you are hand-cuffed by the condo association in terms of what can be done to the property to increase its value. As a real estate investor, you must always ask yourself, "How can I add value to any property I purchase to make it worth more when I sell?" The idea is to buy a property for X, find ways to add value to it, and then eventually sell it for Y. With condominium ownership, however, most associations will not allow you to make any improvements at all to the outside of your unit. They want your unit to look like your neighbor's unit, which looks like his neighbor's unit, and so on. For that reason, any profit to be made buying con-dos is limited to

- Finding a bargain in the market (preforeclosure, foreclosure, desperate seller)
- Appreciation in value over time
- Adding value by doing interior upgrades only

Most people don't buy condominiums to make a profit; they do it to buy their first home. This is pretty smart because, as you can see, there is very little profit to be made here, beyond value appreciation, especially when held up against other real estate opportunities.

On the other hand, if you're looking for a home plus an investment and can afford it, a single-family residence or a small set of units may be a better way to go.

Single-family homes

Most of us with real estate on our minds long to be the king of our own castles. That is, we want to be homeowners. Thankfully, purchasing single-family homes offers a great opportunity to get your feet wet investing in real estate and a chance to create some extra profit as well, provided you're willing to put a little added effort into the mix. Additions to consider in order to add value to your investment might include outdoor shutters, upgraded landscaping, outdoor lighting, new paint, attractive fencing, interior upgrades, and so on.

All of these kinds of additions are possible with single-family homes because there's a great diversity in the properties that the typical single-family home area offers. Unlike condo tracts, there's hardly ever (except in planned communities) a requirement for a single-family home to look just like the neighbor's. With the shackles off, the opportunity to add value to your investment only stops with your imagination.

Knowledge is power

When deciding whether to buy single-family homes as an investment, begin, as always, by researching your local market. Start by identifying areas that have some diversity in the homes and that sell well. Look at potential purchases with an eye toward what could be done to add value to the home. A good rule of thumb is that the more conforming the area, the fewer opportunities to find a bargain. The typical conforming area is a housing tract that has hundreds of homes in it but only three or four different floor plans. You can make money here, but because there is so little variation, it limits the possibilities.

If you are looking to add some value to increase your profit, you should take a trip to city hall. You need to determine how difficult the permit requirements are. Obtaining permits can be easy and inexpensive or costly and time-consuming. Answers to these questions will tell you if buying single-family homes in this area would be worth pursuing or not.

 Bright Idea

Check with the local buildings department to see whether there are any restrictions to improving your property due to zoning regulations. Wealthier communities often impose severe zoning restrictions. Historic districts undoubtedly will have restrictions as well.

When searching for a bargain in the single-famly residence market, knowing the following information will you help you spot homes that are underpriced:

- The seller's motivation for selling
- The amount of time on the market
- The price per square foot
- The price per bedroom
- The value of extra bathrooms
- The value of a family room or den
- The value of amenities (pool, deck, garage, hot tub)
- The premium for condition

You can find even more profit by using other facts from your research. In the following scenario, let's say you've found an older two-bedroom house that has about 1,300 square feet. Your research shows that most of the three-bedroom houses also are about 1,300 square feet, and they sell for about $125 per square foot (1,300 square feet × $125 per square foot = a sales price of $162,500). Here, the house you found could be bought for $110,000 because it only has two bedrooms, it's older, and it needs carpet, paint, and window coverings.

The plan would be to buy this house for $110,000. Give the place a well-deserved face-lift and redesign the interior to turn it into a desirable three-bedroom house. Let's say you have determined that this can be done with a minimum of expensive

 Watch Out!

Be aware that many of the homes or units that you are considering will have termites or termite damage. If either is found, it should be up to the seller to have treatments done and make the necessary repairs or to adjust the sales price accordingly.

structural work because you would only have to move some walls and build a new closet. The budget would look like this:

Construction of bedroom	$15,000
Floor covering	$1,300
Interior paint	$750
Window coverings	$500
Exterior paint	$2,000
Landscaping	$750
Total cost to improve	$20,300

Now you would have a sharp, three-bedroom home that should sell for $125 per square foot just like the other three-bedroom houses in the neighborhood. Your gross profit would look like this:

Value added price	$162,500
Less original cost	−$110,000
Less cost to improve	−$20,300
Gross profit	$32,200

One of the extra bonuses of this type of investment is that you combine this purchase for profit with your desire to live in and own your own home. Many investors have started out exactly this way. They pick a house for the investment and profit value and also live in it as their personal residence during the interim. The main goal isn't the personal desires you might have for a home but the profit you can generate by purchasing a particular piece of property. The property just happens to also provide a temporary place for you to live.

 Moneysaver

Before buying a house with the idea of rearranging the interior, have a licensed contractor make sure he can do the work without any major structural alterations.

Living in this kind of investment provides several advantages:

- You gain an investment and a residence in one shot.
- You become your own boss.
- When you sell it, the profit might become tax free if you meet certain criteria.

The first two advantages are obvious, but the last is a new twist because of current tax laws in effect. As of 1999, you can exclude the entire gain on the sale of your main residence under the following conditions:

1. Up to $250,000, or
2. Up to $500,000 if all of the following are true:
   a. You are married and file a joint return for the year.
   b. Either you or your spouse meets the ownership test.
   c. Both you and your spouse meet the use test.
   d. Neither you nor your spouse excluded gain from the sale of another home after May 6, 1997.

The IRS says you can claim the exclusion if

1. During the five-year period ending on the date of the sale, you have owned the home for at least two years (ownership test).
2. Have lived there as your main residence for at least two years (use test).

This is probably the greatest method of delivering tax-free wealth that the government has ever enacted. Think about it. This isn't a way of deferring your taxes; instead, you have absolutely no tax due whatsoever. What's more, Uncle Sam says that you can take advantage of this technique every two years. This can work for both beginning and experienced investors.

For people just starting out, the message is: When you buy a home, don't buy with the idea that you are going to live there forever. Instead, buy a property that will generate the greatest profit within the two years following your purchase. You might want to consider a house in an up-and-coming location, a place with an extra lot that you can sell off separately, or even a classic fixer-upper—anything that will help create some sweat equity.

After you've lived there for two years, the idea is to sell it, take all that free profit, and start over again. This time, however, you might have made enough money from the sale to buy both a home and a piece of income property. Now think about your portfolio. It would include two great pieces of real estate—a home and, say, a small apartment building. If you're game, you could even do it again in two years.

The plan will work just as easily for people who already have substantial equity in their current residence. It can be particularly helpful to people nearing retirement. A person can make money using the same methods previously mentioned, but a significant portion of the capital gain could be put into cash reserves for his latter years.

A final word on this benefit: Our government uses these kinds of tax benefits to stimulate the economy. Other methods are used to slow the economy. Conventional wisdom says that, because this benefit is so huge, it probably won't be around very long. If you wait, you might be left mumbling, "If only I had . . ."

Single-family homes as rental properties

Single-family homes also can be purchased as rentals and, as such, can generate the same returns previously discussed in this book. There are pros and cons to owning single-family homes solely as rental investments. The primary advantage is that the management and expenses of renting a house should be minimal. Management will be easy because you only have one primary tenant to be concerned with. As for expenses, you should make the tenant be responsible for all of his own utilities and general maintenance. Of course, you have to pay for major items such as new roofs, property taxes, and broken water heaters, but the tenant should basically live in the house as though he owned it.

There also are some disadvantages to buying and then renting single-family homes. The biggest disadvantage is that the financial return on single-family residences in a given area is usually far less than the return on an apartment investment. Go back to our discussion earlier in this chapter about the value of the dirt under any property. Because the land holds a great percentage of the value of any property, the rent you earn is being paid not only for the structure but also for the land. This is the only reason why there's a difference in rental rates for homes in differing economic areas in the same city. People don't pay more for the house; they pay more for the location, which is the land. Location, location, location!

Let's say you have a four-unit building on a 7,500 square foot lot. You have four tenants paying rent on that lot. If you had one house on that same size lot, you would only be getting income from one person. It is true that one house will always rent for more than one apartment a quarter of its size, but it is doubtful that it would rent for more than four apartments put together. In our experience, it is a rare case that the premium for a single-family residence will give you the same return as an investment in apartments in the same area costing the same amount.

> **❝**I own several single-family homes as rentals. On two different occasions, I had tenants skip out on the rent and leave me to pay my entire mortgage without any income coming in from the properties at all.**❞**
>
> —Jillian L., property owner

The second disadvantage is that, when you have a vacancy in a single-family home, your vacancy rate is 100 percent. In times of vacancy, that could be quite a big load to carry. However, if you own a positive cash flow four-unit apartment building, the cash flow from the other three units might be enough to still make the mortgage payment and pay for your other expenses.

Vacation homes

A vacation property can provide an interesting mix of benefits. The primary advantage of buying a vacation home is to have a place to go with family and friends—a home away from home where you can relax and enjoy the surroundings.

Because these properties are purchased primarily for personal use, we hesitate to classify them as truly investment property. But, they do take on the characteristics of investment property for two reasons. First, many owners do rent their vacation homes out, and this can produce income. Second, if these properties are purchased with the intent to sell some day at a profit, they qualify for the benefits of a 1031 exchange.

Many owners offset the cost of ownership by renting out their vacation homes when they can't use them themselves. The tax laws say that if personal use of the property exceeds the greater of 14 days or 10 percent of the total days rented, you cannot take depreciation to help shelter any income earned. This means that this income is taxable just like any other portfolio income we may have. The good news is that the expenses, interest, and taxes may be written off subject to the first and second home limitations.

As far as a 1031 tax-deferred exchange goes, a vacation home qualifies for an exchange even if it isn't rented and is only used for personal enjoyment. The key factor is that it was purchased with the intent of selling some day for a profit when the family no longer wants to use it. The good news is that this means you can trade for another vacation home or any other property that qualifies as investment property, like an apartment building.

It's important to note that all the rules of doing an IRS 1031 exchange must be followed. We will be reviewing these rules in detail in Chapter 10, "Planning for the Tax Man," but for now remember to always have your particular situation reviewed by your CPA before you make any moves.

Two-to-four-unit properties

One step up from buying a condo or a house is purchasing a small apartment building. We will define small as a duplex, triplex, or fourplex. As you may have guessed, we favor residential apartment rentals as investments and believe that they represent the safest form of real estate investing. One reason is because, as you learned in Chapter 5, "Borrowing Big Bucks," these properties fall into the residential loan category. For that reason, they're easy to finance with low down-payment options, which make them affordable for most of us.

Secondly, and maybe more importantly, apartment investing is a winner because you are investing in one of the three basic commodities of life—shelter. Thankfully for all real estate investors, every human being on earth needs a place to call home. This is true whether the times are good or bad. A business, on the other hand, which may operate out of a strip mall, can always close up shop and function out of the owner's garage if times get tough. The people who worked there will be out of a job, but those same people will still need a place to sleep at the end of the day.

The premise is this: By providing shelter, we, as real estate investors, should always be able to stay in business.

The privacy factor

As a property owner, your tenants should feel a sense of privacy when living in their units. If given a choice, most people would opt to live in a single-family house. Because houses rent at a

---

 Bright Idea!

Regardless of what we believe is the best real estate to buy, you can't make any profit unless you do buy some property. In fact, "buying some" is the number-one secret to making a profit in real estate. If you can't buy a four-unit apartment building, buy a duplex. If you can't get a duplex, buy a house or condo. But above all, buy some and get started!

premium, however, most renters can't afford them. The next best thing for them is to pay a premium for a nice apartment that has the feeling of a single-family home. The best way to create that single-family feel is to find properties that have separate units on the lot. Even if fences do not separate the units, these kinds of apartments give the tenants more privacy than, say, three or four units that share common walls between them. As a general rule, the more private you can make the rentals, the less the tenants will call and ask for you to provide extra upgrades to their units. This is because privacy makes the tenants look at the unit as their home as opposed to a temporary residence. In addition, if you can add fences to separate the units, you can save on gardening costs as you make each tenant responsible for his own yard. You will see both of these benefits on the bottom line because your overall expenses will be kept at a minimum.

One lone building

The next best thing to completely separate units is to buy a building that sits on just one level. These properties don't have the inherent noise problems that come with tenants living over one another. Many of these situations offer the opportunity to fence off a private area for each tenant behind or in front of each unit. Again, this gives some private open space, and it should save on gardening costs.

Two + two

If you're not able to find these single-family-style properties, you will have to look for standard apartment-style buildings. Basic apartment buildings are usually two stories with a couple of units downstairs and a couple more upstairs. A parking area usually is either attached or separated, depending on the size of the lot. Although these buildings often do not have the same appeal of the other style properties, don't worry. There will always be a tenant available for a nice unit.

In many older urban areas you have two-family ("Philadelphia" style) houses and three-deckers. You also often find formerly single-family residences split into two to four units. The feel of these residences is somewhere between a single-family house and an apartment building. With growing gentrification, as in New York or Boston, some older neighborhoods with this type of housing could be a wise investment

Finding properties

One of the keys to finding the right two-to-four-unit property is to survey the market and get a feeling for the kind of style and amenities that seem to command the highest rent per square foot. Your goal then will be to acquire that type of property or one that can be converted at a minimum cost.

In finding the right property, it's important to pay particular attention to your potential expenses. If possible, look for units that have all the utilities metered separately. This way, the tenants will pay the utility bills instead of you. Also look for units that have individual laundry hookups versus common laundry rooms. Again, this means that they pay for their gas and electricity, not you. Tenants also should supply their own appliances. Not having to purchase and maintain refrigerators and stoves will save you a lot of money over the years. From a practical standpoint, the bigger the items your tenant has to move in, the less likely he is to move out.

> ❝I bought a four-unit row house in Boston in the '80s, converted it to condos and sold them for triple my investment (purchase plus improvements). Twelve years later, the units were selling for 100 percent more than I sold them for.❞
>
> —Matthew K., investor.

You will be restricted based on what tenants in the area expect when they rent. If you find that you will have to provide most of the appliances to keep up with the competition, make sure you become an expert on the secondhand market and local repair services. This will help you keep costs under control.

Five units and up

When you graduate to the five-unit and larger category, you have moved into the arena of commercial loans and the economy of scale that comes from more units per square foot. The first time you start looking at these properties, this discount usually becomes quite apparent. Again, this is primarily because there is a limited availability of financing for these size properties versus single-family residences and two-to-four-unit buildings.

With five-unit buildings, specifically, there is a good method of creating some added value. Surprisingly enough, it is not by adding bedrooms like we did with the single-family example earlier. Instead, you can add value by turning a five-unit building into a four-unit building. In doing so, you turn a property that required a commercial loan into one that only requires a buyer to obtain a residential loan.

Let's say you find a five-unit building in the same neighborhood as our four-unit example. The four-unit is worth $220,000, and we can buy this five-unit for $175,000. (This kind of discount for bigger, harder-to-finance buildings is not uncommon. Once you start to research the market, you will see it to be true.) The four-unit is made up of all two-bedroom units. The five-unit has three two-bedroom units and two one-bedroom units. If the layout of the one-bedroom units is such that they are located right next to each other, you probably can take out a couple of walls and combine them into one really nice two-or-three-bedroom unit. All of a sudden, you have turned your hard-to-finance (and hard-to-sell) five-unit building into an easy-to-finance (and easy-to-sell) four-unit building.

Surprisingly, it's relatively easy to get a conversion like this through city bureaucracy because you are down-zoning the property, which is a preferred situation to creating more units. You are decreasing the density and increasing the parking on your property, which most cities like.

Of course you will have to do diligent research before you attempt this kind of project. You need to know in advance specifically what kind of permits and costs will be involved. If you find that the city is going to require extensive drawings or engineering work before they issue permits, make sure your contractor and architect are in the loop. Their expert opinion will help you to determine whether the project will be worth the expense.

Big apartment buildings

When you become really successful at this game and begin to buy great big apartment buildings with multiple units, your decision-making becomes entirely dependent on the analysis of the financial operations of the property. The good news is that when you get into this range of properties there are usually plenty of loans available. Know, however, that when it comes to commercial loans like these, you are going to have to come up with a great deal of cash for a down payment. With these purchases, lenders usually require you to come up with upwards of 25–35 percent of the purchase price. Just to illustrate what you'll be up against, 25 percent on a $2,000,000 piece of property comes to $500,000 down.

Tenants who rent in larger properties tend to be looking for a different environment than tenants who like the privacy of

Moneysaver

When buying big apartment buildings, always be on the lookout for any available owner financing. If you can find some, it often can considerably increase your leverage and, thereby, your percentage return on your investment.

smaller two-to-four-unit properties. These tenants have similar thinking to people who want to buy and live in large condo developments. They want the luxury of pools, workout rooms, and clubhouses, but they can't afford or don't want the hassle of paying for or taking care of these amenities themselves. Items that attract tenants to larger apartment complexes include

- An attractive appearance from the street (curb appeal)
- Well-maintained common areas
- A security entrance system
- A secure parking area
- Recreational amenities (pools, jacuzzis, saunas, barbecues, tennis courts, a clubhouse, and so on)
- Laundry rooms
- Large square footage apartments
- Appliances
- Multiple bathrooms
- Walk-in closets
- A private balcony or patio area
- Air-conditioning
- Upscale amenities (wet bar, fireplace, and so on)
- Cable or satellite television services

Note that it is not unusual for tenants in larger properties to move a bit more frequently than those who rent in smaller properties. By maintaining a high degree of pride-of-ownership, you will make it harder for tenants to justify moving for purely emotional reasons.

As you move into progressively larger properties, you will be leaving the "mom-and-pop" phase of real estate investing and entering the "just business" phase. The properties produce good cash-on-cash income, but they need the kind of organized

Bright Idea

Unless you have the confidence and experience to manage a large apartment building yourself, you should hire a property management company before you buy. Make sure you take a company representative with you to look at each and every property you are considering. The representative will provide insight about things that you never even considered.

management that any larger business would need. The principles we will be discussing in Chapters 13–15 will be most applicable to these size properties.

Commercial and industrial properties

Commercial and industrial properties can be a great investment vehicle for you to consider. This is because, like residential tenants, businesses also need a roof over their heads and will pay good money for just the right place to hang their shingle. In fact, you should think of these properties as a "home for a business."

Commercial and industrial properties fall into many categories including

- Freestanding stores
- Small strip malls
- Office buildings
- Mobile home parks
- Mixed-use commercial and residential
- Parking lots
- Garages
- Multistory office buildings
- Specialty commercial (restaurants, gas stations, and so on)
- Small factories
- Larger industrial buildings

Partner up

When you rent commercial or industrial space to a tenant, you really are becoming a partner in their business. If they do well in your location, the odds are good that they will continue to be a tenant and will continually be able to afford your rent.

The fact of the matter is, however, most new businesses fail in the first year or two of operation. If one of your long-term tenants fails, your real estate investment could be in serious trouble. For this reason, you should personally interview all the tenants in any commercial property you consider purchasing. You need to find out the following information:

- The length of time the owners have been in business
- The credit rating of the owners and the business
- Why they left their last location
- Why they chose this location
- The goals of their business
- The type and term of lease they desire

Be especially wary of a property in which most of the leases are coming up for renewal. Many clever sellers have unloaded a prize building with a great long-term tenant because they got wind that the tenant was going to be moving on. You don't want to get stuck owning a great strip mall without any tenants.

Types of leases

The foundation of most commercial properties is the lease as opposed to the month-to-month agreement used in residential property. Having long-term leases with successful tenants/businesses is one of the greatest advantages of owning a commercial property—provided your lease is structured properly. Therefore, it is imperative that you hire a real estate lawyer to help you handle these kinds of transactions.

Generally speaking, leases fall into two categories:

1. Gross leases
2. Triple net leases

The difference in the two depends on whether the property owner or the tenant is going to pay the bills. In a gross lease, the tenant pays the rent, and the property owner pays all the expenses of operation except the tenant's utilities. In a triple net lease, the tenant pays for everything including the rent, the taxes, the insurance, the utilities, and most of the maintenance of the property. In some retail leases, the tenant even pays a percentage of their sales as part of their rent.

Commercial and industrial properties have some distinct advantages and disadvantages when compared to residential purchases:

Advantages

- Long-term tenants
- Limited management
- Consistent return on investment
- Consistent value appreciation

Disadvantages

- Limited availability of tenants
- Limited availability of financing
- Significant holding costs between tenants

Niche markets

There are a couple of interesting trends in this type of real estate. The first is the niche market of providing small office and commercial space for new enterprises. One of the effects of the leaning of our new entrepreneurial economy in the late 1990s is the emergence of the displaced or energetic person who has an idea for how to make a better mousetrap. This started with more and more people working from home. When they outgrow their home office, these workers usually end up looking for a small space to rent where they can have a desk, a copy machine, and maybe a secretary instead of a house full of kids. What's more, young entrepreneurs are usually willing to pay a premium rent per square foot to house their new ventures.

Moneysaver

Many communities offer low-interest loans and redevelopment funds to help investors restore older historical properties.

The other phenomenon is the conversion of older commercial and industrial buildings into loft apartments or live/work spaces. This mirrors the trends in cities such as New York and San Francisco for a hip, open environment for young adults and trend-setting businesses. These older buildings sometimes can be purchased at a very low price per square foot. Then, with a minimum of improvements, they can be rented or sold at a fantastic profit. If the structures are of any historical significance, there are some very attractive tax benefits. In these cases as well as the other commercial/industrial properties, the secret to your success will be staying on top of the market so that you are not caught owning a white elephant.

Just the facts

- A real estate investment in raw land requires two things from you: money and patience.
- Adding value to a condo or a single-family home is the best way to get more out of that kind of investment.
- An investment in a single-family home will never bring you the same return as a unit investment on that same lot.
- Because of the great financing available, two- to four-unit buildings can be huge moneymakers.
- Big apartment buildings require huge down payments and intensive management.
- There are a lot of opportunities to make money by buying commercial and industrial properties.

Whether fixer-uppers are really for you ▪
Mismanaged properties and why they're an
investor's dream ▪ The truth behind the foreclosure market ▪ Getting in on "short sales" ▪
Buying property with little or no money down

Tricks of the Trade

You've seen the ads on late-night TV—the "get rich quick" ads where the *nouveaux riches* testify to the glory of foreclosures, fixer-uppers, and no-money-down deals. Yep, those people sure look like they're living the high life. Perhaps they are, but probably because they made a bundle starring in infomercials rather than investing in real estate. The truth is there are several types of properties that present an opportunity to make an extra profit—that is, if you are an experienced investor with deep pockets. But, suggesting novice buyers go out and invest in these deals right out of the gate is like asking someone to jump off a high dive before they know how to swim. Nonetheless, people have made loads of money (and others have lost bundles) investing in these "sure things." Here are the facts so that you can analyze those opportunities and make an educated decision.

The fixer-upper

The classic property that offers a chance for the investor to make an extra buck is the fixer-upper. A fixer-upper is a property that is in disrepair and needs money and TLC to bring it back to life. The idea, in theory, is to buy a fixer-upper, do any necessary repairs yourself, and then reap the rewards of an investment property purchased below market value. Countless books have been written about these types of investments, and countless people have invested in them only to discover that they are in over their head. To explain, let's look at a variation on our example property and see how fixer-uppers really pencil out.

The facts and the figures

We'll assume that 333 Richmond Street is an average fixer-upper. Here are some estimates for what the necessary repairs will cost:

Exterior

Exterior paint	$2,500
Landscaping	$500
Garage doors	$800
Fence	$750
Roof	$3,000
Total	$7,550

Rehab Unit

Carpet	$750
Interior paint	$350
Misc.	$75
Lost rent	$550
Total	$1,725
Grand total	$9,275

If you recall, 333 Richmond Street was listed on the market for $225,000, but we estimated the value to be $222,500 using the appraisal methods learned in Chapter 4, "Appraising Like an Appraiser." In this instance, because the property needs some fixing up, we were able to negotiate a $20,500 discount from the list price and bought it for $205,000.

Let's take a look at what this means in terms of our potential profit. The first logical assumption is that this fixer-upper will be worth the full $222,500 as soon as we finish the work. Therefore, our estimated gross profit from the project will be

Finished value	$222,500
Purchase price	−$205,000
Gross profit	$17,500

In order to find the net profit, we deduct the cost of the necessary repairs from the estimated gross profit:

Gross profit	$17,500
Less upgrade costs	−$9,275
Net profit	$8,225

In order to determine the percentage return the first year, we then need to add the net profit to the estimated return for the first year of ownership, and then divide by our down payment and fix-up costs. To recap, remember that in the first year 333 Richmond Street had an estimated total return of $13,419. We had $1,080 from cash flow, $300 in equity growth from loan reduction, $11,000 in equity growth from appreciation, and $1,039 in tax benefits (see Chapter 3, "Elements of Return"). After this bit of math, we can calculate our percentage return for the first year is as follows:

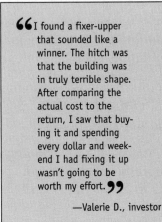

"I found a fixer-upper that sounded like a winner. The hitch was that the building was in truly terrible shape. After comparing the actual cost to the return, I saw that buying it and spending every dollar and weekend I had fixing it up wasn't going to be worth my effort."

—Valerie D., investor

$$\frac{\text{Returns } \$13,419 + \$8,225}{\text{Investment } \$30,000 + \$9,725} = 54.4\% \text{ return}$$

As you can see, a 54.4 percent return isn't half bad. But, remember, on the original nonfixer-upper example, as demonstrated in Chapter 3, we obtained a pretty good return the first year as well, of 44.7 percent. The question then becomes whether the higher return of 54.4 percent on the fixer-upper project was worth the extra time, extra money, and extra energy it took to achieve it? As your parents used to say, "We'll see." Let's keep analyzing:

When you look beyond the first year and examine the return in subsequent years of ownership, you will note that the percentage return on the investment begins to drop at a rapid clip. This is because the extra profit you gain in a fixer-upper is a one-shot increase in value that first year, which requires an additional cash investment over and above the original down payment. Keep in mind that in each subsequent year of ownership you will have to divide your annual returns by a much higher equity position. This will decrease your leverage, and thereby your return, significantly.

Let's illustrate: We'll make the assumption that the profit in the second year would be about the same as it was the first year. If so, look at what happens to our overall return because we now have the extra cash it took to fix up the building invested without any extra return the second year to offset it.

$$\frac{\text{Second year return } \$13,419}{\text{Investment } \$30,000 + \$9,275} = 34.2\%$$

Yes, 34.2 percent in the second year is a sizeable decrease in percentage return from 54.4 percent the first year. Again, this is due to our increased equity position and no fix-up profit this year, which proportionately decreased our leverage.

Many other investors use a different strategy when investing in fixer-uppers. Mistakenly, they (like many before them) fail to

Bright Idea

Compile a notebook with the cost of basic property maintenance items as well as a list of work you have had done on your property. This will come in handy when a crisis arises and you need to know how much it will cost to fix it.

recognize that the real wealth from real estate investing comes from taking advantage all four elements of return over the long haul. Instead, to them, buying real estate is like buying raw materials to produce a product to resell. In real estate, however, this is usually a recipe for disaster. The trouble is that most people with this "flip-it-quick" mentality never do the kind of analysis you are learning here, and thereby never really see the percentage return they are making. If they did, they surely would see the error in their ways.

To illustrate, let's look at the percentage return in this instance. This time, we will assume that you will hold the property for just one year like many investors do, and then sell. Of course, you will get the normal returns as well as the fixer-upper profit, but the rub is that we now have to add in the costs of selling. A good guesstimate of sales costs would be $15,000. Our profit, therefore, now looks like this:

First year return	$13,419
Plus fix-up profit	+$7,725
Less sale costs	−$15,000
Net profit	$6,144

We then divide the net profit by our equity, as follows:

$$\frac{\text{Net profit } \$6,144}{\text{Investment } \$30,000 + \$9,275} = 15.6\%$$

As you can see, a 15.6 percent return isn't a very impressive profit at all. Especially when you factor in the tremendous amounts of time, money, and effort required to fix up and then flip fixer-uppers.

Nine times out of ten, the only way to make financial sense out of a classic fixer-upper would be if

1. You were a skilled contractor and had the resources to drastically reduce the cost of the repairs and the time it takes to do them.

2. You were also a licensed real estate broker and could reduce the costs of selling.

Yes, we are being a little tongue-in-cheek here, but we're trying to prove a point. The truth is fixer-uppers tend to sour the average person on real estate investing long before he ever finds out that they aren't necessary in order to make an excellent return on investment (see the 44.7 percent return on the example property from Chapter 3, "Elements of Return").

Nevertheless, if your goal is to consider a fixer-upper and see an opportunity to make an extra profit, you must thoroughly evaluate whether it will be truly worth the extra risk and extra money. Remember, the added capital investment decreases your leverage. As you are learning, leverage is one of the most significant elements that drive the return on your invested capital. For that reason, the percentage return from any fixer-upper project needs to be pretty darn good to warrant the loss of leverage and increased risk.

From a practical standpoint, it may make better sense to take the extra capital it would take to repair the 333 Richmond Street fixer-upper and, instead, put it toward the down payment on a second building. Remember, if you go with a 3-percent-down FHA loan, the down payment on a $200,000 building

 Watch Out!

You are taking on an extra risk when you buy a property that needs work to bring it back to life. Many times, a job that looks like it will only take a month to complete and only cost a few dollars ends up taking six months and costing four times the original estimate.

would only be $6,000. That's $3,275 less than it cost to fix up the example property.

Management fixer-uppers

As you know by now, real estate, by nature, is not a get-rich-quick investment. You can't (and shouldn't) get in and out quickly like you can when buying and selling stocks or bonds. Unfortunately, many people jump into real estate not knowing this reality and get stuck owning property that they are unwilling to maintain and properly manage. For the knowledgeable real estate investor, however, finding "management fixer-uppers" such as these, is like striking oil deep in the desert.

Unlike standard fixer-uppers that offer very little profit compared to the money necessary to achieve it, management fixer-uppers offer a superb opportunity to add value to your bottom-line. Because they have been mismanaged for one reason or another, they often can be described as properties in which "the inmates are running the asylum." Rents usually are well below market, and they always arrive late or, sometimes, not at all. Often, mismanaged buildings cause their owners so much grief that they discount the selling price dramatically just to be rid of the headache. Thankfully, buildings like these are often priced well below market, but cost very little to turn around; a starkly different story than that that of the standard fixer-upper.

For both part-time and out-of-state owners of small properties, mismanagement of their real estate is a common problem. It also is common with properties owned by partners or groups of investors. Owners of these buildings either get tired of owning property, get tired of the losses their properties produce, or both. The truth is, they have given up on real estate investing all together and are ready to do whatever it takes to get the property off their books.

When individual investors find themselves in this situation, it usually is because they have something more pressing than landlording to attend to in their lives. Many people find out

Moneysaver

Mismanaged buildings are a much wiser choice for the real estate investor than standard fixer-upper opportunities. They generally require less money and very little physical effort to straighten them out.

after the fact that they don't have the time, energy, money, or desire to make their buildings perform. For groups, the problems come from the fact that they usually lack a leader willing to do the job necessary to save the investment. That person would have to put in a larger amount of effort only to receive his proportionate share of the profit.

Your real estate agent will have to do much of the detective work to find a good mismanaged building for you to make a run at. This is because many of these opportunities are sometimes not even for sale on the open market. Instead, your agent will have to network with other agents who have contact with disillusioned property owners who might consider an offer. Other agents might not come right out and say, "Your client can steal this property," but they will give you and your agent hints along the way. Common clues that might lead you to a management fixer-upper opportunity are

- The rents are well under market.
- The partners are having problems.
- The seller can't handle the maintenance problems anymore.
- The partnership is breaking up.
- The owners moved out of state.
- The seller needs the money for (fill in the blank).
- The seller lost his job.
- This is the last property the seller is getting rid of.
- The sellers are separating or getting a divorce.
- There is high vacancy or credit losses.

- The building has a lot of deferred maintenance.
- The exterior looks shabby.
- Expenses are way too high.
- Nobody is watching the property.
- Theft is happening by the staff, tenants, or others.

When you find a property with a motivated seller and some management problems, it's time to sharpen your pencil and do your homework because this is where you can make some real money. The first thing to do is analyze the true value that might be there, provided the building could be turned around. As with the standard fixer-upper, you want to be sure there is adequate profit available for the risk you will take by buying someone else's problem.

Assume that because 333 Richmond Street has been mismanaged, we buy it for $205,000—a bargain, considering we determined earlier that comparable, properly managed buildings in the same neighborhood are worth $222,500.

In this scenario, not only did the listing agent indicate that the owners were anxious to sell, we noticed that they had lost interest altogether. Here is why:

1. **The exterior looks shabby.** Paint is peeling, and the landscaping is terribly overgrown.

2. **There has been a unit vacant for more than two months.** There are two reasons for this: First, the unit isn't rent ready. It needs new blinds on the windows, the carpets need cleaning, and the kitchen and bathroom need painting. The second reason for the vacancy is probably due to the "For Rent" sign stuck in the window of the vacant unit. It can barely be seen from the street, it doesn't say anything specific about the building, and it only lists a phone number that is hard to make out. What's more, we discover that besides the sign, the owner didn't advertise the vacancy in any way.

3. **The rents are all too low.** The market rent for the neighborhood is $550, but the current rents in the three occu-
   pied units are just $475, $490, and $505. The reason it's
   under rented is that the sellers didn't want to rock the
   boat by raising them. In addition, because the sellers were
   reluctant to maintain the property, they didn't want to
   have to worry about cleaning units up if tenants decided
   to move out because of a rental increase (a common problem with uninterested owners).

Before we raise the rents on the existing units, we first
decide to offer some upgrades to ease the pain of the increase.
The budget for all of the repairs and upgrades is as follows:

Exterior

Exterior paint	$500
Landscaping	$250
Total	$750

Rehab vacant unit

Clean carpet	$75
Paint	$350
Misc.	$100
Lost rent	$250
Total	$775

Upgrade to other units

Unit #1: New garbage disposal	$75
Unit #2: New blinds	$125
Unit #4: New screens	$110
Total	$310
Total cost of upgrades	**$1,835**

Bright Idea

Offer your tenants a referral fee if they recommend a new tenant for one of your vacancies. The whole idea of successful landlording is to keep your units full. A small cash outlay to achieve that result will always be well worth it.

Let's review the profit from the purchase and see how this compares on a percentage basis. The gross profit is

Finished value	$222,500
Purchase price	–$205,000
Gross profit	$17,500

Now we deduct the estimated cost of the repairs from the estimated gross profit to find the net profit:

Gross profit	$17,500
Upgrade costs	–$1,835
Net profit	$15,665

Now, in order to determine the overall percentage return on investment the first year, we need to add the first year's return to the $15,665 profit, and then divide by the down payment and the $1,835 it costs to do the fix up, as follows:

$$\frac{\text{Returns } \$13,419 + \$15,665}{\text{Investment } \$30,000 + \$1,835} = 91.3\% \text{ return}$$

A 91.3 percent return the first year is nothing to scoff at. As you can see, for financial reasons alone, the management fixer-upper is the investment of choice for many seasoned investors. The cost involved and the effort needed to fix the problems are minimal, yet the rewards, as demonstrated, are significant. Of course, your return will drop in subsequent years, as it will with any leveraged real estate investment, but an initial return of 91.3 percent the first year on our example property would be a great leg to start out on.

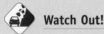

> **Watch Out!**
>
> One drawback to buying REOs is that you will not receive any type of disclo-
> sures regarding the condition of the property. Therefore, you bear all the risk
> of any hidden problems the property might have.

Bank-owned properties

Back in the 1990s there was a rash of bank-repossessed properties on the market. In the business, these are known as REOs,
which stands for Real Estate Owned. Today, you can still find the
occasional REO. These properties can offer the investor an
opportunity to purchase real estate at a substantial discount, but
as is true with most things in life, with a discounted REO, you
often get what you pay for.

Consider how the bank came into possession of the REO.
Someone bought the property with one of two ideas in mind: to
get a nice home for himself or herself or to get a set of units that
was hopefully going to make a decent profit. Along the way things
started to go wrong. It might have had to do with the economy in
general, a problem with the building itself, or perhaps some
issues in the person's own personal life. Whatever the reason,
the borrower stopped making her mortgage payments and the
lender was forced to take the property back. The problem for the
investor is that he will never know why things went sour. This is
because, with a foreclosure property, the bank is not required to
give any disclosures or warranties at all. In fact, with foreclosures,
you will be going into the deal with your eyes wide shut.

The enticement of buying REOs for the layperson is that
these buildings usually have a large discount in price compared
to the average property listed on the open market. This discount, though, can give novice buyers a false sense of profitability. Remember, bankers are not interested in losing money.
They are out to make a profit just like the rest of us. The truth
is, when they set the price of their foreclosure properties, they
do diligent market research just like any other seller would. In

fact, they have their own expert appraisers on staff who can give them an opinion of value based on market research, the property's current condition, and the cost of needed repairs. Although banks might leave a bit of extra profit on the table in order to move the property off their books, don't assume that every REO will make you a windfall profit.

The biggest trouble when trying to buy a bank-owned property is finding adequate financing. On rare occasions you can find a bank that is willing to finance their own foreclosures, but these are buildings that are usually still in good condition (which is harder to find). Additionally, any property that is still in decent condition will certainly be priced accordingly, which, when bargain hunting, defeats the purpose. Remember too, that if a conventional loan was to be had here, it would probably have to be for an owner/occupant only.

You could discover that if a property has a lot of deferred maintenance and has one or many vacancies, it might not be possible to get financing from a conventional source at all. At a minimum, you probably will have to put substantial cash down for a new loan. As an alternative you might have to go to a hard-money lender to get the money needed for the purchase. To add insult to injury, all your financing will usually need to be in place before you make an offer to buy. Just the opposite is true when it comes to financing conventional deals. For most real estate investors, this requirement is really putting the cart before the horse.

As you will come to appreciate, substantial fix-up costs, higher fees, higher interest rates, and—especially—higher down payments, can all make or break the profitability of an investment.

 Moneysaver

When buying any REO property, it is advisable to have a thorough inspection done by a professional contractor or a licensed property inspector before you sign on the dotted line.

Nonetheless, the first thing to do when considering an REO is to do an accurate assessment of the current condition of the property and any management problems it might have. In most cases, you have to purchase the property "as is" and, as mentioned, will not get any reports, disclosures, or clearances from the lender whatsoever. Once you gather all your data, you then will do the same kind of diligent analysis we have been preaching for eight chapters now.

To illustrate, let's revisit 333 Richmond Street. Here, we will attempt to paint a picture that is as close as possible to the typical REO situation you might find yourself in. To begin with we will assume the Richmond Street REO has severe repair and management problems, which is typical with most REOs. In this case, three of the four units are vacant and need a complete overhaul. The last unit has a tenant, but the tenant isn't paying rent and will need to be evicted after you close. We will use the same market value of the finished building ($222,500), but because it's owned by the bank and has some serious problems, we can get it for $170,000.

Some additional facts are as follows:

1. As with many REOs, the rent loss and eviction expense will be significant. One reason is because the clock isn't able to start ticking on any necessary evictions until we actually take possession. In this instance, we will assume that it will cost $300 in legal fees and will take one month to get the tenant out.

2. It will take one month to do the repair work on the units.

3. We will be able to rent one unit in July for an August 1st move in. We will rent two units in August for a September 1st move in. The last unit will be rented in September for an October 1st move in.

Here is a summary of what we're getting into:

Exterior fix up

Exterior paint	$2,500
Landscaping	$500

Garage doors	$800
Fence	$750
Roof	$3,000
Total	$7,550

Interior fix up (four units)

Carpet at $750 each	$3,000
Paint at $350 each	$1,400
Misc. at $100 each	$400
Total	**$4,800**

The timeline of the vacancies, assuming we close June 1st, looks like this:

	Close	End Month 1	End Month 2	End Month 3	End Month 4
Month	June	July	August	September	October
Vacancies	4	4	3	1	0

As you can see, we have lost a total of 12 months of rent (4 months in June, 4 in July, 3 in August, and 1 in September). We also have lost the cost of the eviction plus the cost of the repairs. With an assumed rent on the units of $550 each, our total expenses due to lost rent and eviction costs are as follows:

Rental loss	$6,600
Eviction expense	$300
Total	$6,900

We then need to add this $6,900 to the fix-up costs in order to determine the total cost of the project:

Exterior fix up	$7,550
Interior fix up	$4,800
Rental loss and eviction cost	$6,900
Total upgrade cost	$19,250

Now we will review the profit and see how it compares on a percentage basis. The gross profit is

Finished value	$222,500
Purchase price	–$170,000
Gross profit	$52,500

In order to find the net profit, we then need to subtract all the estimated upgrade costs from the estimated gross profit:

Gross profit	$52,500
Upgrade costs	–$19,250
Net profit	$33,250

Finally, in order to determine our percentage return the first year, we now need to add this net profit to the first year's return, and then divide by the down payment and upgrade costs. We will assume that we were indeed able to obtain a loan with 20 percent down. Twenty percent of a $170,000 purchase price is $34,000; therefore, the return is

$$\frac{\text{First year return } \$13,419 + \$33,250}{\text{Investment } \$34,000 + \$19,250} = 87.6\% \text{ return}$$

As demonstrated by an 87.6 percent return the first year, there can be a lot of profit to be made with REOs. The problem is that in order to achieve those returns you must always sink a lot of extra cash into them. Cash that you could, in essence, throw at a second investment property. In this instance, it took an additional $19,250, which was above and beyond the down payment of $34,000,

> ❝ It all looked good from the start, but completing the work took longer than projected. The negative cash flow because of the lost rents tapped me out and made me rethink this approach to investing. ❞
>
> —Blake M., investor

Watch Out!

When banks are forced to take a property back in foreclosure, they usually do the least amount of work necessary to get the property off their books. As far as they are concerned, peeling paint, rotting stairways, and overgrown landscaping are all just fine.

to get the building running again. Unfortunately, the facts remain: Tons of extra money and hard work are the rules with REOs, not the exceptions.

Remember too, that your return will drop the second year, as it will with any leveraged investment. This is because, like the standard fixer-upper, the extra return is only a one-shot increase, but the extra $19,250 it cost to fix up the building is now equity that you have invested that will decrease your leverage year after year.

Some deep-pocket investors who have cash to spare buy foreclosures with the flip-it-quick mentality. If so, let's demonstrate the kind of profit we would have made on this deal, provided we sold after the first year:

First year return	$13,419
Plus fix-up profit	+$32,750
Less sale costs	−$15,000
Net profit	$31,169

Once you know the net profit, you can determine the percentage profit as follows:

$$\frac{\text{Net profit } \$31,169}{\text{Investment } \$34,000 + \$19,250} = 58.5\% \text{ return}$$

A return of 58.5 percent on your invested capital is pretty decent. So much so, that the flip-it-quick and then do-it-again strategy is an excellent approach, that is, provided you have the management expertise and extra cash on hand to buy, fix up, and carry these properties until you can sell them again.

For most laypeople, however, the allure of buying repossessed properties is that they offer the illusion of a deep discount in price over fair market value. As you can see, though, this deep discount is usually always offset by the necessity of sinking in lots more money out of your pocket. In the end, most purchases of repossessed properties never end up being the gold mine that the average investor had bargained for.

But don't despair; there is another similar class of properties that can bring a smile to anyone's face—that is, the preforeclosure, or "short sale."

Short sales

A short sale is one in which the property has yet to be formally foreclosed on, but the lenders have agreed to take less than is owed on the loans to get a payoff on the balance owed. At this stage, the owners have been doing the best they can to keep the building running. All the units are probably rented, but the owners are still drowning for one reason or another. In situations like this, lenders have found that they can minimize their loss on bad loans by getting the property sold before they have to go through the formal foreclosure process.

In these instances, you will be negotiating with the actual owner, subject to approval by the lender. Most owners in this situation aren't too concerned with what kind of price they accept since the bank is going to get it all anyway.

To get the best pricing, you need to present a well-organized story to the seller and the lender. Your offer should include

- A brief biography of you and your knowledge of real estate
- A complete financial package on you and two years of tax returns
- A prequalification letter from a reputable lender
- A copy of the purchase contract
- A good-faith deposit check

Moneysaver

Lenders who have said they would consider a short sale are already tipping their hand in admitting that they will take a lower amount than is owed on their loan.

A second section of your proposal should include a detailed discussion of the physical condition of the property. It should include the following:

- A professional property inspection report
- Photos of all items that need repair
- A termite report if necessary
- Disclosures on other systems as needed
- Bids to repair any deferred maintenance items

Next you need to give the seller and the lender your estimate of value, which will justify the price you offered. At this point, you could consider hiring a professional appraiser because he could present the valuation in a format to which the lender is accustomed. If this is not practical or cost effective, you can present the information yourself. Make sure you get your real estate agent's help to find the best comparable sales to justify your offer. Your opinion as to the value of the property should include

- Copies of comparable sales with pictures
- Details of how you determined your price via accepted appraisal techniques

You should end the proposal with a strong statement as to why the lender should accept your offer. The format of the following letter should give you an idea of what you might say.

September 27, 2003
Bodian Savings and Loan
410 Hauser Blvd.
Los Angeles, California 90036
Re: Short Sale Proposal Loan # 14283

Gentlemen,

Enclosed you will find my proposal to purchase the property secured by your loan number 14283. As you know, this loan is in default, and I am asking you to consider a short sale to avoid the long and costly process of doing a foreclosure.

I have included my financial information so you can verify that I have the background and capability of closing this transaction quickly if you grant your approval. I have chosen a lender to handle the financing and have included their letter to show their willingness to make the loan.

The price I am offering is based on careful consideration of current sales in the area and a detailed inspection of the property in its current condition. I felt it was important for you to have this information about the current condition because it does impact the value, based on a comparison with current sales. If you were forced to take this property to foreclosure, your expenses would increase significantly, and the condition of the property would no doubt worsen.

I am prepared to close the purchase within 45 days of opening escrow. I urge you to accept my proposal, which will allow you to get this nonproducing loan off your books.

Sincerely,

Spencer Strauss
333 Richmond Street #10
El Segundo, CA 90245

Bright Idea

Many lenders have lists of approved appraisers. You might be able to hire one from this list, which should help you sell your bid to that lender.

Will a strong proposal guarantee acceptance? Unfortunately, the answer is no. We admit that, after 30-plus years in real estate, we are still baffled by some of the decisions made by banks and savings and loans.

Although these properties offer an opportunity to get a great discount in price, that doesn't mean this is the right type of property for you. You will need to do the same analysis that was done for the previous examples to see if the overall returns are worth the extra effort and capital investment.

Low- or no-down deals

When it comes to alternative real estate deals like those mentioned in this chapter, know that it's not always an uphill battle. As you have learned, investing in leveraged real estate is the best way to make a great percentage return on your money. Well, how about being able to buy property with little or no down payment at all? Well, believe it or not, creating that kind of leverage can be achieved. It's done by finding buildings where the seller will carry some or all of a loan for you.

There are several common motivations of sellers in this situation. Some have purchased rental property and then realized that landlording just isn't the business for them. Many are moving out of the area or have had a career change that makes it difficult to continue running the property. Many are just retiring and want to quit being a landlord. No matter what the reason, what they want is someone to take the property off their hands and give them enough cash to pay selling expenses. Some of these owners might even be willing to take money out of their pockets to move the property.

In these situations, the seller's primary goal is to reap the rewards of an installment sale (as mentioned in Chapter 5, "Borrowing Big Bucks"). These sellers know that by carrying a big loan on the sale of their buildings they can still receive a great yield without the everyday hassles of being a landlord.

Properties in this category offer a willing buyer two distinct advantages:

1. Lower down payments

2. Seasoned financing

The first advantage is obvious. If you only need to put closing costs or less down, you are getting into a property with great leverage. This leverage will work to your benefit and will greatly increase the percentage return on your investment in the first few years of ownership.

Second, seasoned financing offers a distinct advantage to you as an investor. It is the nature of conventional financing that there will be very little payoff on a loan balance in the initial years of the life of a loan. In the middle years, this increases; in the final years, principal pays off quickly. What this means is that, if the loan you are taking over was written for 30 years and has 20 years or fewer to go until it is paid off, it is beginning to make some significant reductions in principle.

 Bright Idea

It's not unusual to be able to pay a loan off in 10 years that actually had a 20-year payment schedule by just a small increase in the payment from the cash flow of the building. Collecting the cash flow from a property with no mortgage is a great position to be in during retirement.

A word of caution

The examples in this chapter have given only a broad overview of kinds of special-circumstance properties. Our goal was to expose you to the opportunities and how they give you the possibility to make some extra profit. The most important lesson is that you must look at these special properties closely to be sure the extra profit is worth the increased risk and the increased capital required. Make sure that you do a complete analysis of each special opportunity before you make a purchase.

Just the facts

- Fixer-uppers are better left for the later years of your investment career—after you've made some good money and have had considerably more hands-on experience.

- Management fixer-uppers are relatively cheap and easy to cure and are the vehicle of choice for the savvy investor.

- REOs usually require way too much money out-of-pocket to make them profitable—or feasible—for the average investor.

- A short sale gives the investor an opportunity to buy a troubled property from a lender at a considerable discount.

Setting Your Investment Goals

Building an Investment Plan

When was the last time you heard someone say, "I'm happy just scraping by," or "I don't care if I get ahead in life"? Never, right? This is because that kind of thinking goes against human nature. Instead, as human beings we long to be successful. In fact, we're obsessed with it. We dress for success, read about success, and—above all—we spend money (borrowed at 18 percent) as if each of us was the most successful person on earth. Truth be told, however, most of us aren't any closer to our dreams than we were last year at this time. The question then becomes, how come?

Perhaps there is a piece of the puzzle missing? In Chapter 1, "Planting the Seed," we talked philosophically about taking control of your own destiny. Unfortunately, if you take control but don't have a clearly defined set of goals with a plan, you'll probably spend most of your time simply spinning your wheels. For that reason, the purpose of this chapter

Chapter 9

is to teach you how to turn your good intentions into achievable results through planning. The end result could be a great future you designed yourself.

Good intentions versus planning

Most people's lives are so complicated that they put things off until they absolutely have to do them. This is true whether it's something as simple as taking out the trash or something as vital as planning for retirement. We all might have the best of intentions, but in reality, no matter what the chore is, we put it off until we decide to get around to it.

We learned of a sales tool many years ago that might help you overcome this problem. Get a piece of card stock about three inches square and cut it into a circle. With a red marker, write the following words across the middle of your circle: "to it." After you've done that, put the card-stock circle in your pocket and keep it with you at all times. Problem solved. You no longer have the excuse of being able to wait until you get around to it because you now have one—a round "to it."

In all seriousness, having a plan with stated goals is one of the most important foundations of successful investing. Yet, even people who want to get ahead in life often fail to make a distinction between good intentions and planning. A good intention could be the desire to have the better things in life. For example, declaring that "I want to be worth a million dollars one day," would be a nice, good intention. The problem, however, is that declaring it doesn't bring you any closer to achieving it. This would be true even if you said you wanted to be worth a million dollars with *conviction*.

On the other hand, a person who plans expresses a specific goal or goals and a method on how to get there. A good example of well-thought-out planning would be, "I plan to have a net worth of $500,000 within 10 years by purchasing small rental properties." As you can see, the plan is specific and lays out a methodology for achieving the desired result.

To that end, let's put all our good intentions aside, and learn how to write a winning investment plan for your budding real estate empire.

Writing a winning investment plan

Although a good investment plan doesn't need to start out in minute detail, it should be in writing from day one. Your plan gradually will grow in detail as you proceed though your investment career. To get things started, buy yourself a three-ring binder in which to put your plan. This way, you can change the contents easily as you make progress. Your planning binder should contain the following four sections:

1. **Goals:** Here you will lay out your long-term investment goals and the time frame you have scheduled for their achievement.

2. **General plan:** This spells out how you will achieve your goals over the time limits set forth in the plan.

3. **Detailed plan:** The detailed plan is similar to the "profit plan" of a business. It establishes the year-by-year goals of the plan. This is the measuring stick to determine how you are doing along the way.

4. **Follow-up and goal review:** Here you will enter predetermined dates to periodically monitor your progress. This is a perfect opportunity for equity and property budget reviews.

We'll spend the remainder of this chapter going over each of these sections one at a time.

 Bright Idea

Give copies of your investment plan to people whose opinions and knowledge you respect. By knowing your intentions, your respected confidants will help keep you on track.

Section 1: Your long-term investment goals

The goals section of your investment plan should be divided into the following subsections:

- Cash flow requirements
- Net worth projections
- Tax shelter benefits required
- Cash withdrawal from plan
- Other goals

Cash flow requirements

Cash flow requirements refer to your cash flow projections during and after completion of the plan. The point at which you will begin to achieve a significant cash flow depends on two things:

1. The amount of cash you invest in the plan initially
2. How well you manage your plan

To that end, let's look at some ways of setting cash flow requirements for your investment plan with a few typical examples:

- **Case #1:** You are well employed, expect to remain so for the immediate future, and would like to retire in 10 years. You have available to you between $30,000 and $40,000 for investment purposes. Your current salary is $40,000 per year, and you expect to be making about $50,000 per year in 10 years. To supplement your company-sponsored and Social Security retirement income, you would like to have about $20,000 per year of income from your real estate equities at retirement. Because you feel that you can support yourself and your family adequately until you retire, you will require no cash withdrawal from the plan; however, you would prefer no significant negative cash flows during the life of the plan.

Bright Idea

Make it a habit to read and reread your investment plan. When you look at your goals daily, you keep yourself tuned in to the future you want.

Your cash flow requirements from the plan would be

Cash flow of $20,000 each year after the 10th year. No significant negative cash flow during the plan.

- **Case #2:** You are young, ambitious, and single. You have a good job that pays $35,000 per year. You borrow $10,000 from your parents and are willing to invest that money in real estate. Your plan is to parlay that nest egg into $500,000 in real estate equities in 15 years.

  Your cash flow requirements from the plan would be

  Generate $500,000 in net equities at the end of 15 years. Pay off the loan from your parents from cash flow over the first 5 years. The $500,000 invested at the end of the plan at 10 percent in trust deeds should yield $50,000 per year income.

- **Case #3:** You have been employed in the aerospace industry for 15 years, and your salary is $40,000 per year. Over 50 percent of the employees in your department have been laid off recently due to budget reductions. You suspect that you, too, might someday lose your job, and your prospect for a new job in this field is slim. You have saved $50,000, but you know that amount won't last long without other income to supplement it. With the right real estate purchase, you believe your net equity could grow to $350,000 in 8 to 10 years. If you are laid off after that date, you could sell the property and carry the financing. At a 10 percent interest rate, you would have $35,000 in interest per year. With your company retirement and this interest, you could live comfortably in case you couldn't find other work.

Your cash flow requirements from the plan would be

Invest $50,000 into a four-unit building that will appreciate to yield $350,000 in equity in 8 to 10 years. No cash flow is required during the plan. All cash flow proceeds are to be put back into the property to promote payoff of the financing.

Cash flow is generated from a property in two ways. The first way is from net income from the property after paying all the expenses and loans. This cash flow should increase yearly as you increase rents. By retirement, this cash flow can be significant, depending on the amount of financing you have left on the properties.

The second way to generate cash flow is from the sale of your building and carrying your equity as a note against the property. As a general rule, the cash flow at that time will be equal to the going rate of interest multiplied by the net equity of your property. The great thing about this is that you generally can get a larger percentage yield by carrying the financing than you could get in a typical savings account or certificate of deposit. Another advantage is that you postpone the capital gains taxes due when you carry the financing because the government considers this to be an installment sale.

Let's say you need $20,000 per year cash flow to supplement your retirement income. It normally is safe to plan on a 9 percent interest yield. To find out how much net equity you would need at retirement, you would use the following formula:

$$\frac{\text{Cash flow required}}{\text{Interest yield}} = \text{Net equity needed}$$

 Bright Idea

When it's time to sell, make sure to let your listing agent know that you are interested in carrying an installment note. This way, your agent will make sure to bring you buyers who desire this type of financing.

Or:

$$\frac{\$20,000}{.09} = \$222,200$$

What this tells you is that you will need at least $222,200 in net equity in order to generate the cash flow you need. By figuring out this number for yourself, you will be able to create a target for your own investment plan.

Net worth projections

Your net worth projection will be your second subsection under the Goals category of your plan. Simply put, your net worth projection is the amount of money you want to be worth at the end of a given period of time. As we have previously shown, net worth and cash flow are related. In cases where your investment plan is set up as a retirement vehicle, your net worth projections probably will be about 10 to 12 times your net annual cash flow requirements. This assumes that, at the time of retirement, you will be able to locate savings investments that offer yields of 8 to 10 percent per annum. This is a very reasonable assumption based on the available returns for the last 10 to 20 years.

One of the advantages previously discussed is the installment method of selling property. By acting as a banker and carrying a note when you eventually sell or trade up, you usually can earn a higher interest rate than the market is offering. What's more, you can postpone the payment of your capital gains taxes and can even earn interest on the tax money you are keeping. This is a great advantage, and you need to remember to factor this possibility into your calculation when setting your net worth goals.

If you decide against carrying paper and instead decide to take the profit and run, you will need to make an estimate of the capital gains taxes due when you sell. This is because settling up with Uncle Sam will dilute the net amount you have to invest when you retire. The calculation to determine your net equity for reinvestment looks like this:

Gross equity at sale

−Sale costs

−Capital gains taxes

Net equity for reinvestment

If you decide to use the installment method, you can eliminate the tax from the calculation. Capital gains tax rates have been known to change at the drop of a hat depending on who holds political office. You need to factor in a reasonable tax rate in the event you decide to sell at the end of the plan because it will have a significant impact on your net equity.

You might want to establish your net worth projections for reasons other than just cash flow requirements. For example, you might want to provide a college education for your children, purchase a business to run in your retirement, or you might just have the old American desire to be a millionaire. Regardless, if that is what you want, your net worth projection goal might look like this:

Attain a net worth of $1,000,000 at the end of 15 years by investing in rental properties.

Tax shelter benefits

Your next subsection to your plan will be tax shelter benefits. Recognize that in real estate investments, tax shelter benefits are complicated and can vary widely. Therefore, we are going to devote the entire next chapter to this subject. For now, however, we will provide a few necessary guidelines and warnings for you to keep in mind. Here are some general tips:

- We do not recommend buying real estate for tax benefits only. The tax benefits have been diluted by the tax law changes in the late 1980s.

- It is important to consider the amount of depreciable improvements when making your final decision on a

Moneysaver

Tax-deferred exchanges are best made after you have had a few years of experience in real estate investing. Why? Because the experience with your own properties will improve your ability to judge potential winning trade opportunities.

purchase. All things being equal, the property with the highest improvement ratio will give you the best return because of the higher write-off.

■ We recommend the use of the tax-deferred exchange and the installment sale.

A reasonable tax benefit goal would look like this:

Maximize tax benefits on purchases and use tax-deferred exchanges and installment sales when available.

Cash withdrawal from the plan

Cash withdrawal refers to any lump sum amounts of cash you take out of the plan. By penciling them in at the onset of your plan, you have the opportunity to make provisions for these expenditures long before you will ever have to dip into your pocket to pay for them. What's more, building in perks for you is a great way to stay connected to your plan's ultimate success. You could make provisions for your children's education, a trip to Europe, a new boat, or building a dream home on the lot you own—all of which should bring you a magnitude of pleasure.

Major cash withdrawals can occur either by selling or by refinancing. In some cases, money in your property accounts can adequately cover the withdrawals. Examples of these types of goals are

■ *Withdraw $2,500 in year 2 to go on a fly-fishing vacation with my poker buddies.*

■ *Generate $75,000 in year 5 to pay for an addition to the house.*

■ *Withdraw $15,000 in years 7–10 for Jillian's college fees.*

Watch Out!

Exercise considerable care and thought in setting your goals; they form the
cornerstones of your investment plan.

Other goals

The last subsection is for any other goals you would like to
accomplish with some of the earnings from your real estate
investments. This section could involve helping family and
friends through your investments or perhaps benefiting a charity in the future. Examples of these kinds of goals might be

- *Buy a four-unit apartment building that has a nice owner's unit
  for the folks to live in.*

- *Donate the expected second trust deed from the sale in the 5th
  year to the college scholarship fund.*

- *Buy new carpet for the pulpit at the synagogue.*

Section 2: Determining
your general plan

As we already have seen, setting future net worth at a given
interest rate also sets future cash flow. Therefore, we will concentrate most of our discussion of the general plan to achieving
a given future net worth.

The first step in developing a general plan is knowing what
you can logically expect to achieve. This depends on a few key
criteria:

1. The capital you have available to invest

2. The length of time for which you will be invested

3. The amount of your own effort you can afford to contribute to the plan

In making these projections in real estate, we commonly use the compound interest algorithm. The mathematical formula for this is

$$FV = PV(1 + I)^N$$

Relax, it's really not so intimidating. Nevertheless, in language that the math-challenged student can understand, this translates as follows:

- FV = Future value of the investment
- PV = Present value of the money invested (down payment)
- I = Average interest rate you earned on your investment
- N = Number of years the money is invested

This formula states in simple language that, if you invest an initial amount of money (PV) at a compounding rate of return (I) for a given number of years (N), your total investment will have a future value (FV) at the end of the period. For example, if you invested $50,000 (PV) for 10 years (N) at 30 percent (I) compounded interest, the value of your investment at the end of the period would be $689,292 (FV). The equation would look like this:

$$FV = \$50,000(1 + .30)^{10}$$

The following is a table of various combinations of the compound interest formula. It will quickly give you an idea of the kind of future equities you might expect at various times with differing investment amounts. The compound interest percentage on the following page might seem high and unattainable to you, especially if you are used to the 4–6 percent interest you receive from your bank, but this is where real estate rises head and shoulders over any other investment vehicle. Study the chart, do the math, and see for yourself how the money adds up.

PRESENT VALUE/FUTURE VALUE TABLE

PRESENT VALUE	YEARS	I = 10%	I = 20%	I = 30%	I = 40%
$10,000.00	5	$16,105.00	$24,883.00	$37,129.00	$53,782.00
	10	$25,937.00	$61,917.00	$137,858.00	$289,255.00
	15	$41,772.00	$154,070.00	$511,858.00	$1,555,681.00
	20	$67,275.00	$383,376.00	$1,900,494.00	$8,366,822.00
$20,000.00	5	$32,210.00	$49,766.00	$74,259.00	$107,565.00
	10	$51,875.00	$123,835.00	$275,717.00	$578,509.00
	15	$83,545.00	$308,140.00	$1,023,717.00	$3,111,361.00
	20	$135,550.00	$766,752.00	$3,800,989.00	$16,733,640.00
$30,000.00	5	$48,315.00	$74,650.00	$111,388.00	$161,347.00
	10	$77,812.00	$185,752.00	$413,575.00	$867,764.00
	15	$125,317.00	$452,211.00	$1,535,576.00	$4,667,042.00
	20	$201,825.00	$1,150,128.00	$5,701,483.00	$25,100,476.00
$40,000.00	5	$64,420.00	$99,533.00	$148,517.00	$215,130.00
	10	$103,750.00	$247,669.00	$551,434.00	$1,157,018.00
	15	$167,090.00	$616,281.00	$2,047,434.00	$6,222,722.00
	20	$269,100.00	$1,533,504.00	$7,601,977.00	$33,467,290.00
$50,000.00	5	$80,526.00	$124,416.00	$185,646.00	$268,912.00
	10	$129,687.00	$309,587.00	$689,292.00	$1,446,273.00
	15	$208,862.00	$770,351.00	$2,559,293.00	$7,778,403.00
	20	$336,375.00	$1,916,880.00	$9,502,471.00	

It's important to remember that this is the average expected return on your investment, combining all four components of return: cash flow, equity growth from loan reduction, equity growth from appreciation, and tax benefits.

The underlined portion of the chart is an example of how to use the chart to make a projection for yourself. Down the left column (PV), locate the amount of the original investment of $50,000. Move over one column to the right to locate the number of years of the plan (N), which in this case is 10. The next columns are the future values (FV), based on the range of returns, and (I), located at the top of the chart. For our example, we are projecting an average return of 30 percent, so the final value is $689,292. If you are starting with an amount that isn't on the chart, you can combine totals to estimate the return.

Now let's look at how we use the table to determine what financial goals you can logically expect to meet. Let's say you have $30,000 to invest and require a net worth of $1,500,000. Here, you will have two variables to work with in order to meet this goal:

1. The rate of return on the investment (I)

2. The number of years invested (N)

If you look at the chart, you will notice that you can meet this goal in 15 years at a 30 percent rate of return. These percentage returns might seem high. Surprisingly, however, due to the power of compound interest, they are not unrealistic. Remember, Albert Einstein called compound interest the most powerful force on Earth.

Let's refresh your memory of the return from the example property at 333 Richmond Street. The return components were

Cash flow	$1,080
Equity growth (loan reduction)	$300
Equity growth (appreciation)	$11,000
Tax savings	$1,039
Total	$13,419

Therefore, our percentage return the first year was

$$\frac{\$13{,}419}{\$30{,}000} = 44.7\% \text{ return}$$

Each year, your percentage rate of return will drop a bit from the previous year because your equity in the property will increase significantly faster than your total annual return. For this reason, you should use a percentage return of the compound interest

 Bright Idea

Most business calculators have the compound interest algorithm, which you can use just in case you aren't carrying this book around with you for the rest of your life.

column that is lower than the initial return you expect so as to off-set this decrease. This compound interest number should be the rate you can expect as an average over several years of ownership.

Now that you have a handle on how to use the compound interest chart, let's return to determining a general plan and setting your future net worth goals. Most of us start with the primary constraint of a limited amount of capital to work with. Knowing the amount you plan to invest initially, we will combine the percentage return we can expect with the number of years we are going to invest to estimate our net worth. We are, of course, constrained by the maximum rate of leveraged return (compound interest) we can achieve, but 20–30 percent should be a comfortable rate for the average investor.

> ❝I've learned that when my rate of return drops below 25 percent, it's as if a red light goes off. It's then that I know it is time to refinance or trade out of that property.❞
>
> —Mareeva S., investor

Using the formula, let's review a couple of the cases we used earlier in this chapter when we were discussing setting goals.

- **Case #1:** You have $30,000 to $40,000 to invest and have the goal of having $20,000 per year income in 10 years. This requires approximately $200,000 in equity invested at a 10 percent interest rate. Because this is your first invest-ment, it would be wise to only invest $30,000 and keep the other $10,000 for contingencies. You will see from the table that this goal requires a sustained rate of return of 20–25 percent, which is in our comfortable rate range.

- **Case #2:** You can borrow $10,000 to invest and want to have a total equity of $500,000 in 15 years. Again, using the table, we can see that this requires a rate of return of

30 percent for the 15 years. This is at the top of our range, so our young and ambitious investor will need to devote the energy and sacrifice to attain this goal.

Now we are ready to pull all this work together and set your general plan. There are three steps in this process:

1. **First determine how much cash you have available to invest comfortably.** Always keep some cash in reserve. You can always invest some of your reserves later as your experience and confidence increases.

2. **Next set the feasibility of your future net worth.** You can convert this to a cash flow at retirement by assuming it can be invested at an 8–10 percent interest rate return.

3. **Set the number of years you want for the overall plan.** Using the table, move down the column on the far left (PV) to the amount nearest your available capital. Move across this row until you come to a value at least as large as your future net worth goal. The rate at the top of this column is the rate you will have to maintain to meet your general plan goal. Remember, you can combine two lines and add the totals to get a combination that equals your capital investment if it isn't on the chart.

Your general plan should look something like this:

I am going to invest $_____ for ____ years in real estate investments at a sustained rate of return of ____ percent and be worth $_____ at the end of the plan term.

Bright Idea

If time is not a particularly important factor in your plan, you would be well advised to pick a conservative rate of return and extend the years of the plan accordingly.

Section 3: Establishing a detailed plan

In establishing a detailed investment plan, we will use the $30,000 it took to buy 333 Richmond Street as our capital, and that property will be the beginning investment of the plan. In this instance, let's say we have decided that $350,000 is the target we are shooting for. Therefore, we will have the following general investment plan:

> *We are going to invest $30,000 for 10 years in real estate*
> *investments at a sustained rate of return of 30 percent and be*
> *worth $350,000 at the end of the plan term.*

It's now time to crunch the numbers and make our detailed plan. We (the authors) are fortunate to have a proprietary computerized system for building investment plans that makes this process much easier. For the benefit of those without access to a computerized system, we will demonstrate how to do this manually. It necessitates eliminating some of the fine-tuning a computer is capable of doing, but it will give an adequate plan to measure your progress against. We have included a copy of a computerized investment plan of the four-unit at 333 Richmond Street in Appendix D.

The next step in building your detailed plan is to establish the variables to be used in making the estimates for the future calculations of the plan. You will need the following:

- The appreciation rate
- Interest rates for first and second loans
- Loan-to-value ratios
- Income and expense increase rates
- Buy and sell costs
- Gross rent multipliers for various size properties

You will establish these variables after you have done your research and with the help of your investment real estate agent. Your agent's input will be helpful because the prior history of

Bright Idea

Consider seeking out an investment real estate agent who has access to a computerized planning system. With a simple click of the mouse, any variable in the equation can be changed to suit your needs.

the market helps establish the future trends, and this will help you set the rates for the future years of the plan. Using these variables, you will be estimating the financial performance of the properties that you will be acquiring in your detailed plan.

We will start the detailed plan with the specifics of 333 Richmond Street and then use our estimated rates for the preceding factors for the balance of the plan. The heart of the detailed plan is the accompanying projection worksheet on the next page. The horizontal lines are the year-by-year estimates of the performance of the property we acquire. The vertical columns are the financial parameters of the plan. The most important columns are the last two columns—the return on equity (ROE) and average return on equity (AVG ROE).

The return on equity is essentially the same concept as the return on investment. In the first year of ownership, the return on investment and the return on equity are the same because your equity is your investment. In the second and succeeding years, the equity is the initial investment plus the profit you made during the year. This is why we call your investment in subsequent years your "equity." Recall that in our example, our return on investment for the first year is

Cash flow	$1,080
Equity growth (loan reduction)	$300
Equity growth (appreciation)	$11,000
Tax benefits	$1,039
Total	$13,419

YEAR ____

TRANSACTIONAL POSITION

YEAR	MARKET VALUE $	TOTAL EQUITY $	INCOME __%INC	OPER'G EXP'S __%INC	TOTAL INTEREST $	AMORTI-ZATION __%DWN	CASH FLOW __%DWN	APPRE-CIATION __%M/V	TAX REBATE __%DWN	ROE %	AVG ROE %

The percentage return on investment (ROI) is

$$\frac{\$13,419}{\$30,000} = 44.7\% \text{ return}$$

To make the estimates for the second year of the plan, we will assume there are no changes in the cash flow, loan reduction, and tax savings. The appreciation will be adjusted because the property appreciated $11,000 during the first year of ownership, as we used an appreciation rate of 5 percent. Our investment, now called our "equity," is

Original investment	$30,000
First year profit	+ $13,419
Equity second year	$43,419

This calculation is repeated in successive years to find the equity.

The appreciation for the second year is calculated as follows:

Starting value	$220,000
Appreciation	+ $11,000
Value second year	$231,000

Value second year	$231,000
Multiplied by appreciation rate	× .05
Second year appreciation	$11,550

The profit the second year is now

Cash flow	$1,080
Equity growth (loan reduction)	$300
Equity growth (appreciation)	$11,550
Tax benefits	$1,039
Total	$13,969

The percentage return on equity the second year is

$$\frac{\$13,969}{\$43,419} = 32.1\%$$

The average return on equity (AVG ROE) is

$$44.7\% + 32.1\% \div 2 = 38.4\%$$

The following worksheet shows the calculations through the third year. You'll see that in the third year the average return on equity (AVG ROE) dropped from 38.4 percent to 34 percent. No need to panic. It just means it's getting time to do something to increase the average return. We have two options: We can either refinance or do a tax-deferred exchange. In this example, we'll do a tax-deferred exchange because it is the most common way for investors to reposition their equity.

Now is when the experience of your investment real estate agent will really help with your plan. This is because you will have to make an estimate of what property will sell for and how it will perform years into the future. If you are not fortunate enough to have an agent who tracks value appreciation trends, we suggest using "the world doesn't change that much" method of estimating probable future value.

Let's assume you can make almost the same purchase in the future as you can make today. We will eliminate the cash flow, equity growth from loan reduction, and tax benefits from our calculation as a way of evening up any errors and simplifying our estimate. In some locations, the cash flow and equity growth might be the most significant aspect of the return. In these areas, you will need to keep these elements of return as part of the planning process.

The next step is to estimate the costs of the transaction (selling and then trading via a 1031 exchange) and then build the model of our new property for the plan. Here's how: At the start of year four, 333 Richmond Street is valued at $254,600, and you have $71,907 in equity. Remember that this assumes you have put aside all the cash flow and tax benefits from this investment.

YEAR
TRANSACTIONAL POSITION

YEAR	MARKET VALUE $	TOTAL EQUITY $	INCOME %INC	OPER'G EXP'S %INC	TOTAL INTEREST $	AMORTI-ZATION %DWN	CASH FLOW %DWN	APPRE-CIATION 5%M/V	TAX REBATE %DWN	ROE %	AVG ROE %
1	220,000	30,000	26,400	7,920	17,100	300	1,080	11,000	1,039	44.7	
2	231,000	43,419	26,400	7,920	17,100	300	1,080	11,500	1,039	32.1	38.4
3	242,500	57,388	26,400	7,920	17,100	300	1,080	12,100	1,039	25.3	34
4	254,600	71,900	TRADE UP EQUITY LESS $12,000 COSTS								

The costs of doing this trade will be the sale expenses on the existing property and the purchase costs on the new building.

To simplify this step, we will assume the selling expenses of the existing property to be 5 percent of the sale price, and we will round this off at $12,000 ($254,600 × .05 = $12,730). In addition, we will assume that we get the seller of our new property to pay our purchase costs. This technique usually can be accomplished in the negotiation process by adding the costs to your final offer. The benefit to you is that you get to finance these expenses in the price you pay for the building. The equity left for reinvestment now is

Equity at start of fourth year	$71,907
Costs of transaction	−$12,000
Equity for reinvestment (rounded)	$59,900

For the next step in our plan, we will invest these proceeds in one or two new properties using a 1031 tax-deferred exchange. To calculate the correct size of the next property that will fit in with our plan, we need to use the following formula:

$$\frac{\text{Equity to invest}}{\% \text{ of down payment}} = \% \text{ value of new property}$$

Using our available funds, the value of the next property can be calculated by plugging in these numbers:

$$\frac{\$59,900}{.10} = \$599,000$$

 Bright Idea

When using a manual system for planning, don't hesitate to round off the numbers to make your calculating easier. This plan is just an estimate of where you are going, and the rounded-off dollars will not make a significant difference in the final numbers.

As you can see, we will need to trade into a building worth $599,000 in order to keep our plan alive.

The chart on the following page has the values added for the trade in year four (the trade we just worked together) and the trade that was needed in year seven. The trade was needed in year seven because the average return on equity (AVG ROE) again fell into the low 30 percent range. Through trial and error, we determined that one more year of ownership would make the average less than the target 30 percent. Note that the further into the future your plan gets, the tougher it will become to estimate the smaller components of return. For that reason, when planning for future trades, you can eliminate any estimates for income, operating expenses, total interest, amortization, cash flow, and tax benefits.

Section 4: Follow-up and goal review

Just as important as preparing your investment plan is managing the plan to its successful completion. This involves, among other things, monitoring the progress of the plan to make sure you stay on plan at both the general and detailed levels.

The general review of your plan starts with your goals for your family and how they affect your investments. As things change in your personal life, you sometimes need to make alterations in your financial commitments. A job change might take away some of the time you had to dedicate to the properties. A bonus at work might now allow you to buy another property, which will get you to your goal sooner or will raise the amount of your final net worth. The market might change, which will affect what you buy or sell.

YEAR

TRANSACTIONAL POSITION

YEAR	MARKET VALUE $	TOTAL EQUITY $	INCOME %INC	OPER'G EXP'S %INC	TOTAL INTEREST $	AMORTI-ZATION %DWN	CASH FLOW %DWN	APPRE-CIATION %M/V	TAX REBATE %DWN	ROE %	AVG ROE %
1	220,000	30,000	26,400	7,920	17,100	300	1,080	11,000	1,039	44.7	
2	231,000	43,419	26,400	7,920	17,100	300	1,080	11,500	1,039	32.1	38.4
3	242,500	57,388	26,400	7,920	17,100	300	1,080	12,100	1,039	25.3	34
4	254,600	71,900	TRADE UP EQUITY LESS $12,000 COSTS								
4	590,000	59,900						29,500		49.2	
5	619,500	89,400						30,975		34.6	41.9
6	650,475	117,400						32,500		27.6	37.1
7	682,975	149,900	TRADE UP EQUITY LESS $34,000 COSTS								
7	1,160,000	116,000						58,000		50.0	
8	1,218,000	174,000						60,900		35.0	42.5
9	1,278,000	234,900						63,900		27.2	37.4
10	1,342,800	298,800						67,000		22.4	33.6
11	1,409,800	365,800									

As for reviewing your detailed plan, this book started out by recommending that you gain knowledge about the market and property. The secret of a successful plan is to never stop that education process. Monitoring your plan at a detailed level requires that you stay in touch with the market. It is easy to get involved in the day-to-day operation of your property and forget to look at what is happening around you. In the review section of your planning binder, you should keep a blank copy of the projection worksheet previously shown in this chapter. At the end of each year, make it a point to meet with your investment real estate agent and do an estimate of value based on the current market conditions. Discuss how the market is doing and where it looks like it is going in the next 12 months. Use the new value and the actual performance figures from the year's operation of your property to complete the next line of your worksheet.

Now compare what really happened in that year with the plan you laid out 12 months earlier. How did you do? If there are any significant changes—good or bad—go back, revise your plan, and get ready for next year. This will force you to stay involved in reaching your final goals. There is no doubt that many changes will occur over the life of a 10–15 year plan. Some changes will be positive; some will be negative. The secret is to take full advantage of the positives and take the necessary steps to minimize the negatives. This requires staying informed by monitoring what is really happening.

Just the facts

- A written plan with stated goals is critical to successful investing.
- Installment sales are a great method to help you achieve a desired net worth.

- The compound interest formula demonstrates how your equity will rapidly multiply in real estate.

- Your detailed plan will give you a year-by-year projection of where you are headed.

- It's advisable to revise your plan as necessary along the way.

Planning for the Tax Man

As the cost of government increases, the burden of individual taxation increases proportionately. Built into the framework of federal, state, and local tax laws, however, are certain techniques whereby investors can legally defer their taxes due for an indefinite period of time. To take advantage of these techniques, you need to have an understanding of certain taxation rules.

There is no beating around the bush; these rules can be complicated. To that end, we suggest you seek the advice of your accountant, tax attorney, or other tax expert from the outset. You do need to have a basic understanding yourself, however, because it is not practical to have professionals review every transaction under consideration.

There are two broad areas in which knowledge of taxation is important. The first is during the ownership and management of the property. The second is upon the sale of the property. In this chapter we will examine both of these areas in great detail, making them easy to understand and almost enjoyable.

Deductions, deductions, and more deductions

As a real estate investor, a number of tax benefits are now yours for the asking. They are

1. The deductibility of your purchase costs
2. The deductibility of your operating expenses
3. The corresponding annual depreciation allowance that Uncle Sam provides

Purchase costs

As a general rule, most of the costs incurred at the time of your purchase are tax deductible in the year of the purchase. The following list covers some of the most common:

- Prepaid interest on the loan
- Fire and liability insurance
- Property tax prorations
- Escrow fees
- Title insurance costs
- Miscellaneous fees from the lender and escrow company

You'll notice that loan fees and points are not in the preceding list. The rule is that any money paid to secure a new loan for income property must be written off over the period of the loan. If the loan for our example property at 333 Richmond Street required a loan fee of 1.5 percent and the loan was a 30-year loan, the yearly deduction would be calculated as follows:

Loan amount	$190,000
Loan fee rate	× .015
Fee (points)	$2,850

Watch Out!

Be sure to check with your tax expert each year to see if there have been any changes in the tax laws. It would be a shame to miss out on opportunities for write-offs because you were uninformed.

To calculate how much of a deduction you could take, you then would divide the loan fee by the term:

$$\frac{\text{Loan fee } \$2{,}850}{\text{30-year term}} = \$95 \text{ per year}$$

In the past, points could be written off in the year of purchase, but after years of abuse, this loophole was closed.

Operating expenses

In addition to the purchase costs, all the expenses you incur in the operation of the property also are deductible. The biggest problem in determining deductibility is distinguishing between expense items and capital items. As a general rule, if you incurred the expense by fixing a problem in your building or merely by maintaining the value of the property, it should be considered an expense item. These normal operating expenses are deductible in the year you spend the money. Examples of these include

- Utilities
- Interest on loans
- Insurance
- Taxes
- Gardening and cleaning expenses
- License and city fees
- Roofing, plumbing, electrical, and miscellaneous repairs
- Management fees
- Advertising and rental commissions

- Mileage, postage, and phone expenses associated with the operation of the property
- Any other noncapital expenses

On the other hand, if the improvement increases the value or completely replaces a component of the property, it should be considered a capital expenditure. With capital expenses, the cost needs to be depreciated rather than expensed in the year the money is spent. The tax code says that capital items must be written off over the period of time they contribute to the usefulness of the property. Capital expenses include

- Carpeting
- Drapes or window coverings
- New roof, plumbing, or electrical systems
- Building additions
- Major appliances or furnishings
- Major repairs—a new driveway, replacing stucco or siding, replacing landscaping, and so on

It's important to note that the principal paid each month on your loan payment is not a deductible expense. It actually is one of those returns on your investment that you must pay tax on, but you never see the money because you have to give it to the bank to pay down your loan. If you have a positive-cash-flow property, you are paying off your loan with the income you are receiving from the tenants. The rule says that you cannot deduct the portion of your payment that goes toward paying off the loan. Note: You don't need to worry about calculating the principal. Your lender will send you a statement at the end of each year showing you how much of your payments went toward principal and how much went toward interest.

The depreciation allowance

As the owner of your own real estate business, you now are able to deduct a certain amount of expenses for the loss of value on

Moneysaver

Keep detailed records of each expense related to your property. This way, you will be able to take advantage of every single deduction to which you are legally entitled. We would rather see you keep your money than give it to Uncle Sam.

the improvements (improvements = the structures on the land) of your property—things such as wear and tear from aging. Remember that, because the dirt does not depreciate, this depreciation expense is only for the physical structure of the building and other improvements, not the land.

The most important point to remember is that the depreciation schedule you originally calculate will be with you as long as you own that property. If you sell the property and pay your taxes, you can start fresh with the next property. If you trade via a 1031 exchange, however, that basis and its schedule stays with you.

As you learned in Chapter 3, "Elements of Return," the most important component of the depreciation schedule is the land-to-improvement ratio. (See the section, "Inflationary appreciation," also in Chapter 3.) For any improved property, part of the value is for the land and part is for the improvements. Because you can't depreciate the land, a property that has a high ratio of improvements has a high depreciation deduction. To set your ratio, you must make sure to use an accepted method. If you don't, the IRS might disallow your schedule, force you to set a new one, and probably end up sending you a bill for additional taxes and penalties.

Limitations on deductions

To calculate the tax benefits from a property, you need to understand the rule changes adopted from the Tax Reform Act of 1986 (TRA '86). These new rules affected the amount of depreciation that property owners can take per year, and they also defined investors into different classes depending on the amount of their involvement in their properties. The new tax code recognizes two classes of investors: passive investors and active investors.

Passive investors

Generally, you are a passive investor if you buy property as a limited partner or with a group of more than 10 partners. As a passive investor, you can use the depreciation deduction to shelter any profit from the property. It's like having a savings account of tax benefits that can be drawn upon to cover future profits.

Active investors

You probably are an active investor if you purchased your property alone or with a couple of partners and are active in the management of the building. The IRS calls this "materially participating" in the management. This means that you have a say in how it runs, how the bills are paid, and how much you are charging for rent. You might not actually run the property if you have hired a company to do this, but the key is that you have the ultimate responsibility for it. There are two classes of active investors:

1. Those who consider real estate investing and management as their primary career

2. Those who invest in real estate as a secondary career

Rules for active and passive investors

If you are "in the business" of real estate and it is your primary career, you have no restrictions whatsoever on the dollar amount of losses you can claim against earnings.

 Bright Idea

If your spouse doesn't work outside the home, he or she can help you qualify for unlimited deductions by obtaining a real estate license and handling the management of your properties. This may qualify your spouse as a full-time property investor.

Most people, however, fall into the category in which real estate is a secondary career. If this describes you, your real estate losses are limited to $25,000. If your adjusted gross income before real estate deductions is $50,000, for example, and your losses from property are $30,000, you can only deduct $25,000 of the $30,000. You don't lose the remaining $5,000. Instead, it goes into that tax shelter bank account previously mentioned. What this deduction means is that, instead of paying tax on $50,000 of income, you only pay tax on $25,000. The tax you save is profit and therefore is included in the overall return from your investment.

The earnings limitation

A second code change from the Tax Reform Act of 1986 limits your ability to use the losses from your real estate against the earnings from your regular career. This limit occurs when your earnings exceed $100,000. For every $2 you earn over $100,000, you lose $1 of deduction. This means that, at $150,000, you have no deduction against your income. Remember that these are not lost; they're just saved up for future use.

Calculating capital gain

Capital gains taxes are taxes on the profits you make when you sell your property. To understand capital gains and how to calculate them, you first need to be familiar with some new terms:

- **Sale price:** The price for which you sell the property
- **Adjusted sale price:** The net price after deducting sale costs
- **Cost basis:** The original purchase price plus capital expenses
- **Adjusted cost basis:** The cost base minus depreciation

To estimate your capital gain, you would complete the following calculation:

Sale price
− Sale costs
_____
Adjusted sale price

Cost base
+ Capital expenses
− Depreciation
_____
Adjusted cost base

Adjusted sale price
− Adjusted cost base
_____
Capital gain

To illustrate this formula, let's use the Richmond Street property that we bought for $220,000. We've depreciated the property for five years at $5,090 per year for a total depreciation of $25,450 ($5,090 × 5 = $25,450). We also just put on a new roof for $5,000 (a capital expense). We can sell it for $320,000, and our total expense to sell will be $20,000.

Knowing this information, we can calculate the capital gain as follows:

Sale price	$320,000
Sale costs	− $20,000
Adjusted sale price	$300,000

Moneysaver

Before you decide to use one of the tax-deferral methods, you first should determine your capital gain and what the tax implications are. You might actually be better off in the long run if you pay your tax now and start fresh with a new property.

Cost base	$220,000
Plus capital expenses	+$5,000
Less depreciation	− $25,450
Adjusted cost base	$199,550

Adjusted sale price	$300,000
Adjusted cost base	−$199,550
Capital gain	$100,450

As you can see, the capital gain of $100,450 is a sizable chunk of money to have to pay tax on. Instead of giving it to Uncle Sam, let's learn about some methods of deferring or reducing these taxes.

The 1031 exchange

As far as saving on taxes is concerned, the IRS 1031 tax-deferred exchange is probably the single most important technique available to the real estate investor. An exchange enables you to pyramid your equity while deferring the payment of taxes. In effect, Uncle Sam becomes your partner by letting you use the taxes you owe on your capital gains as a down payment on the buildings you trade into. When you trade into larger properties, the government figures that, in turn, you will make more profit. By making more profit, you eventually will owe more tax. It's a win-win situation.

You must be aware of the three rules to qualify for a tax-deferred exchange:

1. You need to trade for like-kind property. Like-kind property in this instance would be a property you are purchasing for investment purposes. You can't trade a duplex you've been renting out for a new dream house. This is because the duplex is income-producing property and the dream house would be a primary residence. You can, however, trade the duplex for an office building or a

strip mall. The idea is to trade income-producing property for other income-producing property.

2. The property should be of equal or greater value than the existing property, hence the phrase "trading up."

3. You should not receive cash, mortgage relief, or "boot" of any kind in the transaction.

Note: In an exchange, "boot" is the term used to describe something of value given in addition to the like-kind property, as in "this acre and cash to boot."

Three categories of exchanges

Most 1031 tax-deferred exchanges fall into one of three categories:

1. The straight exchange

2. The three-party exchange

3. The delayed exchange

The straight exchange

The straight exchange occurs when two parties get together and simply trade properties. At the end of the transaction, each party goes his separate way. This scenario doesn't happen very often because most investment property owners either trade up or just get out altogether. By trading straight across the board, one party probably ends up with a lesser property, which fails to meet the requirement of trading into a property of equal or greater value.

The three-party exchange

The most common type of tax-deferred exchange is the three-party exchange. As its name suggests, three different parties are involved in the process. One of the key elements of doing a tax-deferred exchange is that the party trading up never receives the equity in the property being traded. For that reason, the party cannot just sell the property, collect the proceeds, and go out and buy a larger property. Because most people with bigger properties don't want to trade into anything smaller, these three-party exchanges have evolved so that each party can get what it wants and stay within the framework of the law. Here's an example of how one might work:

Facts:

- Party A owns a four-unit building and wants to trade into an eight-unit building.

- Party B owns an eight-unit building and wants to sell, pay the taxes due, and retire to Florida.

- Party C is just getting started investing and wants to buy the four-unit building of Party A.

   Solution: Parties A and B enter into an exchange escrow in which Party A gets the eight unit and Party B gets title to the four unit. In a separate escrow, Party B agrees to accommodate the exchange and deed the four-unit building to Party C immediately after he acquires title from Party A. Both of these escrows contain contingencies stating that they must close concurrently. This means that if Party C can't buy the four unit for some reason, Party B will not have to take Party A's four unit in trade for his eight unit.

   Result: At the close, Party C owns the four unit he wanted, Party A owns the eight unit he wanted, and Party B is sipping margaritas at his beach house in Florida.

   Recap: In case you're wondering, Party B doesn't pay any tax by taking the title to the four unit because it is sold for the same price at which it was taken in trade. This is what is called a non-taxable event.

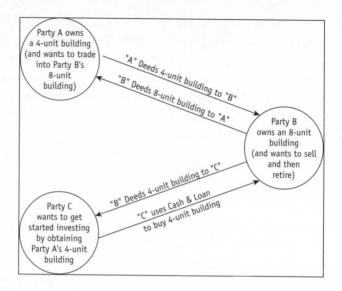

The delayed exchange

The final category of exchange is the delayed or Starker exchange. Starker refers to one of the principles in *T. J. Starker v. U.S.*, a case in the Ninth Circuit Court of Appeals. In this case, Starker exchanged some timber acreage for 11 different parcels of property owned by Crown Zellerbach. As was agreed between the parties, Starker selected the properties and they were transferred to him by way of the exchange. This was called a delayed exchange because the transfer spanned more than two years.

Because of the two-year delay, the IRS questioned whether this was an exchange at all and took Starker to court. Fortunately, for all investors, the Ninth Circuit Court approved of the process, and this has since been codified nationally for use by all U.S. investors. The Starker court held that

1. A simultaneous transfer of title was not required.

2. IRS Section 1031 should be broadly interpreted and applied. Treasury regulations under IRC 1001 to the contrary were deemed invalid.

In an effort to update the rules concerning exchanges in light of the new rulings, a number of additional changes were made to IRC 1031. These changes included

1. Partnership interests are no longer of "like kind" for exchange purposes.

2. To identify the potential replacement properties, the taxpayer much complete a written 1031 Property Identification Statement by midnight on the 45th day after escrow closes. More than one property may be identified with the following restrictions:

   ▪ Three or less properties without limit on their value or on the percentage of the identified properties, which must actually be acquired

   ▪ Four or more properties provided the combined fair market value of all the properties does not exceed 200 percent of the price of the property sold

   ▪ The purchase of 95 percent of the total value of all replacement properties identified should the total values of four or more properties exceed the 200 percent limitation

3. The taxpayer must receive the identified property within the earlier of 180 days after the date he transfers his property in the exchange or the due date of his tax return for the year of the exchange including extensions.

To accomplish a delayed exchange, an accommodator is used. An accommodator is an unrelated party (or entity) that holds the exchange proceeds. These proceeds are called "exchange valuation credits," or "EVCs." The EVCs are contract rights allowing the investor to use the net proceeds being held by the 1031 accommodator to purchase a replacement property. The investor will find the replacement property, and the accommodator will fund the purchase with the money that the EVCs represent. The accommodator can even take the title to the property that the investor trades into in order to complete the exchange.

Watch Out!

Before you do a 1031 delayed exchange, you should be very sure of your next purchase. If you miss the 45-day or 180-day deadlines imposed by the IRS, you will have to pay the capital gains tax on the sale.

In choosing an accommodator, make sure you check their credentials, business history, and insurance coverage. Remember that the accommodator will be getting all your funds from the sale of your property. He or she holds it for you until it's time to purchase the replacement property. Be sure to choose your accommodator wisely. Over the years, some unscrupulous ones have been known to close up shop, pack their bags, and get the heck out of Dodge—taking the trust funds with them.

Since the first edition of this book was published in 1999, we have seen a surge in property values. This surge has created a renewed interest in buying property, and—conversely—a marked decrease in the inventory of properties to purchase in most areas. This increase in prices has produced more capital gain, which most property owners would like to shelter by using the benefits of the 1031 exchange.

As you can well imagine, more profit and less property, combined with a 45-day window in which to identify potential up-legs have created some tense moments for investors who have closed escrow without properties to trade into. It's important to note that these delayed exchanges offer many advantages over the straight or three-party exchanges, but there are also additional risks involved. If you close your delayed-exchange escrow 181 days after your down-leg property closed, you will owe the capital gains tax due and will probably not have the cash to pay for it.

There are some additional complicated rules associated with completing a successful delayed exchange. To that end, make it a point to consult with your tax advisor before making any decisions in this regard. The net result of an ill-informed decision could be costly.

Exchanging versus paying your taxes and buying another

An additional problem created when you do a tax-deferred exchange is that you limit the depreciation deduction on your new property. Part of the exchange process is that you carry forward your profit and your basis from the traded property. Whatever the depreciation schedule was on the old property now becomes the schedule for that part of the new property.

We'll illustrate this using our example property. Assume that 333 Richmond Street can be sold for an adjusted sale price of $300,000. We will net $80,000 from our sale, and we'll use that $80,000 as a 15-percent down payment (with a seller carrying another 10 percent) on a new property worth $550,000. This new property has a land-to-improvement ratio of 80 percent. The depreciation deduction we will be carrying forward is $5,090 per year. This means that, if we started fresh, the depreciation deduction on the new property would be

Price of the property	$550,000
Percentage of improvements	× .80
Depreciable improvements	$440,000

In order to find the depreciation deduction, you do the following calculation:

$$\frac{\text{Depreciable improvements } \$440,000}{\text{Useful life 27.5 years}} = \$16,000 \text{ depreciation deduction}$$

 Watch Out!

None of these tax-deferral methods get you out of paying your taxes. Instead, these techniques simply help you put the taxes off until sometime in the future.

Now let's see what the deduction will be if we trade up via an exchange. Because we carry the depreciation schedule with us from the old property, we are only allowed to calculate a new schedule on a portion of the new price. Therefore, the portion of the new value we can depreciate on a new schedule is

Purchase price	$550,000
Value transferred in	− $300,000
New cost base	$250,000

New cost base	$250,000
Percentage of improvements	× .80
Depreciable improvements	$200,000

$$\frac{\text{Depreciable improvements } \$200,000}{\text{Useful life 27.5 years}} = \$7,272 \text{ depreciation deduction}$$

To find the total deduction, you add the old and the new schedules as follows:

Prior deduction	$5,090
New deduction	+ $7,272
Total deduction	$12,362

As you can see, trading up represents a $3,638 decrease in the annual depreciation ($16,000 − $12,362 = $3,638), as opposed to a new purchase that had nothing to do with the trade. Remember, it is important to review the impact of a proposed trade on your annual depreciation because this new schedule will be with you for the life of your holding period for the new property.

One last problem that should not be overlooked is related to your goals from your investment plan. Although the use of the exchange allows you to pyramid equities, it also pyramids the tax liability on a future sale. If you have plans of cashing out at the end of your plan, paying your taxes, and then retiring, this could leave you with a very large tax bill. If this is your goal, you might consider paying your taxes as you go along or consider the next alternative, the installment sale.

The installment sale

The installment sale is another significant technique for deferring payment of capital gains taxes. In an installment sale, sellers elect not only to sell property but also to put up some or all of the financing needed to make the deal work. Because the property is being sold now but is being paid for later, such deals are called installment sales. As far as taxes are concerned, it differs from the 1031 exchange in that you actually sell the property without getting a new one in return, but you still delay paying some or most of your capital gains taxes due. Here's how:

With an installment sale, instead of taking all the cash and walking, you become one of the lenders on the property. You find a qualified buyer, he takes over your existing loan, and you carry a note (and your profit from the sale long term), all the while receiving interest-only payments. The idea is to keep earning a high interest on the taxes due for many years and put off paying the capital gains until the contract is complete. The wonderful thing about an installment sale is that you don't owe Uncle Sam a penny until you actually receive the profit from the sale. If you structure it correctly, that could be years down the road.

The rules for qualifying for an installment sale were significantly modified by the Installment Sales Revision Act of 1980. In the past, there were rules regarding the amount of the down payment and the number of years needed to qualify. These rules no longer exist. The advantage of an installment sale now is that you are only required to pay capital gains tax on the amount of the profit you receive in one year. You pay the balance of the tax due as you collect the profit in subsequent years.

Because an installment sale can be relatively complex, we need to simplify our example. Let's assume you are selling 333 Richmond Street and need to decide how to handle the tax on the $100,450 capital gain we calculated earlier. We'll estimate the tax rate at 28 percent. To find your after-tax net equity, use the following formula:

Capital gain	$100,450
Tax rate	× .28
Tax due	$28,126

Capital gain	$100,450
Less tax	− $28,126
Remaining profit	$72,324

As you can see, your profit is $72,324. If you have no plans to spend the money and you want to invest it in a passive, cash-flow-generating vehicle, the installment sale is for you. The only tax due will be on the amount of cash you take as a down payment.

Let's assume you take a 10 percent down payment on the $320,000 sale of 333 Richmond Street; this would be $32,000. You then carry the rest of the profit as a note due on an installment contract. See how this affects the net cash profit:

Down payment	$32,000
Tax rate	× .28
Tax due	$8,960

Down payment	$32,000
Less tax	− $8,960
Net cash profit	$23,040

Capital gain	$100,450
Less down	− $32,000
Installment note	$68,450

In this example, we have a net cash profit of $23,040 and an installment note on the property of $68,450.

The real advantage of the installment sale comes from what you can earn from the installment note versus what you can earn by putting your net cash in another investment vehicle. Let's say that, by putting your cash into a certificate of deposit or a savings account, you could earn 6 percent on your money. Conversely, by carrying the financing on the Richmond Street property, you could earn 9 percent on your money. The contrast would look like this:

Outright sale:

Cash out profit	$72,324
Interest rate	× .06
Profit	$4,339
Per month	$362

Installment sale:

Installment note	$68,450
Interest rate	× .09
Profit	$6,160
Per month	$513

Net down payment	$23,040
Interest rate	× .06
Profit	$1,382
Per month	$115

Installment total	$7,542
Per month	$628

As you can see, the difference of $628 per month by carry-ing an installment note versus $362 per month at 6 percent interest is quite dramatic. There are two main reasons for the difference:

1. You usually can get a significantly higher interest return on your money by carrying financing versus putting it in a bank or a comparable investment.

2. You are earning interest on the capital gains you have yet to pay the IRS.

You can increase this profit even more by varying the amount of down payment you accept. In theory, because you are the banker on your loan, you could agree to no down payment at all. By doing this, you would not have to pay any tax, and all the down payment money could earn the same 9 percent inter-est you were earning on the rest of the note.

Refinancing your loan

There is one more technique to avoid paying the taxes due on some of the profit from your real estate. This technique is to secure new financing to pay off the existing loan, netting addi-tional cash at the closing because of the increased value of the property. Let's use our example to illustrate.

Time has passed and the Richmond Street property is now worth $320,000 with an existing loan balance of $185,000. Our current lender tells us that it will make a new loan of 80 percent of the appraised value, and the fees will be about $3,000. This new loan will generate the following cash for us:

 Bright Idea

An alternative to down-payment money is to require additional security on your loan by securing it with not only your property but another property of the buyer that has significant equity. In this instance, the buyer gets a prop-erty with no down payment, and your note is secured by two properties, not just one.

Appraised value	$320,000
Loan amount	× .80
New loan	$256,000

Loan amount	$256,000
Loan fees	− $3,000
Payoff on existing loan	− $185,000
Cash generated	$68,000

As you can see, you now have extracted $68,000 of equity to spend any way you want without selling your property. If we are still in the equity-building years of our plan, we probably will use that money to acquire an additional property.

One of the great advantages of getting at some of the profit by using this method is that there is no tax due on the money. Because we borrowed the money from the bank, we are obligated to pay it back; therefore, no tax is owed. What's more, we also can write off the interest as a deduction on the property you refinanced.

If you've done your job managing the property, the increased rents should more than cover any increased mortgage payments on the refinance. As you can see by comparing the net cash from an outright sale ($72,324) versus the cash you can generate by refinancing ($68,000), the bottom-line numbers are pretty comparable. The advantage of refinancing is that you will still be receiving rents, will still be building equity, and can still be taking advantage of tax benefits.

Refinancing, however, can create a future tax problem you should know about. The IRS doesn't make you pay tax on borrowed money because you have to pay the loan back. What if you were to take most of your profit out on a loan, however, and then sell the property and let someone else take over the loan? This is a situation in which you are taxed on the boot you receive. Remember that boot is something you receive in addition—something extra in a real estate transaction.

To illustrate the problem, let's assume we held 333 Richmond Street for five years and took the depreciation deduction of $5,090 each year. Our adjusted cost base would be

Purchase price	$220,000
Less depreciation	– $25,450
Adjusted cost base	$194,550

When the buyer assumes the new loan, we are relieved of the obligation to pay the $256,000 loan back; however, it creates the following mortgage relief obligation:

Loan amount	$256,000
Less adjusted cost base	– $194,550
Mortgage relief	$61,450

Remember, as long as you keep this property, there is no tax to pay. Once you sell, however, you have to pay tax on the boot.

A tax lesson summary

The information in this chapter is designed to give a basic understanding of real estate taxation and some deferral methods. The goal is to make you aware of the complexity of this area so that you will seek the advice of professionals before you make, what could be, a costly mistake. To cover all your bases, we recommend a three-stage process when contemplating a move with one of your properties:

Moneysaver

Before you select a tax-deference method, you should consult an expert so that you can pick the method that best suits your long-term financial goals. Because of the current liberal tax treatment of capital gains, it is not always advisable to postpone paying the tax as the rates might someday increase.

1. Schedule a general review meeting with your tax consultant before you list your property for sale. Review your
   goals, discuss all the alternatives, and get a general idea of
   your position.

2. When listing the property, make clear to your real estate
   agent and in the listing contract that any transaction must
   be reviewed and approved by your tax consultant.

3. When negotiating a potential sale or exchange, include
   a contingency that gives you the right to have the final
   purchase agreement reviewed and approved by your tax
   consultant.

Just the facts

- As an owner of improved real estate, you can deduct most
  of the purchase costs and operating expenses from your
  taxes.

- The depreciation deduction allows you to take a deduction for the wear and tear from aging on your property.

- Several great techniques are available from the IRS that
  allow you to delay paying your capital gains tax.

- The 1031 tax-deferred exchange lets investors trade into
  new properties and postpone paying any capital gains tax.

- An installment sale can defer taxes due and also can bring
  in significant cash flow for years after the sale of a property.

- A smart way to extract cash from your property is to refinance your loan.

Putting Your Money on the Line

GET THE SCOOP ON...
Real estate agents and whether they are friends
or foes ▪ How to find the perfect agent for you ▪
The keys to narrowing down your search for
property ▪ Determining the seller's motivation
and why it is critical to your success ▪ Winning
methods of writing offers

PART V

Purchasing Your Investment

You've come a long way in your education. Among other things, you have learned why real estate is the best choice for your investment dollar. You also know how to appraise property, finance your deal, create an investment plan, and make Uncle Sam a partner in your business. It's now time to put all the pieces of this puzzle together and buy yourself a piece of property.

For many investors, this is when emotions take over. When first looking at property, many people see a building with an attractive appearance from the street and decide that they just "have to have it." At this point, their goals and well-thought-out investment plan go right out the window. Be careful, this kind of thinking is a dangerous trap to fall into. If your emotions dictate your investment choices, they might keep you from acquiring the very property you need to get the best start.

Chapter 11

One of the best ways to stay focused on your plan is to remind yourself that there are lots of properties out there, any one of which should make you a fortune over the long haul. To that end, think of the buying process as a shopping excursion. Remember the times you set out to buy that new TV or living room set? Those were big purchases, too, but you made the decision to buy long before you left the house. In fact, the trip to the store was only a formality to find the best value for the item you already had decided to purchase. An equivalent premise holds true here. You already have decided to invest in real estate. You have read books, taken notes, and analyzed properties with a keen eye toward the bottom dollar. Now you only need to find the right fit for your plan.

> 66 As soon as we started looking at property, our plan fell by the wayside. The first building we wanted to make an offer on was beautiful, one that we would've lived in ourselves. But we wised up when our agent showed us that the return it generated didn't justify the added cost. 99
>
> —Kevin H. and Cindy B., investors

Real estate professionals

Throughout this process, one of the key players in the hunt for available properties is likely to be a licensed real estate agent. In the beginning, his job will be to sift through all the buildings on the market to find the ones that best suit your goals. Once you have found a property, he then will become the primary negotiator in communicating the terms of your offer to the seller. Once you have a signed deal, he will start to put all the wheels toward closing in motion. In short, his job will be to guide you every step of the way, from the moment you first consider investing to the day you close escrow on your first property. With some luck, you'll have found one who is so good he'll be the one you call on to help you buy your next property, and your next one, and so on.

There is no rule, however, that says you have to use an agent to buy property. Many times, buyers and sellers do a fine job of finding each other and negotiating great deals themselves. The problem is that the vast majority of properties available are under contract to be sold through real estate companies. What's more, the only place those properties are advertised is on a multiple listing service (MLS), which only real estate professionals have access to. (Note: The MLS is a real estate agent's most powerful tool. It is an online computerized service that provides up-to-the-minute information about available properties. Only a few years ago, the MLS was an antiquated service. It was published in hard copy and, in some places, was updated only once a month. As you can see, the Internet has changed real estate, too.) Therefore, unless you have access to properties that no one else knows about, in order to get a good look at all the available properties, you're probably going to have to work through an agent.

This news, however, should be welcomed and not rebuffed. Like any professional in his chosen field, a licensed real estate agent is trained specifically to help people buy and sell property. Just as you wouldn't use yourself as a lawyer if you were being sued, or extract your own tooth if you had a toothache, so too should you not invest in real estate without the guidance of a trained professional. True, some don't take their job seriously and are in it only to make a quick buck if they can, but the vast majority of professional agents are highly skilled and experienced. Your only job is to find the right one by separating the wheat from the chaff.

Given this fact, let's learn about the two types of real estate agents out there and figure out how to find the very best one for you.

Seller's agent versus buyer's agent

When an owner decides to sell her property, she usually hires an agent to give her an opinion as to value. This agent is called the listing agent or seller's agent. Once they agree to work together to actually market and sell the building, the seller and the agent sign a listing agreement. This agreement outlines the price and terms at which a seller is willing to sell. It confirms all the vital statistics about the property including the mix of the units, the size of the property, the income it generates, the year it was built, and so on. It also serves as an employment contract between the seller and the agent. Most listings are then put on a local MLS, to which all the other agents looking for property have access.

It's at this point that the listing agent offers a commission (usually half the total commission that the seller contracted for) to a second agent who can bring in an offer acceptable to the seller. The idea is that once buyers' agents see a listing on the MLS, they in turn tap into their resources of willing buyers. When one is found and an offer is made on a piece of property, counteroffers usually are exchanged until the parties come to a meeting of the minds. At that time, a deal is consummated. For many years, it was not uncommon for the same agent to handle both sides of a transaction (and this is still legal and common in most states); that is, the agent who obtained the listing also brought in a buyer to buy it. This created a dual-agency relationship. In some circumstances, a dual agency might work just fine, but in most business situations, it is tough work to look out for the interests of both parties in a transaction. When was the last time you saw an attorney effectively represent both sides in a legal dispute? It's a conflict of interest.

The following are the best ways to locate potential agents to represent you:

- **Signs and advertisements for property:** When you start looking for property, you'll find that ads and For Sale signs on small two-, three-, and four-unit apartment buildings will begin to jump out at you. Most will give you an idea about pricing, and they all will tell you which agents are dealing specifically in income-producing property. Keep notes about which agent's ads and signs you see most often.

- **Property management companies:** Get to know the property management companies in your area because you might need to hire one someday. In the interview process, ask for references of agents who specifically handle income property.

- **Escrow and title companies:** Escrow and title companies have the most contact with agents in your area. Most should be willing to give you some recommendations for good agents who are easy to work with.

- **Referrals from other income property owners:** Other owners are probably the best resource. When you are getting to know your market, you will be visiting a lot of properties. In many cases, you will be talking to the property owner rather than the manager. Ask them if they can recommend an agent or company that could help you. Once you've compiled your list of names and numbers, start making phone calls. These calls will be like phoning someone before a blind date. You don't know him and he doesn't know you, but you might have something to offer each other.

The following is a list of characteristics you should look for in a good real estate agent:

- You feel you have a rapport with the agent.

- The agent has time to work with you.

- The agent has access to the MLS.

- The agent has knowledge of the market area in which you are interested.

 Bright Idea

Once you have compiled your list of potential agents, consider checking them out with the Better Business Bureau, the local real estate board, and even your state licensing bureau. They may get high marks from your research, or in the alternative, they may fail the test. If so, keep looking.

- The agent is willing to teach you about the market.
- The agent deals in investment property and not just home sales.
- The agent understands your goals in investing.
- The agent owns or manages rental property.
- The agent has made investment property sales or has listing experience.

And, most important:

- The agent's actions speak louder than his words.

If you start looking for a good agent when you first begin researching your market, you will have the best chance of finding someone with whom you feel comfortable by the time you're ready to make a purchase. The bottom line is that you want an agent who can best help you acquire the building you decide to buy. That's his job.

Paying your agent

Most professionals, like doctors and lawyers and so on, get paid per job or per hour. Real estate is different. Real estate agents earn a commission based on a percentage of the price of the property they sell, regardless of the amount of work they put into the deal. Easy deals combine with tough ones, and transactions that never work combine with some that do. These all even out and result in a commission for the agent now and then. The good news is that the seller usually pays any commission your agent receives due to a consummated transaction. In fact, because of the way the system is set up, as the buyer you shouldn't have to dip into your pocket to pay for your agent's help at all.

Nonetheless, many times near the end of negotiations, the principal parties find themselves only a few dollars apart on price. Invariably, they start looking to the agent(s) and what they see as their "big commission" as the perfect source to make up the difference. This might be tempting for the seller

Moneysaver

If you are buying a lot of property and don't like the job your agent is doing and/or don't like paying commissions, consider obtaining a real estate sales license. You then can find and negotiate your own deals and can keep the commission for yourself.

(because he is the one who is really paying both agents), but if you're smart, you should steer clear of trying to do business this way. Remember that your agent is the person who is going to help make you your fortune. If you have been lucky enough to find a good agent, you will need her to help you buy and sell many properties over the years. Don't alienate her by dipping into her paycheck to make one deal work. In the end, your agent will save you—and make you—a lot of money, especially if you respect her way of earning a living.

Comparing apples to apples

At this point, you have learned enough about the market, have developed a workable investment plan, and have found an agent with whom you feel comfortable working and who understands what you are trying to accomplish. It is now time to narrow down the field of available properties and buy the one that best suits your needs.

This can be accomplished by making some estimates of value based on the financial picture of each property and how the market looks to you and your agent. Once your estimates of return are complete, you can rank your list so you can determine which property to make a run at.

Make sure you do an apples-to-apples comparison when comparing properties. In other words, don't make the property you personally like most look the best by using a lower expense ratio compared to the other properties. Yes, maybe one is more pleasing to the eye than another, but that does not mean it will run at lower expenses or make you more money. Only an analysis of the numbers will yield that information.

Bright Idea

When deciding between property A and property B, ask your agent to bring in a colleague for his or her opinion. An unbiased third party might shed some light on something you have yet to consider.

Your list of potential buildings should only have properties on it that have the capability to satisfy the goals of your investment plan. Many times, you will run into great opportunities that are outside the goals of your plan. Even if they are affordable, stick to your plan, especially in the beginning; it's your best guarantee of success.

You should rank your list based on two pieces of information:

1. Bottom-line return and value based on estimates

2. Your personal opinion of the property

The first criteria is how the numbers look. By this point you and your agent should have had plenty of experience in determining that. The second factor is how you would feel about owning the property. Yes, your feelings do matter, and this is the time to take that into account. When you have boiled the list down to a few final choices, the bottom-line numbers probably are fairly close. Don't hesitate at this point to make the final decision based on your personal feelings about the property. You probably will do a better job of running the building if it starts out as one you really want to own. Just don't base your whole decision on your gut feeling about a property.

Determining a seller's motivation

As you have learned, many variables go into determining the right property for your investment plan. It took careful thought about your own dreams and goals to put it together. Now that it's time to buy a property, you need to consider the seller's goals as well. This is where your agent turns into his own version of Dan Rather. His job will be to do some investigative reporting and determine why the seller is selling and what he wants out of the deal. This knowledge will be key to structuring a winning offer.

You will discover that the best transactions are the ones in which everyone comes away feeling as if they won. Winning means getting what you want. Getting what you want depends on clearly defining your motivation as well as the seller's and finding the best way to satisfy both people's needs.

The following is a list of some of the kinds of information you and your agent need to know before you start writing offers. Answers to these questions and any others your agent might ask will help you achieve your ultimate goal—being able to acquire the property you want. You should discover

- How long has the seller owned the property?
- Does the seller own other income property?
- What are the seller's plans for the proceeds from the sale?
- Have there been any other offers?
- If so, what were the terms and what happened?
- How flexible is the price?
- Will the seller consider carrying any financing?
- Is the seller easily offended?
- Is the seller willing to negotiate on price and terms?

Recognize that most of the owners you will be dealing with are not sophisticated real estate investors, and they often have a lot of emotion attached to their properties. We have found that understanding the emotional side of real estate transactions can mean the difference between making the deal or missing out on an opportunity. Here are a few examples to help illustrate how helpful this kind of insider information can be.

Case #1: Seller needs a quick close

Facts: You find a four-unit building that is in good condition and that appears to be priced at market value. It has a large assumable loan on it with a better-than-market interest rate.

Seller's motivation: In talking to the listing agent, your agent finds out that the seller has been transferred out of the area and needs to sell now. He would like to get cashed out but might consider carrying some paper if the transaction will close quickly.

Result: Knowing that he is desperate, you can make a low offer guaranteeing a quick closing provided that you can assume his loan and that he will carry a portion of the financing.

Case #2: Seller's previous deal fell through

Facts: The price on the building seems a little high, but the property is in excellent condition.

Seller's motivation: Your agent talks to the listing agent and finds out that the sellers have owned this property for almost 20 years. They are selling so that they can buy their daughter and her husband their own home as a wedding present. The last offer was 15 percent below the asking price, and they accepted it. The buyer in that transaction didn't qualify for the financing, however, and the deal fell apart.

Result: You can make an offer well below the asking price, include a glowing prequalification letter from a lender, a better-than-average good-faith deposit, a thorough comparative market analysis justifying your price, and promise a 30-day or less closing time. This closing date, coincidentally, is a week before their daughter's wedding.

Case #3: Seller wants to carry an installment note

Facts: This four unit is in a good location and is in decent condition. The rents are really low, but the price is close to market value.

Seller's motivation: Your agent learns that the seller is retiring and doesn't need any cash from the sale. He would rather have the monthly income that comes from carrying a note than pay any capital gains tax.

Result: You can offer just enough cash down to pay selling costs and can ask the seller to carry the balance. You could even ask for reduced payments for the first two years to give you a chance to increase the rents.

Writing an offer

Now that you have found a building to make a run at, you still have some decisions to make. The first is what kind of format to use for writing your initial offer. Because you will be signing a legally binding contract, this decision is an important one. The process of trying to reach an agreement on price and terms with a seller can vary from state to state, and even within some states. Part of your education process will be to learn the specific procedures used in your area. Generally, offers are made in one of three ways:

1. Using a standard preprinted contract supplied by your agent (often called a deposit receipt or purchase contract)

2. Having an attorney draw up a contract of sale

3. Using a simplified letter of intent

Let's look at these three types of mechanisms for writing offers one at a time.

Preprinted sales contracts

In most real estate transactions, deals are put together using preprinted sales contracts provided by the real estate agents. If you are using an agent who is a Realtor, the contract probably will have been drafted by the state or the national association with which the Realtor is affiliated. We (the authors) are located in Southern California, so we use the forms provided by the California Association of Realtors. These contracts have been drawn up by attorneys with the goal of equitably protecting the interests of each party in a real estate transaction.

If you are using the preprinted forms, make sure you use the form designed for the type of property on which you are making an offer. Look for the following types of forms:

Bright Idea

If you are using a preprinted form and you find that it contains language you don't like or that does not apply, don't worry. There is a solution. Simply cross out the part you disapprove of, initial the change, and write in what you want.

- Residential (single-family homes and condominiums)
- Residential income property (2–4 units)
- Income property (5 units or more)
- Commercial and industrial property
- Exchange forms
- Lease with an option to buy

The goal of each of these contracts is to include all the necessary clauses so that you and your agent can make offers without having to hire an attorney each and every time you try to acquire a building. However, recognize that writing offers via these forms will constitute a binding contract if the seller accepts your offer. Therefore, make sure your agent is skilled enough to be able to explain all the clauses in the contract that you are signing.

An offer via your lawyer

Although the purchase of a piece of property usually is one of the most important financial decisions in our lives, an attorney rarely is used to draw up the initial contract. This probably stems from the fact that it often takes many counteroffers before parties come to terms. It can get fairly expensive to have an attorney draw up and review what sometimes amounts to countless contracts.

This doesn't mean that you shouldn't have an attorney review your transaction before it becomes binding. As part of your initial research on real estate, you should ask around for referrals of good attorneys. It is best if you can find one who specializes in real estate. He or she might charge more per hour, but a specialist usually will be able to give you a quick answer, which is what you need after you have negotiated a deal.

Attorneys primarily are used in the purchase of larger properties with complicated financing and intricate leases. You will definitely want to have an attorney review your documents in the following situations:

- There are many complicated changes to the preprinted contract.

- There are complicated leases on the property.

- The seller is carrying the financing using an unusual format such as a land contract, AITD, or lease option.

- You need the seller to subordinate the financing to a new loan in the future.

- There are potential title problems.

- There are potential problems with easements, hazardous waste, or issues with the city.

- Your agent can't explain the clauses in the purchase contract to you.

If you sense any potential need for a review of the contracts by an attorney, you will need to have a contingency in your original offer. It should be something to the effect that the offer is contingent upon review and approval of the final agreement by your attorney. Additionally, it should note that your acceptance of the purchase contract is contingent upon

> 66 Each transaction is different. Choosing how I will make an offer depends entirely on who I am dealing with on the other end. 99
>
> —Adam F., real estate agent

that approval. As your deals and the properties you buy get bigger and more complicated, you might want to include this type of language in all your offers.

Moneysaver

A contingency clause requiring review and approval by an attorney will ensure that you get your deposit back if the attorney finds the deal you negotiated to be unsatisfactory.

Letters of intent

Many novice sellers get scared off when they receive offers written on preprinted purchase contracts or from lawyers. This is because these contracts often are lengthy and always are complicated. For this reason, many offers to buy begin with a much simpler format known as a letter of intent. A letter of intent is meant to be a simple, straightforward expression of the buyer's desire to purchase a particular piece of property. It usually outlines on just one page how much the buyer is willing to pay and the kinds of terms for which he is looking.

> 66 As a property owner, I prefer to get offers written on preprinted forms rather than a letter of intent. I know that lots of investors like them, but for me, a letter of intent doesn't carry the weight that a formal contract does. 99
>
> —Chris Y., investor

By eliminating all the initial legal mumbo-jumbo, the principals can find out quickly whether they can put a deal together. Sometimes the fact that the agreement is not meant to be legally binding allows the parties to concentrate on working out the important issues that solidify a transaction. It would be a good idea to have your attorney draw up a standard form that you can use again and again. (See the sample letter of intent on the following page.)

If you plan on making your initial offer via a letter of intent, it would be best to warn the listing agent beforehand. This is because some agents or sellers who are not familiar with them

LETTER OF INTENT TO PURCHASE REAL ESTATE

This letter covers the basic price and terms under which the undersigned, _____ (buyer), agrees to purchase the property located at_____ _____.

PURCHASE PRICE:_____.
DOWN PAYMENT:_____.
FINANCING:_____.
CONTINGENCIES:_____

_____.

ADDITIONAL TERMS:_____

_____

_____.

PURCHASE AGREEMENT: Within three days of acceptance of this basic agreement, buyer and seller agree to formalize their understanding by completing and signing a standard purchase contract and receipt for deposit.

This letter is written with the understanding that no party will be bound by any of the terms of this agreement unless and until the standard form mentioned above covering all the foregoing matters and such additional considerations as any of us deem appropriate has been executed by both parties.

This letter of intent shall expire on ____/____/____.

_____   _____
BUYER   SELLER

_____   _____
DATE   DATE

might not take your offer seriously if you use one. In fact, have your agent fax them a blank letter of intent in advance. This way, there won't be any surprises if they are not familiar with this kind of agreement.

The good-faith deposit

No matter which method you use to make an offer, you still need to decide how much of a good-faith deposit to include. That is, how much money are you going to put down as an initial deposit on the property? There is no law that says you need to include a deposit at all, but the idea of a good-faith deposit has evolved into an integral part of the offer process.

The deposit serves two functions: Psychologically, it plays into the old adage of putting your money where your mouth is. If you want the property, putting some cash on the line makes a powerful statement to the seller about your level of commitment. Second, it puts some money at risk after the due diligence is completed, which any reasonable seller would require.

Once you put up a deposit, the issue becomes who will hold the money. Unless you specify otherwise in your offer, the check usually becomes the property of the seller. As you can imagine, this might cause some problems if the deal goes sour and you want your money back. Therefore, you must always address this issue when you write your first offer on the property. There most likely will be a custom in your area that addresses this issue, but here are a couple of general guidelines to keep in mind:

1. Even though you should include a copy of your check with your initial offer, there is no need for the seller to cash the actual check until you have a basic agreement in place. It's a good idea to write into your offer that the deposit is to be held uncashed by your real estate broker or a neutral third party until the offer is accepted by the seller and communication of that acceptance has been made to the buyer.

Watch Out!

Make sure your deposit is credited toward the purchase price. In other words, if you are paying $200,000 for a property and a $5,000 deposit accompanies your offer, then $195,000 should be due at closing.

2. When it comes time to cash your check, it's best to put the funds into the hands of a neutral third party. Your purpose in doing this is to protect your money until the transaction closes. Many states have escrow companies and title companies that assist in closings and will hold the funds in their trust accounts.

Once an agreement is negotiated, the due diligence, or "free-look," period begins. This period of time allows you to do an interior inspection and a thorough analysis of the property and any other contingencies without risking any of your deposit. (The next chapter is devoted to this subject in its entirety.)

Be aware that if you decide not to buy after the free-look period has expired, most contracts are written so that you will forfeit your deposit. This is one reason sellers usually want large deposits. They want it to be big enough so that when the due diligence period has passed, you still feel committed to the deal. It could cost them a lot of time and money if you back out at the eleventh hour because you find something that looks better down the street.

Specific performance

When making offers to buy property, you need to make sure you are taking the game seriously. If you decide to back out of the purchase after the due diligence period without good cause, the seller can sue you for specific performance. If you get sued for specific performance and a court rules for the seller, you will be ordered to complete the purchase under the terms to which you originally agreed. To avoid the possibility of this result and the expensive litigation that most certainly would come with it, many contracts offer buyers and sellers an opportunity to agree to liquidated damages in lieu of specific performance.

The idea behind a liquidated damage clause is to let the parties decide ahead of time what the amount of the damages will be in the event of a dispute. In a real estate transaction, damages are the money forfeited by the buyer in the event that the buyer fails to complete the purchase in the manner in which he contracted. Remember that this doesn't refer to the termination of the contract if one of the contingencies isn't met or is disapproved of. This only applies when the buyer fails to close the transaction for any reason other than a contingency. In other words, the buyer just backed out. A typical liquidated damages clause will read something like this:

> *If the buyer fails to complete this purchase by reason of default of the buyer, the seller shall retain, as liquidated damages for breach of contract, the deposit actually paid.*

In some areas, the amount of the deposit is limited to 3 percent of the purchase price if the property is four units or less. If the contract for a four unit were $200,000, a buyer would have to pay a maximum of $6,000 to the seller for backing out of the deal as outlined in the contingencies in the purchase contract.

Presenting an offer

Let's say you find a property and you decide to make an offer. If your offer is way below the asking price and is not presented gingerly and with some tact, you may insult the seller. Hurting his feelings is one thing, but having him tear up your offer and refuse to make a counteroffer on a property you want is an entirely different matter. The following scenarios will illustrate how to best present an offer at less than the seller's listed terms:

Case #1: An overpriced but nice building

Facts: This four unit is listed at $220,000. Your analysis indicates a value of $195,000, but you might even go to $205,000 due to the good location and condition of the property.

Watch Out!

You run the risk of losing out on a deal if you make a low-ball offer without sufficient data to justify your offered price. Sellers are emotional about their properties. If you insult them, they might refuse to sell to you altogether.

Presentation: To begin with, your agent insists that he present your offer in person to the seller. Once they are face to face, your agent first gives the seller some background on you and what your goals are in real estate with a prequalification letter from a lender. The agent lets the seller know that you have decided to make an offer on this property because you are impressed with the way the seller has maintained it. As a lead-in to the offer with the lower price, your agent reviews with the seller a thorough comparative market analysis of value based on other sales in the area. He includes copies of the MLS information and pictures of those properties, so there is no doubt in the seller's mind that the data is correct. The agent finishes the presentation with the following statement, "I would have brought you an offer at your listed price, but this is the value that was indicated by the recent sales in the market. It wouldn't do any of us any good to put a deal together only to have it fall through because the value couldn't be justified by the lender."

Result: The seller doesn't like the lower price but wants to sell. We get a counteroffer at $205,000 because the seller says, "This property is in much better condition than the ones in the agent's market analysis." We gladly accept.

Case #2: Perfect building, but you can't afford the down payment

Facts: This building is just what you want, and the asking price of $200,000 is in line with the market, but you can't afford to put 20 percent down, so you will need the seller to carry some financing. The listing, however, indicates that the seller wants all cash.

Presentation: Again, your agent presents the offer in person with the background on you and your goals. The presentation goes something like this:

> The buyer has made you a full-price offer, which is rare in this business. This is because this buyer needs some extra help from you to complete the purchase. The buyer needs you to carry a small loan and would like you to consider two options. Option number one would be for you to carry the loan yourself. We believe that, if you discussed it with your accountant, you would find that there are great tax advantages in carrying a note. Not only will you save some taxes, the interest rate the buyer has offered is well above the current bank rates. The second option is that, at the outset, we would ask you to carry the note, but then we would look for an investor to buy it from you at a small discount. The buyer asks that you absorb the discount because his offer was full price and most buyers would have offered you less.

Result: The seller likes that you offered him full price and agrees to carry or sell the note and absorb the discount.

Keep in mind, we're not suggesting that every low-ball offer gets accepted. Of course not. Rather, we're just trying to point out that there are techniques available that, if you are willing to learn them, can help you get the building you want. To that end, the important things to remember in presenting offers are

- Know the seller's motivation before writing an offer.

- Have a thorough comparative market analysis or an appraisal in hand to justify low offers.

 Bright Idea

Sometimes your agent will have to educate a seller and his listing agent about the benefits of carrying a loan. If he does, make sure he works the numbers out on paper so that the seller can actually see how much money he can make by carrying the loan.

- Your agent should insist on presenting your offer in person to the seller.

- Have a glowing prequalification letter available to give to the seller from your lender.

- When presenting your offer, your agent should give the seller your personal history and should review the reasons you want to buy the property.

Just the facts

- You must look at your real estate agent as the bridge to achieving your goals. He is friend, not foe.

- Knowing the seller's reasons for selling will give you a marked advantage when writing an offer.

- A letter of intent is a great way to begin a negotiation and to eliminate hard-to-understand legalese.

- Your deposit usually is refundable during the free-look period and usually is not after that time has expired.

- Structure your offer so that, when your agent presents it, it looks like you are accommodating the seller's every wish.

The Due Diligence Period

O nce you have a property under contract, it might seem as if the toughest part of the job is over. After all, you weeded through all the available properties in your market and finally found the perfect fit for your plan. You then made an offer, probably got a counteroffer, and might have made a counteroffer or two of your own. In the end, you successfully negotiated the purchase of a piece of rental property. As far as you're concerned, it's now time to get on with collecting rent and being a landlord.

But hold on; it's not quite that easy. You still have to make sure you get what you bargained for. In most cases when buying income producing property, you will have to agree on price and terms without ever having seen inside any of the units. In addition, you will have to make profit projections based on estimated operating data. You haven't been flying blind, but now that you have a property under contract,

Chapter 12

you get an opportunity to study the seller's books, review the rental agreements, and to inspect the interiors. The truth about your deal will either solidify it or set you free.

Due diligence and contingencies

Once you are under contract, you enter the due diligence or free-look phase of a purchase. This period of time is built around questions that have yet to be answered about the property. These questions should have been expressed in your offer as "contingencies." A contingency is legally defined as a future event or condition upon which a valid contract is dependent. In other words, once you have an agreement in place, your contingencies put the seller on notice that you will be researching specific items pertaining to the deal. In addition, you will be making a final decision to buy based on that research.

The most important contingencies of your deal will be

- Physical inspection of the property, including the interior of all units
- Reviewing financial details of the property, including expense statements and profit and loss statements
- Inspection of all rental agreements and rental applications of existing tenants
- Getting a seller's warranty
- Securing financing
- Obtaining clear title

After jumping through all the necessary contingency hoops, if you determine that everything checks out okay, you then can go ahead and move the financing along so that you can close the transaction as planned. If some hidden land mines pop up, which is not uncommon, you probably will go back to the seller and ask him to clarify or fix the problems you discovered. After all, if you go ahead with the deal with newfound knowledge of some outstanding issues, you will be getting less than what you originally had agreed to.

When you go to a seller and ask for some clarification or repair requests, a number of results could occur:

1. The seller could fix all the problems with no questions asked, and you close the deal as planned.

2. The seller could tell you that he won't correct any problems, and you could choose to cancel the deal.

3. The seller could tell you that he won't correct any problems, and you could choose to stay in the deal.

Or, most likely:

4. You and the seller go through a small renegotiation regarding any problem areas, you shake hands, and you close the deal as planned.

It's important to think of the due diligence phase as an extension of the original negotiation rather than as a "take it or leave it" proposition. With income-producing property, many items of the decision-making process are left up in the air until after your deal is made. For example, interior inspections are usually one of the items not done until after the buyer and seller sign a purchase contract. This might seem like a silly way to proceed, but in truth, it makes the most sense. You must remember that this is a business. It would be bad for business if every prospective buyer were allowed to traipse through the seller's units beforehand only to decide that they weren't really interested in buying anyway. Tenants would get nervous and the seller's apple cart would get upset.

Rather, the more logical way to proceed is to give a buyer access to all the things he needs to see during this free-look period. Only then, after there is a deal in place, are buyers usually allowed to see inside the units and review the rental agreements and books. These items may or may not impact the decision to move ahead. In actuality, most of the things that come up shouldn't be deal breakers. Instead, they'll probably just need some clarification or a little renegotiation here or there.

To protect buyers from hidden surprises, most of the preprinted purchase agreements include a contingency clause that says

> *If, during the time periods provided in this contract, the purchaser provides the seller a reasonable written disapproval of any item for which the purchaser has a disapproval right, the seller shall respond within _____days after receiving the purchaser's written notice. If the seller is unable or unwilling to make the correction, then the buyer has the right to cancel the contract.*

This means that if you encounter something unexpected during the due diligence period (like the discovery of a two-foot hole in the wall inside unit #4), you need to put it in writing and ask the seller to fix it. If he doesn't fix it or come to an amicable solution with you, you have a right to cancel the contract and walk away unscathed.

Requesting repairs

The one key to getting a seller to comply with your repair requests is to be reasonable. Let's say you found a property and you came to terms with the seller. That first night you probably toasted to your future wealth with a bottle of champagne. Now the due diligence period is here, and it is time to do your interior inspection. What happens next? You get to see the units and panic sets in. The carpet smells a bit and looks like it hasn't been vacuumed in a year, dirty dishes are overflowing from the sink, and laundry is laying everywhere. All of a sudden, you

---

 Watch Out!

Be careful not to go back to the seller with a laundry list of repair requests. This is a red flag that you are a beginner, and it makes the seller think he might be better off cutting his losses and selling to someone else. Remember, you are buying a "used" building. A little wear and tear should be expected.

Watch Out!

If you find yourself worrying about all the small details, you probably haven't done enough homework before making your offer. If this is the case, go back to the learning and research phases of the five-point plan we laid out in Chapter 2, "The Profits and the Plan." At this point, more education will probably be the thing that gets you to truly move forward.

begin to think, "I would never live here. In fact, I want out of this deal!" The truth is you're probably just nervous about the big step you're taking. Unfortunately, "buyer's jitters" aren't reasonable grounds for the cancellation of a contract.

Realize that the jitters are natural, especially for first-time buyers. Backing out of a deal because a tenant doesn't keep a nice house, however, or because you think the kitchen cabinets in unit #3 look dated would be considered by a court to be unreasonable. Contingencies are not designed to give you an easy out from a transaction. Their purpose is to protect you in case you come across an unforeseen material issue that can't (or won't) be corrected. Material, in this case, means something significant, not minor (see the garage floor example that follows).

The magic word

In case you haven't figured it out by now, the magic word is "contingency." Therefore, when writing an offer, it's important for you to use this word for all the items on which you will be basing your final decision to buy. Most preprinted forms have contingencies structured correctly, but if you or your agent decides to add any clauses to the contract yourselves, you might make what could be a costly mistake.

Let's assume you have a nice four-unit building under contract, but when you first looked inside the garage, you noticed that the floor in one corner looked like it wasn't level with the rest of the floor. There isn't anything in the preprinted contract that directly applies to this situation, so you decide to add a clause that says, "As part of the exterior inspection, I will be checking the floor of the garage to see if it is level."

During due diligence, you hire a contractor to have a look at the garage. He does a quick survey of the elevations and confirms what you had thought. The lot in the left rear corner of the garage is lower on one side. He says that this area probably will flood during heavy rains, making it hard for the tenants to get into the two parking spots on the left side. It can be corrected, but it requires raising the grade of that corner of the lot and possibly the floor of the garage.

This is something you hadn't planned on. What's more, you consider a garage that will flood to be a significant issue that goes directly to the heart of the deal. You decide that, unless the seller pays to have the problem corrected, you want out. Unfortunately, the seller refuses to compensate you or fix the problem, so you are forced to call the escrow office and call the whole thing off. The seller then informs you through the escrow officer that he will be keeping your deposit because you defaulted on the contract. He says he let you inspect the floor as you wanted, but you never let him know that having the garage floor level was a contingency of the transaction. The end result is that the large deposit you made probably will be held in trust until the ensuing legal battle between you and the seller can be resolved.

This legal battle could easily have been avoided if you simply had written into the contract that your offer was contingent on the inspection and approval of the garage being level. This would have put the seller on notice from the outset that his response to your requests for a repair (if one were needed) would directly determine the outcome of the deal.

Some examples of proper wording for your contingencies might be

- "This deal is contingent on the buyer's approval of the interior inspection."
- "This deal is contingent on the seller fixing the broken railing surrounding the front patio."
- "This deal is contingent on a licensed pest-control company determining that the property is free of termites and termite damage."
- "This deal is contingent on the seller filling the vacancy in unit #2 at $550 per month or more."

By wording your concerns this way, you will ensure that the outcome of the deal (and the safety of your deposit) hinges on satisfactory resolutions to your own contingencies.

Inspecting the units

Two big contingencies usually get quick attention by buyers as soon as the due diligence period begins. These are

- Inspection of the interiors
- Inspection of the overall physical structure of the property

These inspections usually aren't as important as many novice buyers make them out to be. In truth, you're buying a used apartment building, and that's what you are going to find once you go and do the inspection. But, because it's the nature of the beast to ink a deal before you actually see much of what you are bargaining for, the built-up anticipation often becomes of paramount importance.

Professional inspections

There are two ways to perform a property inspection. You can either hire a professional property inspector or do it yourself. We recommend that, unless you have expertise in this area, it's best to hire a professional. The peace of mind you get from a professional's opinion will be well worth the small expense.

Moneysaver

Reduce the cost of your inspections (and any other service you require) by negotiating in advance with the inspector. Almost everyone expects you to haggle over prices, so don't disappoint them.

The scope of a professional inspector's report should cover all of the following areas:

1. Roof

2. Structural

3. Electrical system

4. Plumbing system

5. Heating/air-conditioning system

As of the printing of this book, the property inspection business is in its infancy, and most states are just beginning to work on guidelines and licenses. The most important thing is that you find an inspector who is affiliated with a local or national organization of building inspectors. If you are unable to locate one of these professionals, find a local contractor that has experience with the type of building you are buying. You should be able to find a reputable property inspector or licensed contractor by asking other property owners, contacting your local apartment owner's association, through a referral from your real estate agent, via a search on the Internet, or by looking in the Yellow Pages.

Refer to Appendix E for a sample professional property inspection report done on our example property at 333 Richmond Street.

Do-it-yourself inspections

The other way to do inspections is to do them yourself. Unless you have extensive experience in contracting, however, we recommend that you refrain from taking this route. Rather, you should do your own inspection in *conjunction* with a professional's inspection. A professional inspector is going to determine and note the condition of every aspect of the property. He might find that the systems work fine, but your job is to take his information and couple it with your own judgment to make determinations about potential upgrades or repairs you will need to make in the future. This information will let you know how accurate your estimated budget was for maintenance. This

> ❝I have always accompanied the inspector on his tour. That way, I can take notes and ask questions while he's inspecting the property. ❞
>
> —Matt K., investor

will be important in establishing a long-term budget for replacements, which we will discuss in Chapters 15, "The Big Picture of Management," and 16, "So What's Stopping You?"

The items to consider in your own property inspections are

- The same items listed above that a professional inspector would look at, including the roof, structural, electrical system, plumbing system, and heating/air-conditioning system
- Property dimensions, footage, lot size, boundaries, age, permits, and so on
- Sewer and water systems
- Zoning, building restrictions, city inspections, and so on
- Geological conditions
- Neighborhood conditions, adequacy of services, hazards, and so on

It would also be wise for you to sketch the layout of each unit. Knowing the size, the general floor plan, and the amenities will help you determine its future rentability compared to the competition. You also should use a checklist to make the job easier. Here is a checklist that you can use for yourself. Feel free to add to it or adapt it as necessary to meet your own needs.

ADDRESS_____

UNIT #_____

CONDITION:	BAD	AVERAGE	GOOD
Paint			
Drapes/blinds			
Vinyl flooring			
Kitchen cabinets			
Kitchen counters			
Stove			
Refrigerator			
Dishwasher			
Garbage disposal			
Faucets			
Sinks			
Doors			
Windows			
Heater			
Water heater			
Air conditioner			
Bathroom cabinets			
Tub/shower			
Shower door/curtain rod			
Toilet			
Vanity			
Bedroom 1			
Bedroom 2			
Bedroom 3			
Closets			
Tenant			
Notes			

Bright Idea

You can use this same uniform checklist for new tenants to inform them of the condition of the unit when they move in. When you give them a copy, make sure you get them to sign it.

Sometimes, inspections give you an opportunity to meet the tenants even before you take over ownership. This can be good, or it can be bad. It's natural that, once you meet them, you'll begin to form an opinion about whether they fit into your overall plan for the property. Make sure you couple your first impression with a few months of property ownership before you make up your mind. First impressions can be deceiving.

To protect your privacy, you might also want to consider introducing yourself as a prospective property manager, rather than a prospective new owner. That way, during the time that you are the owner of the building you can always say that you're just doing your job.

The exterior inspection

As opposed to interior inspections, when you should get in and out with as little intrusion to the tenants as possible, you can take all the time in the world for your inspection of the exterior. This inspection is critical. If there's a big problem that you miss in the due diligence period, you could get stuck footing the bill. As you walk around the property, take notes on everything you see. Jot down notes about rusted railings, peeling paint, overgrown landscaping, fire escape access, gutters, downspouts, and anything else you see.

> ❝At one property we were considering, the inspector pointed out that the acoustic ceiling might contain asbestos. The seller refused to pay to have it removed, let alone tested, so we decided to walk away from the deal.❞
>
> —Kirk M., investor

You also should make a rough sketch of the lot and the lay-out of the building as well as any structures on the property such as garages or driveways. This kind of diagram will make it easier for you to give directions to contractors or potential tenants throughout the tenure of your ownership. You should label the location of items such as

- Water meters
- Gas meters
- Electric meters and breakers
- Furnace or boiler
- Water heater
- Shutoffs for all utilities
- Shutoffs for all equipment in the building
- Pool equipment room
- Drain clean-outs
- Sprinkler system controls
- Cable TV panels
- Layouts of the units
- Garages, carports, or space numbers
- Tenant storage units
- Laundry rooms and laundry utility meters

Seller's warranty and maintenance responsibility

After you complete the inspection of the condition of the prop-erty, there are a few additional things you can do to ensure that you will get what you bargained for.

If available in your area, you should insist on obtaining a real estate transfer disclosure statement. These disclosures essen-tially outline the seller's knowledge, or lack thereof, about the property. By making the seller fill out a transfer disclosure as a contingency of the deal, it forces him to think about most aspects of the property and to make written representations about those aspects. If you have trouble finding this disclosure, contact the Department of Real Estate in your state and ask for one or have your attorney draw one up.

Along with a transfer disclosure statement, you should get the seller to give you a warranty about the condition of the property as of the date of your inspection. This also should include a stipulation that the seller

> ❝ If I can meet the seller at the inspection, I try to establish a rapport. I also ask if we can communicate after escrow in case I have any questions about the building. In my experience, most sellers are willing to be helpful. ❞
>
> —Jeremy L., investor

is to maintain the property in that condition until closing. This warranty should read something like this:

The seller warrants that on the date of the inspection of the property:

1. *There are no known leaks in the roof.*

2. *The tub and shower enclosures and pans are free of leaks.*

3. *All plumbing, electrical, heating, and air-conditioning systems are operative.*

4. *All appliances that go with the property are operating properly.*

5. *All screens will be in place and any broken or cracked glass will be replaced.*

6. *The property in its entirety will be maintained in substantially the same condition until the closing as it was on the date of the inspection.*

Many sellers will want you to purchase the property in "as is" condition. This is a legal issue you might want to discuss with your attorney. If it's a property you really want, and the price and terms are right, you probably are safe in doing this as long as you get a professional inspection done first so that you know what you're getting for your money.

As previously mentioned, you should also make sure you get a signed transfer disclosure statement from the seller. In doing this, your goal is to protect against the cover-up of a known problem by the seller. If you have a signed transfer disclosure and you discover a problem later that the seller knew about, you probably are in a good position to hold him liable.

Inspecting the books, records, and rental agreements

One of the most important items to analyze during the due diligence period is the inspection of the books and records of the operations of the property. Your purchase agreement should have a contingency that reads something like this:

> *This offer is contingent upon inspection and approval of the records of income and expenses of the property. The seller warrants that these are the income and expenses used by the seller in completing state and federal tax returns. Expenses are to be for the prior 12 months of operation and should include copies of the actual bills for all utilities, city fees and licenses, property taxes, insurance, service contracts, and any other bills associated with the operation of the property.*

If possible, it's important for you to see the actual bills rather than an operating statement or even the schedule from the seller's tax returns. Many part-time investors are not very consistent in the way they handle their books for tax purposes, whereas the actual bills tell you exactly what's happening with the operations of the property. From this data, you will be able to see how close your projections are to reality. If your numbers

 Bright Idea

Try to review the books and records before your scheduled interior inspection. If the building's books fail to meet your exectations, you can save yourself a lot of time and money by canceling the inspection (and the deal).

Bright Idea

If you have trouble determining when a tenant began his tenancy, check the electric meters when you do your inspection. If the tenant pays for his own electricity, the meter might verify the move-in date.

are off, it might be that you can spot a problem that can be corrected. We'll elaborate on this contingency in greater detail in Chapter 14, "Managing the Expenses."

As part of your review of the income and expenses of the property, you need to get copies of all the current rental agreements as well as the original applications filled out by the tenants before they moved in. You also should ask for a summary of any delinquent rents and a detailed payment history of each tenant. Though you won't be in a position to do anything about the data you get, the information will give you a strong idea of who will survive the storm and who will not.

Verification of terms

As a new landlord, you legally are required to honor any leases signed by the previous owner. One problem that can come up after a deal has closed is any special arrangements made between the tenants and the former owners. Even though you've seen the rental contracts, that doesn't mean there aren't other verbal agreements that the seller failed (or forgot) to disclose to you.

To avoid any problems in this regard, it's a wise idea to have the seller provide signed estoppel certifications from all the tenants before closing. A signed estoppel gives you a current statement verifying the main points of the rental agreement. If there are any additional terms that are in the minds of the tenants, the estoppel is their opportunity to mention them or forever hold their tongue. You can either obtain a blank estoppel form from your real estate agent, or use the one shown on the following page.

1. Unit number _____.

2. I have a month-to-month agreement/lease (circle one) and pay $_____ per month rent.

3. The last rent I paid was for the month of _____.

4. My security deposit is $_____.

5. My last month's rent is $_____.

6. The appliances I own are (check all that apply):

   stove_____ refrigerator_____

   washer_____ dryer_____

   other_____.

7. The names of the other tenants on the agreement or living in the apartment are

   _____.

8. I do have a pet_____.

   I do not have a pet _____.

9. Other agreements I have are

   _____.

10. Any problems related to my tenancy are

    _____

    _____.

    (Write "none" if applicable.)

    Signed _____

    Date _____

Service contracts

Along with your inspection of the operating details of the property, you also need to review any service contracts currently in place. These might include any of the following:

- Laundry equipment and service
- Pest control service
- Boiler or furnace maintenance
- Air-conditiong service
- Garbage and trash disposal
- Pool or spa maintenance
- Intercom or alarm systems
- Elevators
- Superintendent, porters, and doormen
- Cable or satellite TV
- Water treatment systems
- Gardening and landscaping
- On-site property manager
- Off-site property management

Many of these services are under long-term contracts, and breaking these agreements could cost you a bundle. Make sure you at least review them with representatives from each company, however, so that you know what terms you will be living with.

Changes during escrow

Your closing might take some time, usually because you are waiting for financing to come through. Therefore, it's important that the seller not make any material changes to the property without notifying you. You should have a clause in your purchase agreement that gives you the right to review and approve any material changes the seller wants to make during escrow. Remember that a material change is anything considered to be significant. The changes you should be concerned with are

Watch Out!

Thoroughly review the applications of any new tenants the seller finds during the escrow period. Some sellers have a tendency to fill last-minute vacancies with less-than-qualified tenants.

- Renting or leasing a vacant unit to a new tenant
- Beginning legal proceedings on a nonpaying tenant
- Changing the terms of any existing rental agreement or lease
- Making changes to any existing service contracts
- Any material change in the condition of the property
- Any violations or notices of violations or disputes

Financing and appraisal contingencies

Make sure specific details about the loan you are trying to obtain are contingencies. A typical financing contingency might look like this:

> *This offer is contingent upon the buyer obtaining and qualifying for a new first loan of not less than $_____, payable at $_____ per month including interest at ____ % (fixed/adjustable, circle one) amortized for ____ years, all due in not less than ____ years. Loan fees not to exceed $_____. Maximum adjustable interest rate to be ____ %. Additional terms: _____*
>
> *_____.*
>
> *Buyer agrees to act diligently and in good faith to obtain the above financing.*

If you notice how this contingency is worded, you'll see that it's designed to protect you regarding all the important aspects of your loan. One line says that you will obtain a new loan for no less than a certain amount of money. (You fill in the blank.) By having this line, the clause protects you in case a lender refuses to loan you all that you need. Another example is the line that stipulates when the loan is due. If you write in that it will be due in 30 years, but the lender will only give you a loan for 10, again you are not bound. Finally, there is a line that protects you from being hit up for loan fees that exceed the amount you budgeted.

Having the property appraised for the negotiated purchase price is another contingency that usually needs to be met. Sometimes, however, the appraised value of the property may come out to be less than the price you negotiated. Most standard contracts contain a clause that protects you in the event that this happens. In these instances, the clause will allow you to cancel your purchase contract without forfeiting your deposit.

There are two other options available when this happens. First, you can use the appraisal as ammunition to get a lower price. With a lower appraisal in hand, you can go back to the seller or his agent and renegotiate the purchase price to make it equal to the appraised value. Second, if you really want the property, you can simply put down additional money needed to complete the purchase. This way, the bank will be satisfied with the final loan-to-value ratio that they are lending on and can thereby justify approval of the loan you are seeking.

Note: It isn't unusual in an escalating market for appraisals to come in low. This doesn't mean that the value isn't there for the investor. It just means that the appraiser's formula didn't work in that particular instance. In the long run, if you have done your homework properly, having a building fail to

 Watch Out!

Contingencies have time limits set for their completion. If you're not able to complete your due diligence by the time they expire, ask for extensions and get any new agreements in writing. For example, the lending process always takes more time than you think it will. If you fail to notify the seller that your loan approval is going to take a few extra days, the deal may go awry and you could be left out in the cold.

appraise usually has little to do with the profit you can earn from your business. As always, do your own homework so you can make educated decisions along the way.

Obtaining clear title

Once you have opened escrow, you should receive a title report, a title opinion, or some type of chain of title for your review. Any of these reports will let you know whether there are any recordings against the property that might adversely affect your plans. It is not uncommon to have federal or state tax liens, local property tax liens, or judgments that have been recorded. Most of these items are usually rectified by sellers before closing. Nonetheless, you must have a contingency that requires the seller to give you clear title. A typical title contingency might be

> *The seller shall provide at the seller's expense a preliminary title report for the buyer's review and approval. At closing, the seller shall provide the buyer with title insurance and shall transfer title, free and clear of all liens. Unless otherwise agreed to in this agreement, title shall be free of other encumbrances, restrictions, easements, or other rights or conditions that are of record or known by the seller.*

Most title reports or opinions do not cover boundary issues, city zoning, or building issues unless they are recorded against the title. For that reason, if you have any concerns about property lines, fences, or where a structure is built, you might need to hire a surveyor or a civil engineer to answer these questions for you. If you have any zoning or building-code concerns, you need to check with the local departments that handle those issues.

 Moneysaver

Title insurance is one of those items that usually gets paid according to the norms and customs of the area. In some areas, the seller pays; in others, it's the buyer's responsibility. Regardless of the custom, you can always ask the seller to pay for title insurance because it can only save you money. The worst she can say is "no."

Other contingencies

Years ago, when offers were made to purchase real property, the preprinted form was only 1 page long. Today, in California, for example, that same form is 10 pages long, and it includes enough contingencies and disclosures to fill a small book. These agreements have evolved due to hard lessons learned in the courts and the desire in the real estate profession to provide full disclosure. These forms and disclosures help jog everyone's memory on the important issues in a transaction.

Space prevents us from reviewing all the current issues we see in these agreements. This chapter has touched on the major issues and contingencies that should concern you. The following list, however, contains some others to consider:

- Agency disclosure
- Smoke detector and water heater compliance
- Natural hazard disclosure
- Environmental hazards
- Environmental survey
- Lead-based paint
- Earthquake safety
- Megan's Law
- Military ordnance locations
- Tax withholdings
- Americans with Disabilities Act
- Pest control

You probably will be doing business with a real estate agent who is a Realtor. This means she is affiliated with the National Association of Realtors in her state. If this is the case, it is in your best interest to use the preprinted forms she provides that correspond to the type of property you are buying. These forms will cover all the specific issues you need to be concerned with in your area.

Removing contingencies

We've discussed, at length, the importance of contingencies in protecting your rights in a real estate transaction. Now that you're up to speed on how to handle the most important contingencies, let's learn how to remove them so you can get on with closing your transaction.

Removing a contingency means that the problem or issue has been corrected so that the deal can proceed as planned. Most of the preprinted contracts require you to choose one of two methods for removing contingencies:

1. The active method of removing contingencies

2. The passive method of removing contingencies

The active method of removing contingencies says that, if you find a problem during the due diligence period, you need to put it in writing and deliver it to the seller. It also means that, once there has been an amicable solution to the problem, you need to put that in writing, too. Once you do, that contingency will be removed, and you will be one step closer to closing your deal.

The California Association of Realtors defines the passive method of removing contingencies in this way:

> *If purchaser fails to give written notice of disapproval of any item or of a cancellation of this contract within the strict time frames specified in this contract, then the purchaser shall conclusively be deemed to have completed all reviews and inspections of the documents and disclosures and to have made the election to proceed with the transaction.*

This simply says that written notice to the seller is not required. Instead, you need to negotiate a correction of the problem within the time periods specified in the contract; otherwise, the seller will deem your silence on the issue to mean that the contingency has been waived or removed.

Bright Idea

It's more work to remove all your contingencies in writing, but it forces all parties involved to pay attention to the details.

Regardless of the method of removal, keeping track of the time period for removal of contingencies is critical. Once you have a property under contract, you must calendar any deadlines that have been agreed to. Naturally, the goal of most sellers is to get this free-look period over as soon as possible and to find out whether you are "in" or "out." Your goal is to complete your reviews in a timely fashion and to either accept the property as you find it or go back and ask for clarification or an adjustment to the deal.

Just the facts

- Many transactions require some extra give and take once the due diligence period begins.

- Contingencies aren't designed to give you an easy way out; they are there to protect you from unforeseen material problems.

- You always should hire a professional inspector to check out any real estate purchase you are considering.

- Insist on seeing at least twelve-months worth of income and expenses before you make your final decision to buy.

- Make sure that obtaining sufficient financing and clear title are worded as "contingencies" of your deal.

Property
Management Essentials

PART VI

GET THE SCOOP ON...
The first things to do after you close escrow ■
How to determine the market's vacancy rate ■
Surefire techniques for finding new tenants ■
Getting your unit rent ready ■ How to keep your
tenants happy and your units full ■
Raising the rent

Managing the Tenants

You have just closed your deal, and sweat is starting to form on your brow; now is when the real work of owning property begins. It's time to take over management of the building and begin the job of running your new business. We know that closing your first escrow and taking on this new challenge can be a daunting prospect, especially when you think of dealing with vacancies, bounced rent checks, and late night phone calls about overflowing toilets. Don't worry, be happy; this chapter is for you. Here you will get a jump-start on some key tenant-managing techniques before you ever close on a property.

Meet and greet

It might sound trite, but this really is a people business. Many investors tend to lose focus when they buy a couple of buildings and forget that to make money in any business, you must continually strive to keep your customers happy. As a real estate investor you will have two customers to worry about. One is the person who will ultimately buy your properties when it comes time to sell. You don't need to worry about him for a while. The second customer is the one you need to concern yourself with now because he is the one who is going to help you make your fortune. He is your tenant.

Provided that you haven't hired professional property management, you will need to meet your new tenants as soon as you close escrow. Either mail them a letter or post one on their door that very day introducing yourself. Let them know that you would like to meet with them personally and that you'll be calling in a day or so to set up an appointment. This request always brings up a tenant's worst fears. He thinks you're going to raise his rent (which you might), tell him to shape up or ship out (which you might), or tell him you want his first-born child (which you don't). In truth, all you want to accomplish is to gain the tenants' trust, review any concerns or problems they might have, and if they are on month-to-month tenancies, get their signature on a new rental agreement.

When you get a new agreement signed, you can discuss with the tenants how and when you want the rent paid. This will be one of your first management decisions. If it's common practice in your area for the rent to be paid on the first of the month with a three- or five-day grace period, that should be your policy as well. You might, however, end up making some concessions on this issue, especially if tenants you inherited had a different arrangement with the former owner due to a payday issue. If you decide that these are tenants that you would like to keep for a while, you should continue to honor their former arrangement. In the future, you will be able to exclude tenants that cannot pay on the day you want rent paid.

Beware of falling into the trap of becoming friends with your tenants. Yes, certainly you should be friendly, but for the most part you should keep your contact with tenants on a strictly

Bright Idea!

Make sure you get new rental agreements signed and dated by your tenants as soon as you close escrow. The new agreement will ensure that the tenant will not be able to sway the judge with any stories about other agreements with the former owner.

business level. This way, if their child gets sick or they get laid off from their job, you will be able to ask for rent without guilt. Keep in mind, McDonald's doesn't give away free hamburgers, nor should you ever be expected to give away free housing.

Protecting the privacy of you and your family should also be of paramount importance to you. There are a number of proactive steps that you can take to achieve this goal, including

1. Picking up the rent in person or having it mailed to a post office box or other place of business.

2. Setting up your post office box before you purchase any property. This way, your home address will not show up on any recorded documents or utility bills.

3. Having an unlisted phone number and caller ID blocked.

4. Never giving out your home address to anyone who lives at the property. This includes resident managers and superintendents.

5. Getting either a voice-mail service or a pager to answer ad calls and emergencies. This way, you can stay available but still protect your privacy.

Think how you would run your business if you owned a restaurant, or were an accountant, for example. In those instances, and rightly so, your customers would only know how to reach you at your place of employment. Well, the same principle should hold true for you in the apartment rental business. Most of us would never think of asking for our accountant's home telephone number or, even worse, calling our accountant at his home in the evening to get a question answered. Rather, use the suggestions above to help eliminate any potential invasion of your personal privacy. Your longevity and ultimate success in this business will depend on it.

A policy on checks

It's a fact of life that sometimes tenants bounce their rent checks. Occasionally it's on purpose; usually, however, it's not. Nonetheless, now that you are the landlord, this problem directly affects you. Therefore, you need a policy regarding the acceptance of personal checks for rent. Have a firm rule that, if a tenant bounces a rent check, you no longer can accept personal checks from him, and he must now pay his rent by either cashier's check or money order. His bank will probably charge him a nominal fee for this, but this is a business and it isn't your problem. You also should never allow your tenants to pay cash for rent. Besides the inherent bookkeeping problem it poses, accepting cash can make you an easy target for a robbery. Finally, you should have a reasonable late payment policy. Make sure the tenants know that you expect them to pay a late fee and any bank charges if and when they pay their rent beyond the agreed upon due date and grace period.

Housekeeping duties

During escrow you should have received information from the seller about who does the regular maintenance work on your building and the names of the local utility companies. Make sure you contact each utility company and maintenance contractor long before you close. Sometimes utility companies require deposits from new owners in order to maintain the service. It would be an ominous beginning to your tenure as the landlord if the utilities were turned off the very day you took over.

Insurance concerns

Before your loan was funded, you surely were required to purchase insurance for the building to protect against fire. But, maybe beyond that, you should also consider buying additional

Moneysaver

Consider buying comprehensive general liability (CGL) insurance. It can cover most of the cost of a legal defense as well as any damages you might have to pay as a result of a lawsuit.

coverage. One area of coverage to consider is insurance to protect your manager and the workers that come on the property in case of injury. You might not think you have any employees for your modest three- or four-unit building, but, in the eyes of the law, maybe you do. The guy who cuts your grass, the handyman who fixes the broken garbage disposals, and the tenant who shows the unit for you from time to time all may be considered employees by a court of law if they get hurt while working on your property.

The workman's compensation insurance laws aren't very forgiving. For that reason, you should check with your insurance agent to see whether your existing policy covers these casual workers. If not, you need to get a policy to cover them. One way around the law is to only use contractors who can prove they have their own workers' compensation insurance. The flip side of using these contractors is that they usually charge the most because they pay all the fees and obtain all the licenses for the work they do.

Apartment owners associations

One of the best organizations you can join at this time is a local apartment owners association. If there isn't one in your own community, see if you can find one in the closest major city. (See Appendix B for a state-by-state list of apartment owners associations.) Experienced apartment owners and professional property managers usually run these organizations, and their sole purpose is to give time-tested advice to other owners and managers like you. Most associations also have monthly newsletters that will keep you up-to-date on current events and changes in your market. They also carry advertisements for contractors who

Bright Idea!

Consider taking a course from your local apartment owner's association on property management before you close escrow. The price is usually right, and the information you will learn will be invaluable.

can give you help when you need it. In addition, many associations will supply you with various forms you might need, and some have access to credit reports to check out potential tenants. Some associations even give seminars and classes on property management and specific classes for resident managers. These are all well worth attending.

Neighborhood watch

The next order of business is to get to know the competition. You probably did some initial investigation before you bought, but now you need to begin keeping a log that will contain ongoing specific information about what's happening in the neighborhood around your building. Things to note should include

- The number of units in the surrounding buildings
- The number of properties on the surrounding streets
- Phone numbers from "For Rent" signs
- Amenities in the other properties
- Rental rates and terms on the vacancies
- The overall condition of the streets
- The location of the local police and fire departments (Get to know them.)
- Any new construction you see

Don't wear yourself out trying to fill up your logbook in one day; the idea is to just begin the process and to keep it going for as long as you are a property owner. Remember, this is a working notebook; it doesn't have to be anything fancy, just something that you can keep under the seat of your car.

The first thing to note is how many units are in the surrounding buildings. By knowing this number, you can determine a general vacancy rate at any given time and will thus be able to monitor changes in vacancy trends. The easiest way to estimate the number of units is to just count the number of mailboxes you see in your neighborhood. It isn't necessary for you to be 100 percent accurate; you just want a general estimate of how many units are out there. Once you know the number of units, you can estimate the vacancy rate by counting the number of "For Rent" signs in the neighborhood and then dividing that number by the number of mailboxes. Your calculation will look like this:

$$\frac{\text{Number of "For Rent" signs}}{\text{Number of mail boxes}} = \text{Vacancy rate}$$

Know that this method of determining the vacancy rate is an inexact science. It should be close enough, however, to help you determine a general vacancy rate at any given time.

Giving over the reigns of control

Although you might want to turn properties over to management right after you purchase them, it would best if you could manage your first buildings yourself. We know, however, that this isn't always practical for every investor. If you do opt for management, the key to double-checking their effectiveness is to "manage the managers." One great way to do this is to always be aware of what the market rate for the rent should be. By being keenly aware of the local rental rates, you will always be sure that you are getting the right amount for your rentals.

 Watch Out!

Make sure your management company always calls you first when they think major repairs need to be done. It's not uncommon for a management company to call an expensive plumber when a plunger could have easily fixed the problem.

It's pretty easy to do a rent survey. Whenever you see a "For Rent" sign in your neighborhood, jot down the phone number in your logbook and call on the unit as if you were a prospective tenant. Make sure you ask all the pertinent questions that any would-be tenant would and then note the details in your logbook. Things to ask would include

- How much is the unit renting for?
- How many bedrooms and bathrooms are there?
- What is the square footage of the apartment?
- What amenities are included?
- Do they accept pets?
- Can you see inside the unit?
- How much will it cost to move in?

By routinely doing this exercise, you will have ample ammunition to guard yourself against a complacent management company. Sure, it's easy for them to turn in good numbers if they never raise the rents to their full potential. However, this is a business and your cash-on-cash return depends on them selling your product for the correct price. Your tenants will never complain if your rents are too low, and they probably won't ever move either. Keep in mind, however, that when it comes time to sell or refinance your building, any lower-than-market rent will directly affect the value of your building.

Losing tenants

As a landlord, you will wear many hats. The very day a tenant gives you notice that he is moving out is the day you put on your salesman's hat. That's because it's now time to market your rental to someone new.

The first thing you should do when you get notice is to find out why the tenant is leaving. Maybe there was a job transfer or perhaps he wants to move his children to a better school district. In these instances, there is nothing you can do. Sometimes the move might be directly related to other tenants in the building or to the way you run the show. If that is the case, your ears should perk up because that is the kind of feedback that will help you improve your product the next time around.

It's said that one bad apple can ruin the whole bunch, and one bad tenant isn't any different. You'll find that most tenants won't complain about a bad neighbor; instead, they often will just decide to move out to get away from an unwelcome situation. The same premise holds true for maintenance issues that go unattended. Rather than complain, many tenants will just find another place to live where the owner takes care of things. If you ask your tenants why they are moving, it might be as simple as, "The building on the corner of Holly and Richmond has two washers and two dryers, as opposed to just one of each." This news might be hard to take, but it should serve as a wake-up call that you have fallen behind the competition.

Filling vacancies

The key to filling your vacancies as quickly as possible lies in doing the right kind of advertising for the soon-to-be-available unit. The major methods are

- Posting rental signs or banners
- Offering a referral fee to existing tenants
- Holding open houses
- Posting fliers at local businesses
- Placing ads in the local papers
- Sending direct mail to tenants in similar buildings
- Registering with rental agencies
- Contracting with a management company
- Creating a Web site on the Internet

Remember that your goal should be to fill the unit so that there is no lost rent. Keep in mind that if you wait until the current tenant has vacated to do any advertising, you probably will lose a month of rent. The secret to minimizing any lost rent is to start your advertising campaign the day you get notice from the tenant that he is moving. Even if the market is strong and you only need a "For Rent" sign out front to attract someone, get it up right away. The sooner your rental is on the market, the better chance you'll have to get the best selection of future tenants. You don't want just a replacement tenant; you want the best-qualified tenant currently looking for a unit.

"For Rent" signs

Nice signs and banners out front are an easy way to find prospective tenants to rent your vacant units. Sadly, we have seen plenty of attractive properties over the years that advertise their vacancies with cheap-looking, poorly worded, plastic signs just stuck in a front lawn. This is hardly the message you want to convey about your property. Instead, take a bit of time to make a legible sign that shows you care about your building. It doesn't have to be a Picasso, and it doesn't have to cost much, but it should show that you are taking some pride in your business.

Don't forget that the sign should have enough information so that potential tenants can decide whether the unit could work for them. The important information is

- Size of the units (bedrooms and bathrooms)
- Cost to rent it
- How to see it
- Who to call for more information

 Moneysaver

By having a legible "For Rent" sign in front of your building, you will attract some people to your property that actually are driving around the neighborhood searching for units being advertised by others. Sometimes, by piggybacking off someone else's ad, you will save a few bucks on advertising and might even attract some new tenants at the same time.

Keep in mind that many people won't bother to call if you don't list the size or the price. Others might be seriously looking, but you don't want them to waste your or the manager's time if they can't afford your unit or if it is the wrong size for them. Additionally, you might want to consider utilizing a toll-free phone number to advertise your rentals. In many larger cities, the local phone company issues several different area codes and charges long distance rates to call from one area code to the other. You might not ever give this a second thought, but someone on a tight budget might hesitate to call on your vacancy if they think it may be a toll call. Contact a local pager or answering-service company in your area to find the best rate for toll-free numbers.

Posting fliers

Posting multiple fliers in the neighborhood about your upcoming rental works well, too, especially if you are close to some commercial centers that have community bulletin boards. In this case, make some nice fliers with photos of the property and some tear-off tabs at the bottom that have the address and phone number of your building. More often than not, the fliers will stay on the boards even after you have filled the vacancy. This is an excellent way to get the word out about your great building.

Offer a referral fee

Offering a modest referral fee to existing tenants is another great way to attract new tenants. It is less expensive than other paid methods of advertising, and by having your current tenants refer their family, friends, or co-workers, you have a high probability of finding compatible people that might stick around for a while. Make sure you make it clear that they will only get the referral fee if you rent to the person they referred. You're not offering money for just a list of names.

Moneysaver

The most expensive newspapers aren't always the best choice for your advertising dollar. In a lower economic area, an ad in a throw–away-type paper might indeed draw more calls than an ad in a paper that the prospective tenant has to buy.

A bang for your advertising buck

If you need to pay for advertising and are placing several different ads, make sure you keep track of the calls you get and document how those callers found out about your rental. By doing this, you will learn two things:

1. Which papers produce the greatest number of calls
2. What works and what doesn't when it comes to writing rental ads

Before you run an ad, check the newspaper and review the ads that other owners are placing. Notice which ads catch your eye and which do not. You will see that the size of the ad isn't always the most important feature. Instead, what is said in the ad is most important. When placing your ad, try to list the key features about your property. Limit the sale job; instead, give enough facts to give people a reason to visit your property.

Showing your unit

Having the unit available to show at the hours potential tenants are looking is the most important aspect of this process. The easier you make it to view your vacancy, the better your chances of getting the best tenant. Generally speaking, prospective tenants will be out looking for apartments in the early evenings and on weekends, primarily Saturdays. These are the times that you or your manager needs to be available for a showing.

Beginning landlords always ask, "Can I show a unit before the current tenant moves out?" The answer is yes, sometimes. Most rental agreements have, or should have, a clause that allows you to enter the unit with 24-hour notice. This gives you the right to show the unit to a prospective tenant, but make sure you don't abuse this right. We have found that most tenants are pretty helpful when it comes to organizing convenient times to show their units, especially if you have been an amenable land-lord up until that point. As always, if you treat your tenants well, the odds are good that they'll do the same for you.

Be aware that most states have laws governing the showing of rented apartments. Therefore, be sure to stay in touch with your local apartment owners association and stay current on the most up-to-date rules for your area. Although it would be preferable to show your unit before it's vacant, be careful of doing so if the tenant presently living in the unit protests. Odds are that the situation will leave a sour taste in the mouth of your prospective tenant, and losing a live prospect before you ever had a chance to sell to them would be a shame. Under these circumstances, it might be best to wait until the unit is vacant to show it. At that time, you can make the best impression and will probably be able to command the most rent.

Web sites

Web sites are a great way to advertise your vacancies. Many Internet providers offer private Web sites for little or no cost. This can be a great way to show your units without disturbing your current tenants. A prospective tenant probably won't rent your unit based on your Internet ad alone, but this sneak peek might be just enough to get them to call you so that you can seal the deal in person.

Cattle calls

One way to make it easy on both you and the tenant moving out is to hold an open house for your upcoming vacancy. Let all qualified prospects know that you will have the unit open on an upcoming Saturday from 12 to 1 p.m. If they are interested in renting from you, this is when they should show up. As far as you're concerned, the more the merrier! This technique is the least intrusive on your current tenants, and it creates a great sense of urgency in your prospects because they see lots of other people looking at the same great rental.

"Rent-ready" apartments

The biggest stumbling block in getting a unit rented quickly is getting it cleaned and ready for the next tenant after the previous tenant moves out. The key to this job is finding out ahead of time what has to be done and lining up the proper people to do the work. When a tenant gives notice, you or your manager should meet with him right away and walk through the unit to see what needs to be done to get it "rent ready." Things such as dirty carpet, scuffed walls, torn screens, and so on should be written down on your repair list. What's more, doing this walk-through with the tenant who is vacating will help prevent any disputes about keeping all or part of their security deposit.

Once you have a list to work from, you can set a schedule so that the work can be finished in a timely manner. In most instances, many small items that need to be replaced can be purchased ahead of time—such as switch plates, towel bars, light fixtures, and so on. This way, you will avoid any delays while waiting for your contractor or handyman to make a run to the hardware store to get a small item.

Sometimes completing the finishing touches that make a unit really sparkle is what keeps you from renting your vacancy in a timely manner. The paint job gets done, but there is a missing switch plate. The new carpet is in, but it hasn't been vacuumed yet. The blinds aren't up yet, there's a half-empty soda in

 Watch Out!

You might not want to show a unit if it needs extensive work or if the current tenant keeps a messy house. Instead, show the prospective tenant the manager's unit as an example of what the vacancy will look like when they move in. After the messy tenant vacates, get in there immediately and make the unit sparkle again.

the refrigerator, and you have yet to put up a new shower curtain. Buttoning up all the final details will go smoothly if you have someone you trust do a final walk-through on your unit. They should think of themselves as a prospective tenant and look for things that would discourage them from renting the unit. Armed with this information, you can correct any outstanding problems with your unit and will soon be on the road to collecting rent again.

Two key points to remember are

1. If you have tenants ready to move in, they usually want to move in as soon as possible, so get the unit rent ready as soon as possible.

2. If you don't have a tenant lined up, it's much easier to rent a unit that is clean and ready to move into.

Discrimination

Whether you're the manager of a 100-unit apartment complex or the owner of a small duplex, federal anti-discrimination laws apply to you as might several state and local ordinances. The federal Civil Rights Act and the Fair Housing Act prohibit landlords from discriminating on the basis of race, ethnic background, national origin, religion, and sex. The Americans with Disabilities Act (ADA) effectively prohibits discrimination against someone with a disability.

The law says that, if you are faced with two equally qualified tenants, it is legal to pick one over another for no other reason than you liked one better; there is nothing discriminatory in that. If you have a pattern of not choosing African Americans,

 Bright Idea

From a business standpoint, the only form of discrimination you should practice is one based on a tenant's ability to pay the rent.

Jewish people, women, or other minorities, however, you leave yourself open to an expensive discrimination lawsuit.

Even if you are not discriminating, as a landlord, you should be equally concerned with the appearance of discrimination. If you have an apartment complex occupied only by whites, for example, you might appear to be discriminating even if you are not. The key to minimizing that risk is to set up objective, legitimate business criteria when looking for new tenants and to stick to them. What you must do is look consistently for such things as two positive references, stable employment, and a good credit history. Treat people equally and use the same criteria in every case. It would also be wise to write down your criteria and keep it on file. Above all, be consistent and document your reasons for denying someone a unit.

> 66 "The only color that matters to me when I rent my apartments is the color of money. Green! 99
>
> —Jack B., landlord

Rental agreements

You have picked a new tenant, and now it is time for both of you to sign a new rental agreement.   As mentioned in Chapter 12, "The Due Diligence Period," it's advisable to use a rental agreement that you get from your apartment association because it will have all the proper protection clauses for both you and your tenant. Never use one of those preprinted forms you get at your corner stationery store. These forms usually are very general and lack the specific details that will protect you legally. Also, the apartment association's form should cover most legal issues for your area.

You will find that local custom often will dictate the kind of tenancies you will have. In some areas, month-to-month agreements are preferred. In others, leases are more common. Each has pros and cons attached to them. In short, month-to-month agreements allow landlords and tenants to terminate the agreement with just 30-days notice. Leases, on the other hand, lock both parties in at an agreed-upon rental rate for an extended period of time (usually one year at a time on residential income property). Therefore, the type of tenancies you ultimately decide on will depend on the amount of flexibility you desire.

In addition, you should have any other necessary agreements ready for signature when you're closing the deal on a new tenant. Some properties, especially larger buildings, have tenants sign a list of house rules. Most states have required disclosures regarding lead-based paint and other environmental concerns. Finally, you should have an interior-condition checklist for review by you or the manager and the tenant. (Adapt the checklist from the "Do-it-yourself inspections" section in Chapter 12 to meet your needs.) Walk the unit and go over the checklist together. When complete, make sure you both sign it. This will eliminate most arguments over deposit refunds in the event you need to charge the tenant because of any damage above and beyond normal wear and tear. This form should cover the following areas:

- The condition of the carpet
- The condition of vinyl and other floor coverings
- The condition of the paint
- Any holes or cracks in the walls
- The condition of the ceilings
- The appliances and their condition
- The condition of doors, windows, and screens
- The condition of carports, garages, and storage areas
- Keys and accessories (garage door openers)
- Other

Help from Uncle Sam

There are some special groups of tenants of which you need to be aware. Because many people in our society lack the ability to afford adequate housing, the government has several programs available that assist them in paying for a place to live. The most common program is through the office of Housing and Urban Development (HUD). This division of the government provides assistance to people who cannot afford a place to live. The original goal dates back to the Housing Act of 1949, the purpose of which was to provide "a decent home and a suitable living environment for every American family."

Section 8 is the program under which this rental payment assistance is administered. Some cities get Section 8 assistance; others have an office that administers the housing assistance programs for needy families in the community. Individuals and families must apply to these organizations and be qualified according to HUD criteria to receive the rental assistance. If qualified, the applicants will have part of their rent paid by the program, and they will be responsible for the balance. In most instances, the tenant's share of the rent doesn't exceed 20–30 percent of their income. As you can see, the advantage of having Section 8 or voucher tenants is that the government pays a major portion of the rent. What's more, the government usually is very prompt in payment. Now that's the kind of tenant we all like.

Part of HUD's job is to establish the general market rent for various size apartments and houses in the community. This rent schedule becomes the top rent the tenants are able to pay including any subsidies by HUD. If you have rentals in an area with HUD subsidies, you should find the rent they set to be more than reasonable. These rental rates are based on the market rent in the area, the size of the unit, any utilities that are included, the appliances provided, and so on.

One hurdle you'll need to face with a HUD-assisted tenant is the inspection of your property by a HUD official. Their goal is to provide decent, safe, and sanitary conditions for the tenants.

Watch Out!

When choosing HUD tenants, it's important for you to do the same due diligence checking of their references as you would with any other potential tenant. HUD makes no guarantees concerning the tenants' ability to pay their portion of the rent.

As long as the unit passes inspection, it will pass the program's requirements. Note that your units will need to be re-inspected every year by a HUD official.

Be aware that there is always plenty of paperwork to fill out when having your building approved for HUD. This is because HUD is a government entity. Long before you ever start collecting rent, you will have to have all the i's dotted, t's crossed, and then some.

Finally, when you take over a property with a HUD tenant, you will need to prove to HUD that you are the new owner and complete new rental agreements before you start receiving rent from them. Make sure that you tackle this issue as soon as possible upon taking ownership, as any delay might cause you to lose a month or two of rent, which defeats your whole purpose.

We say yes to pets!

Should you rent to tenants who have pets? We think so. Most landlords handle the problem by just saying no to pets. This might be the easiest solution but perhaps not the wisest.

When you buy your building, you will inherit a pet policy from the previous owner; he either allowed pets or he didn't. Now that you're the new sheriff in town, you have to decide how it is going to work under your watch. Here are some good reasons to consider taking a tenant who has a pet:

- Because the general method of handling the pet issue is not to allow them, it makes it tough for someone with a pet to find a new residence. By considering these tenants, you will have a pool of grateful tenants to pick from.

- Pet owners generally stay in an apartment longer than non-pet owners. This is because it is so tough for them to find a landlord who will take them, and, when they do, they want to stay put.

- Accepting tenants with pets is an excellent method of combating periods of high vacancy.

- Most pet owners are willing to put down a large security deposit if you accept them as a tenant. If the pet damages the unit, you have the money to fix it after they move.

- You can command a premium rent from someone with a pet.

In these instances, it wouldn't be unreasonable to increase the security deposit 50 percent and add 10 percent to the rental rate. If you decide to consider pets, advertise your unit just that way: "Will consider pets; call to discuss." Finally, it's important that, if you rent to a tenant with a pet, you check out their references thoroughly with their previous landlord. If their pet ruined their last apartment, you would want to know about it.

Also, make sure you fill out the checklist previously mentioned indicating the condition of the unit before the tenants and their pet move in. This list will be invaluable if you need to withhold a security deposit to repair damage caused by the pet. What's more, you can protect yourself further by taking pictures of the unit before they move in. These photos will help out just in case you ever have to prove a point in court.

Note that if you inherited tenants on leases, you will have to wait to change your policy regarding pets until the contract term has been fulfilled. Also, a landlord cannot legally prohibit

 Bright Idea

When considering renting to a pet owner, make sure you interview the pet as well. Their dog might be small now, but even Great Danes are small when they're puppies.

an animal that is used to assist someone who is blind, deaf, or disabled.

Keeping tenants happy

Once you have a building full of tenants, you need to keep them happy. Of course, your main goal from real estate is to make the most profit you can, but to do this, you need to keep the customers (tenants) content. Your ability to do this over the long haul will be reflected in the bottom line.

The most important aspect of keeping tenants happy is being sure they're getting their money's worth. This is how all good businesses must operate; but in the apartment rental business this becomes easy to forget. Think about any good restaurant: Management works hard to put out the best product and service it can because if the customer has a bad experience, odds are he won't come back. So, too, in the apartment rental business. Once a unit is rented, the tenant still needs to be catered to, just like a restaurant patron.

It's easy to buy a property, fix it up, fill it with nice new tenants, and then let it slip back to its old tired condition over time. This doesn't have to happen. If you want to have a thriving rental business with a great tenant base, buy a building, fix it up, manage it properly, and keep the property up at all times. Remember that most restaurant customers don't complain about bad food; they just don't come back. With rentals, if you let the building deteriorate over time, the tenants will probably just find another place to live rather than complain.

 Bright Idea

From the very first meeting, give your tenants a clear sense of your guidelines and expectations. You should let them know what you will do for them as a landlord and what you expect from them as tenants. This way, you will avoid setting any false expectations on either side.

Addressing tenant requests

It's important to address tenant requests as fast as possible. Again, most people don't like to complain, so when they do, assume that the problem has been going on long enough that it is really starting to bother them. It's not your fault that they waited so long to call, but as they say, the customer is always right. In addition, it doesn't hurt to ask your tenants when you see them if everything is going okay in the building. They might forget to mention that little leak under the sink unless you ask. Nipping small maintenance issues in the bud will always save you money in the long run.

It's a good idea to have some form of check system to be sure tenants are remembering to let you know about any issues that come up. A good way to handle that is to put a clause in your rental agreement about maintenance problems. Here is a sample of what it might say:

> *It is the owner's goal to handle your maintenance problems as soon as possible. To assure that your request is processed quickly, please do the following. Promptly report any problems to the resident manager. Follow this up by turning in a written request when you make your next rent payment. Please submit any major upgrade requests to:*
>
> *Rocha Rental Properties*
>
> *PO Box 444*
>
> *Sacramento, CA 95816*

At some point, your tenants might want you to do some big upgrades to their unit—things like new appliances or kitchen cabinets. Rather than doing those kinds of upgrades while the unit is occupied, we recommend that you save these kinds of major changes for turnovers; that is, unless you have a great long-term tenant that you want to keep around for a long time. On the other hand, you might consider making smaller changes, such as new linoleum, window coverings, or fresh paint while your tenant is in the unit. Agreeing to any reasonable request should make it that much easier for you to raise rent when the time comes.

Painting

Be careful when it comes to handling requests for interior paint. All things being equal, agreeing to paint during the term of a tenancy can cause you a slew of troubles. The problem is that painting doesn't really have any value to you because you will most likely need to paint again when the tenant eventually moves out. Also, problems occur because painting is messy; therefore, there is a risk of damage to the tenant's property. For that reason, we recommend two creative ways to handle this kind of request. Provided that you are willing to have the unit painted,

1. Offer to buy the paint and have the tenant do the work.

2. Give the tenant a credit for the amount you normally would pay for new paint, but have the tenant contract directly for the painting work themselves.

In both cases you have kept your tenants happy, but removed yourself as far as possible from the liability due to any damage.

Window coverings

Window coverings are the easiest request to fulfill because you usually can just have the drapes cleaned or order replacement blinds and then have them installed. These items will hold their value when the tenant eventually moves, and there isn't much opportunity for liability. What's more, new blinds or clean drapes are relatively inexpensive and will certainly add to the value of your rental.

Floor coverings

A tenant's request for new carpet can be handled in one of three ways. If you determine that the carpet doesn't need to be replaced, one way of handling the request is to just say no. A second solution would be to have the carpet professionally steam-cleaned. The process is fairly inexpensive, and it has a couple of

Moneysaver

If replacing the carpet needs to be done, but money is an issue, consider replacing it only in the living area and just cleaning the carpet in the bedrooms.

good benefits. First, it improves the appearance of the apartment at a nominal cost. Second, frequent carpet cleaning prolongs the life of the carpet. Like all things related to maintenance, if you take preventative action along the way, it will save you money in the long run.

If cleaning won't do the trick and the carpet needs replacing, this will require a significant capital investment from you. Carpet lasts for several years, of course, so the benefit of the improvement will not be lost on the one tenant alone. You also should raise the rent to help recover the cost. We recommend a three-year recovery period for new carpet. If the carpet replacement costs you $1,200, the monthly increase in rent can be calculated like this:

$$\frac{\text{Carpet cost: } \$1,200}{\text{Recovery period: } 36 \text{ months}} = \$33.33 \text{ rounded to } \$30 \text{ a month}$$

This is only a recommended amount. If you are in an area where rents are lower, you might have to give tenants a more modest increase so that you don't lose them.

New vinyl or linoleum

It's tough to clean vinyl or linoleum beyond what you would expect the tenants to do on his or her own. If it needs replacing, you should make the decision based on your desire to keep the tenant in the building. This is another item that should last for many years, so it's not a wasted improvement. You usually can include a nominal rent increase with an expense like this. Use the preceding calculation to help you decide how much to raise the rent.

Raising rent

Raising rents is always a sensitive issue with owners and tenants alike. The problem with most small property owners is that they get overly friendly with their tenants, making the job of raising rents that much tougher. The bottom line, however, is that this is a business. Your cash-on-cash return and your building's ultimate value depend on the amount of your rents. Therefore, raising rents on nice tenants comes with the territory.

The first secret to raising rents is to know what the competition is doing. If the competition is getting more than you are for comparable units, a rent increase is in order. Don't worry. You probably won't lose a tenant because of a nominal rent increase, especially if you are only taking the rent to the new market rate for the area. Your tenants certainly won't be happy about it, but it would be too much work for them to move and pay the same rent down the street just to get even with you.

> ❝I quit having a problem raising rents when I realized that every dollar I didn't get from them was a dollar missing from my wallet. ❞
>
> —Kevin C., landlord

The second secret to raising rents successfully is to be consistent. If you plan to raise rents on a regular basis, do it every year at about the same time. Most people that work understand a cost of living adjustment, so they will take regular modest increases in stride.

To ease the pain, consider doing something extra for the tenants when you raise the rent. We already have discussed specific increases for items such as carpet or new linoleum. It doesn't hurt to follow or precede the cost of living increase with some upgrades to the building. A general upgrade might be new furniture in the patio area or new doormats in front of the apartments. You could also have all the outside windows washed, or you could have all the living room carpets steam-cleaned one

Saturday morning. Even a $10 gift certificate to a local coffee-house would remind them what a great landlord you are.

The best way to get the message about rents to existing tenants in an increasing market is to prominently display the current rental rate on your "For Rent" signs. When existing tenants see apartments being rented at a much higher rate for anyone new coming in, they will be far less apt to object when they get their increases, especially if they are paying less than the market.

Just the facts

- As soon as you close escrow, you need to get all your tenants' signatures on new rental agreements.

- You must make it a habit to do ongoing diligent research about the buildings and vacancies in your neighborhood.

- When a tenant gives notice to move out, begin your marketing campaign to fill the vacancy that very day.

- Discrimination in housing is illegal.

- There are ways to offset the expense of fixing up a unit while the tenant is still there.

- Keeping rents at market rate will help maintain the value of your building.

GET THE SCOOP ON...
Methods of determining expenses before you buy
■ How to manage your books effectively ■ The
difference between fixed and variable expenses ■
Why a great handyman is worth his weight in
gold ■ Proven techniques for keeping utility
costs to a minimum ■ Making capital expenses
and turnovers economically painless

Managing the Expenses

When you put on the bookkeeper's hat, you become the chief financial officer of your company. As you know, CFOs do not make the widgets. Their job is to stay on budget and to make sure the profit margin is as good as it can be. Without the CFO watching the money, overtime costs run wild, workers knock off early, and expense accounts spin out of control.

If you own 100 units, you know how difficult being in charge of the books is. If you are just starting out with a three-or-four-unit building, however, managing your expenses effectively is really not too hard, even for the novice investor. To understand how to become proficient in this area, we have broken down this chapter into the following three areas of study:

Chapter 14

1. How the property operates

2. How to keep the books

and, most importantly,

3. How to control the expenses

How the property runs

Finding out how a specific property runs should take place before you ever close on a transaction. As mentioned in Chapter 12, "The Due Diligence Period," when you make an offer to buy, you should include a contingency asking for review and approval of all expenses related to the building. Reviewing the true costs in advance of any purchase will not guarantee how the property will run for you, but it should give a reasonable facsimile. Items you need to see before you consummate a deal include

> 66 My husband couldn't balance a checkbook if his life depended on it. In our business, he manages the tenants and I'm in charge of the money. 99
>
> —Leslie R., investor

- Bills from the previous 12 months for all areas of operation of the building including, but not limited to, the following:
  1. Property taxes
  2. Property insurance
  3. All utility bills including water, trash, sewer, electric, gas, and so on
  4. City licenses and other city fees
  5. Any ongoing maintenance expenses
- Current rent-roll (list of all tenants and agreed-upon rents and security deposits)

- Rental agreements and applications of tenants
- Copies of all service contracts (laundry, elevator, pool, boiler and heating oil, gardening, and so on)
- Copies of any furniture or equipment leases
- Copies of any major expense items over the last 12 months
- Copies of any guarantees and warranties in effect on major improvements
- List of any personal property "owned" by the building such as stoves, refrigerators, or air conditioners

Add any items to this list that you or your agent feels is necessary, especially if you are buying in a location that requires upkeep that is out of the ordinary. In areas where it snows a lot, for example, it might be necessary to pay for snow removal in the winter to clear walkways or parking areas. In this case, you would need to see the bills from the winter months for this expense.

Sometimes, however, sellers might refuse your request to see the expenses for reasons that are innocent enough. Perhaps he throws the bills away after he makes his payments. If this is the case, ask for copies of his canceled checks and then double-check these figures by talking to the people he wrote them to. If he is being honest in his dealings with you, he should be willing to comply. If he is unwilling to supply you with his expenses, however, you might consider moving on to the next deal, as it is possible that he is hiding some material facts. In the alternative, consider contacting the utility company or service provider directly. Many times they will be willing to help you determine the true costs of running a particular building.

 Bright Idea

Utility companies usually are willing to cooperate with someone trying to get information about utility costs for a building. If you are pleasant, the odds are good that they will give you the information you need.

You might think it would be easier to just ask the seller for a copy of his tax return and review the expenses that way, but this is a bad idea. A tax return may or may not give you accurate information. If a seller is having trouble controlling expenses and decides to sell, it would be easy enough to report fewer expenses to paint a better picture of the property. What's more, your seller may just be a lousy bookkeeper. In any event, the best way for you to find out what is going on is to get copies of the actual bills and do your own accounting during the due diligence period.

Keeping the books

The least enjoyable part of your real estate job will be writing the checks and actually paying the bills. After all, you're doling out most of your rental income to others when you'd rather keep it for yourself and spend it as you like. Nonetheless, paying bills is a fact of life for any business owner. If you learn to do it efficiently, you can save yourself time, money, and aggravation along the way.

The checkbook

The simplest system for keeping books is to have one separate checkbook that you use only for your real estate business. It might be tempting to mix your business and personal checking accounts, but we advise against it. Mixing personal checks and business checks creates a bookkeeping nightmare, especially at tax time.

Many people use credit cards to pay for down payments and property upkeep. To avoid tax hassles at the end of the year, we suggest that, if you are going to be using credit for these purchases, you obtain just one card that you use solely for these purposes. Besides the thanks your accountant will give you, it will also provide a paperwork backup on expenses in case you lose a receipt coming from the lumberyard. Remember, credit card purchases are not deductible until you pay the credit card bill, so be careful toward the end of the year on the expenses you claim.

Moneysaver

If you have a tendency to use cash, always make sure to get a receipt and then attach the receipt to your checkbook. Otherwise, you might miss out on the many expense-related write-offs you can claim at the end of the year.

You should use the larger style checkbook that has three checks per page. These checkbooks have a couple of advantages. First, they give you ample room to write notes regarding each check. Second, a big three-check-per-page checkbook doesn't lend itself to fitting easily in your back pocket. This will help reduce the chances of using money in this account for personal expenses. Another good idea is to see if your bank offers a one-write accounting system. These checkbooks give you a carbon copy of all pertinent information. This simple checkbook system will work just fine for most small properties. As your business grows and you get a second and then a third property, make sure you open new accounts for each one.

You also need to get a three-compartment filing folder in which to keep your records. These folders are available at any office-supply store. One compartment is for the bills that come in, one is for all your expense receipts, and the last is for your canceled checks, statements, and the checkbook itself. At the end of the tax year, this simple and organized system should help you put your tax return together fairly quickly.

One-page spreadsheets

You might want to use a spreadsheet to keep track of your finances. If so, we recommend that you buy spreadsheet paper with at least 20 lines per page and then copy the following list exactly as written down the left-hand side. This list is taken from the IRS Federal Form E, which is the form you will use to file your taxes at the end of the year. The description for each expense item is worded exactly as the form reads. By keeping track of your expenses this way, you will have an easier time come tax season.

Income							
Rents received							
Royalties received							
Expenses							
Advertising							
Auto/travel							
Cleaning/maintenance							
Commissions							
Insurance							
Legal/professional fees							
Management fees							
Mortgage interest							
Other interest							
Repairs							
Supplies							
Taxes							
Utilities							
Other							

Manual accounting systems

If the single-checkbook system isn't working for you and spreadsheets aren't sufficient, many manual accounting systems you can purchase will work just fine. One of the best is called Property Management D-12 by Safeguard Business Systems. This system, and others like it, is based on a one-entry pegboard system. You keep two cards on each property. The first contains all the vital information you might need, including tenants' names, important phone numbers, and so on. The second card is the

Moneysaver

No matter how you choose to keep track of your expenses, make sure you organize your books to correspond with the format you need for filing taxes. Your accountant will thank you for it, and his bill will reflect that.

ledger card. It is used to keep track of all the financial details of the property. These details include all money coming in and all money going out. With this kind of system, you can run all your properties out of one checkbook. The simple coding of the properties and the expenses enables you to develop the reports you need at the end of the year.

The modern method: computerized accounting systems

For those of you with computers, many simple spreadsheet and bookkeeping software programs are available. Most of these property management systems can handle multiple properties and can generate any number of customized reports. You can find these programs advertised in the flyers and booklets put out by apartment owners associations. You also should be able to find them at any office or computer supply stores, as well as via a search on the Internet.

Controlling expenses

There are many expenses associated with the running of a property, and keeping them within reason, even for an experienced investor, is an ongoing struggle. Expenses can be either fixed or variable. Fixed expenses do not fluctuate with rental income. Examples include insurance or property taxes. Variable expenses, on the other hand, increase or decrease with the rent level and the occupancy level of the building. Variable expenses include items such as property maintenance and utility costs.

Let's first spend some time talking about controlling fixed expenses.

Fixed expenses

There aren't too many fixed costs associated with income property, and this actually is good news. Because most expenses are variable, you can use your management skill to curtail costs. There are, however, a couple of big fixed expenses that you need to know how to approach. Your biggest fixed expense will probably be your loan payment, to which we devoted an entire chapter (Chapter 5, "Borrowing Big Bucks"). Beyond your loan payments, your tax bill will probably come in a close second.

The tax man's share

Your property tax payment will be a large fixed expense. Even though taxes are not billed monthly, you should think of them as if they were and should set the money aside so that you can pay them accordingly. This way, you'll have the funds available when it is time to make the payment.

Another way to ease the pain of having to come up with a large lump sum of money for taxes is to have your lender set up an impound account for you. An impound account is like a forced savings account. You pay your property taxes into this account on a monthly basis along with your mortgage payment, and the lender makes your tax payment for you as it comes due. Some lenders even give you a break on your interest rate if you have an impound account because you are showing yourself to be a responsible borrower, and that is the kind of customer lenders like best.

 Watch Out!

It can be tempting to use money set aside for taxes for other purposes, but as you can imagine, this can cause major problems. In fact, most real estate loans include a clause that requires you to pay your taxes when due; otherwise, the lender can call your loan due and payable immediately.

The costs of protection

The other major fixed expense is property insurance. You pay insurance just once a year, but like taxes, you should set the money aside for this bill each month. In fact, if you have money impounded each month for your taxes, you probably can include the funds for your insurance in the same account. Make sure you ask your lender about this option before the close of your escrow.

If you shop wisely, you can save a lot of money on insurance. We recommend the following three ways to find savings:

1. Shop around and compare prices of major insurance carriers as well as independent brokers.

2. Vary the dollar amount of the deductible on losses.

3. Vary the dollar amount of liability coverage.

Be sure to get quotes from all the major carriers as well as several local independent agents because the rates will vary. If you belong to an apartment owner's association, they will probably be able to recommend several agents that have a good handle on insurance for apartment buildings. You should repeat the process every year because rates change depending on the type of business the insurance companies want to attract. It's not uncommon to find cheaper insurance elsewhere even after a year or two of property ownership.

For an apartment or commercial building, you need to get a package policy. A package policy includes fire and extended coverage but does not include flood or earthquake coverage. Most package policies also include some type of loss-of-rents coverage. This is important to have because lenders will require you to make your mortgage payment even if the property is damaged due to some unforeseen reason, and rent isn't coming in.

You also need to be aware of the co-insurance issue. Most policies have a clause that requires you to carry a certain percentage of the replacement cost of the structure; an average number is 90 percent. The clause says that, in the event you carry less insurance than this percentage, you become a co-insurer with the insurance company if there are any losses. Simply put, this means that, if you have a loss, the insurance company will pay their share, and you will have to pay yours.

Keep in mind that if you don't properly insure your property for the correct replacement cost, the effect of a loss can be costly. For example, let's say you have a 90 percent co-insurance clause. In that case, if the cost to rebuild a property after a loss is $200,000, and you have decided to only carry $150,000 worth of insurance, your share of a $25,000 loss due to a fire will look like this:

Reproduction cost	$200,000
90% value	$190,000
Actual insurance	$150,000

$$\frac{\text{Actual coverage } \$150{,}000}{\text{Reproduction cost } \$200{,}000} = 75\% \text{ co-insurance rate}$$

Cost of fire repairs	$25,000
Insurance pays (75%)	× .75
Dollar value	$18,750

Cost of loss	$25,000
Insurance payment	− $18,750
Your share of loss	$6,250

Note that this $6,250 is in addition to your out-of-pocket deductible on the loss. The theory is that you can lower the price of your policy by raising the deductible and by covering less of the value of the structure. This problem usually doesn't surface unless you have a loss. When it does surface, however, property owners and insurance agents invariably point the finger at each other.

When buying a single family home, this situation doesn't present itself very often because most of these policies have a guaranteed replacement clause. Apartment policies, however, aren't usually structured that way. One way to protect yourself is to make sure that your insurance agent actually goes out and measures the square footage of the property before he sells you a policy. This way, he can accurately calculate the building's current replacement cost. If the cost means you will have to buy more insurance than the price of the property, which is not unusual, bite your tongue and pay it. You cannot count on the lender catching this problem (being under-insured) because most only worry about enough insurance to cover their loan. Another alternative is to review the replacement cost section of the appraisal and provide it to the agent or compare it to the agent's figures.

Insurance coverage is a constantly changing product. In recent years, property owners, and—therefore—their insurance companies, have had to deal with potential losses from perils like mold and terrorism. As owners, we want the coverage, yet the insurance companies want to limit their exposure from potential losses. In truth, because most states have fairly strict laws about limiting or changing coverage, many companies just go out of business until the insurance commission allows them to limit their coverage. This can play havoc when trying to obtain affordable insurance for your properties. Of course, you can always get insurance, but it might cost you more until the major carriers get back in the market. However, don't let this higher premium keep you from buying property. Yes, the insurance industry will win; they're just too powerful. But remember, you will win too. You'll win by owning property. You don't make long-term profit waiting for insurance rates to come down. You make it by owning real estate.

Watch Out!

Make sure your insurance agent properly insures your building for the current replacement cost. Otherwise, you could get stuck paying a large sum of money if you file a claim and it turns out that you don't have enough coverage.

Other fixed expenses

Other minor fixed expenses can be associated with real estate such as pool or spa service, pest control, and gardening costs, all of which you can take steps to control. The first thing to know is that these kinds of expenses usually save you money in the long run because they treat potential problems when they are minor, thus keeping them from becoming major. As with any other costs, shop around so that you can get the best rates. Don't be afraid to switch services if you find one for a lower cost. Many times, your existing providers will lower their fees to keep your business if they find out that you are considering changing companies.

Variable expenses

Many variable expenses come into play during the management of a property. Remember that a variable expense is one that changes; it will increase or decrease with the rent level and occupancy level of the building. Two keys to keeping variable expenses at a minimum are to make sure you shop around and avoid hiring overqualified contractors for basic fix-it jobs.

The handyman can

The best way to save money on variable expenses is to get a good handyman—someone who can do most of the minor repairs around the property but doesn't have the knowledge (or license) to do major repairs. This can mean the difference between paying $15 per hour versus $50 per hour. Another advantage is that a handyman can take care of more than one type of problem when he goes to the property. This will save you from paying specialized professionals a minimum fee just to show up.

Your savings could look like this: The plumber comes to fix a leaky faucet in unit #1 and the bill is $45. You get an electrician out to fix the broken light switch in the laundry room. His minimum fee for a service call is $65. Finally, you need to replace an interior door on unit #3, and your general contractor charges you $120 for the parts and labor. Total cost for all the work is $230.00.

Now let's contrast this with what it could cost for one handyman to do the same work:

Parts

Faucet washer and seats	$2.50
Light switch	$1.50
30" door	$29.00
Door handle	$9.00
Hinges	$6.00
1 quart of paint	+ $4.95
Total parts	**$52.95**
Labor at $15 per hour × 4 hours	+ $60.00
Total for handyman	**$112.95**

Cost for professional contractors	$230.00
Cost for handyman to do the same work	− $112.95
Savings by using a handyman	**$117.05**

It will take some trial and error to find a good handyman because most of the good ones are kept pretty busy. Some advertise in local papers; others find work by word of mouth. One good place to find workers is at your local home-improvement center or hardware store because this is where handymen purchase their supplies and, thus, the employees get to know them

Bright Idea

Using a handyman to handle all minor repair work always will save you time. This is because you or your manager only has to meet one person at the property rather than one for every little job that needs attention.

as regular customers. Additionally, make it a point to visit larger buildings in your area that have resident managers. They might know of a good handyman who is eager to make some extra money working on your building as well.

One great secret to keeping a good handyman happy is to pay the bill for his services immediately. Most small service providers like this work from paycheck to paycheck and don't have the reserves to finance 30 or 60 days of receivables. By paying your handyman right away for his work, you will probably find that his work consistently gets done in a timely manner.

Bargain hunting

One basic, but often overlooked, method for reducing costs is to shop around. There is a vast difference in what various contractors charge and what parts can cost for your property. You don't need to get three or four bids for every job, but you should get in the habit of always shopping contractors and suppliers, even when you don't need anything done.

You'll find that materials can be 50 percent of the cost of any repair job. Many retail stores advertise loss leaders. A loss leader is a product advertised at a reduced rate to bring customers in the door. You can save a lot of money on materials by seeking out advertised loss leaders and stockpiling things you will need along the way. When things need fixing, you will only have to pay a handyman for labor.

Water bills and water damage

A big drain on your wallet can be your water bill. Although you have no control over the price of water, you can control how much is used. Toilets are the worst culprits when it comes to water waste. The classic problem is a toilet in which the flapper valve no longer seats properly, and it allows a slow, almost imperceptible trickle of water to run day and night. In communities with higher water costs because of supply issues, this can double or even triple your bill quickly.

Worn washers on faucets are another big water waster. As the washers in faucets age, they wear out and become brittle. This leads to small breaks that show up as annoying drips from the faucet. The problem is that tenants do not mind minor drips, and they usually will not want to bother the landlord because of one. This constant leak, just like the toilet, can drive your water bill sky high. Again, get in the habit of asking your tenants how things are going in their unit whenever you see them. That way, you'll be able to nip small problems in the bud before they become major issues.

> **66** When I first started out as a resident manager, I wasn't very good at fixing things. But after watching electricians and plumbers and handymen do work at the property, I can now do most of the repairs myself. **99**
>
> —Adam F., resident manager

There are two other classic water-related problems that tenants don't tell you about until the damage is done. The first is a leak in the seal around the toilet. The seal only costs about $1.25, and your handyman probably would charge you less than $25 if you catch the problem early enough. If not, you will need to replace the subflooring and the floor covering, and then fix the problem. The total cost could be upwards of $250.

The other problem is the deterioration of the caulking around showers and bathtubs. As caulking ages and cracks, it allows water to migrate to the drywall or plaster outside the shower door. A tube of caulking costs about $2.00, but a wall repair can cost $100 or more. In addition, these leaks usually affect the flooring, and we've already seen what that can cost.

The most annoying and recurring plumbing problems are clogged toilets and drains. Unless you're smart, they invariably can cost you time and money, again and again. Clogged drains and toilets fall into three groups:

1. Tenant-caused problems
2. Tree roots growing into the pipes
3. Mystery problems

Far and away, tenants cause most of the clogged drains and toilets, even if there is no way to know for sure. For that reason, you should have a clause in your rental agreement addressing this issue. Make sure tenants initial this clause so that you both will have proof that they read and understood their responsibility. It should read

> *Tenant will pay for any drain stoppages caused by their own negligence. Owner will provide tenant with a copy of the bill showing the cause found by the plumber.*

The second method of controlling water problems is to have a handyman or plumber do a checkup on your building once a year. Have him go through all the units, check all the fixtures, and make any necessary repairs. It will be well worth the expense. This also will give you a chance to check the units in general to see whether there are any other problems you need to address.

Finding a reliable drain-cleaning specialist who works 24 hours a day also is important. Their rates can vary, so do your shopping and check references. Also, set up your billing ahead of time because the stoppage will inevitably occur late at night, over the weekend, or on a holiday. Make sure the worker understands to always write the cause of the problem on the bill because you can use this to collect from the tenant if he or she was at fault.

Finally, buildings with steam or hot-water heating systems are prone to leaks. Because these leaks often are at floor level and sometimes are behind radiator covers, they can go undetected.

Tenants also fail to report such leaks because they tend to affect the apartment below more than the one with the leak. Make sure you check these heating systems annually and keep them in proper working order.

Cutting electricity costs

If you are paying for electricity on your property, it probably is for the outside lights, garage, carport, and/or the laundry room. You cannot eliminate these lights because they are needed for security, but you can work to cut down on your bill.

To begin with, you should replace the current fixtures and install low-voltage florescent lights. These will save you money on the bill, and the bulbs actually last longer than the nonfluorescent bulbs. You also should put the lights on a timer so that they don't have to run all day. For areas that aren't

> 66 We encourage our tenants to keep us informed of even the little things that need fixing. It's really not a bother because it allows us to save money by fixing problems before they get out of hand. 99
>
> —Kerry and Mia D., investors

used much, you should have motion-detection lights that only come on if movement is detected. Not only do they cut down on costs because they are not on very often, they also help prevent crime by scaring intruders away.

Nipping gas bills

Usually, the only gas you will pay for is for the laundry room and sometimes, if the building is master metered, for the hot water in the units. In the laundry room, you can do two things to cut costs. First, make sure there is an energy-saving blanket on the water heater. These fiberglass coverings go around the heater to provide insulation and can easily be installed by your handyman. The second way to save money is to always keep the thermostat on the hot water heater at a modest level. Most tenants only do laundry on the weekend or at night, so there is no reason to keep the water scalding hot for all those extra hours when the equipment isn't in use.

If you are the one paying for hot water in the apartments, make sure the heater has an energy-saving blanket as well. In addition, if the hot-water heater holds 100 gallons or more, it should be equipped with a recirculating pump. Recirculating pumps move the hot water through the pipes continually so that the apartments farthest away from the heater get hot water just as quickly as the apartments closest to the heater. Otherwise, the tenants farthest away will waste a lot of water (and money) waiting for the hot water to get to their unit.

If your water heater is approaching the end of its useful life, you should start planning for its replacement before it goes out. An emergency water heater repair on a Sunday afternoon will cost you a lot more than a planned replacement. This is especially true if you have purchased the heater at a sale from your home improvement center, and you only need to pay your plumber or handyman for the labor. Thankfully, the efficiency of water heaters has greatly improved in recent years, which will surely help to create a significant savings.

Heating and air-conditioning

In many areas of the country, the property owner provides heating and air-conditioning for the tenants. This can be a significant expense. A couple of ways to keep these costs under control include

1. Review 12 months of utility bills before you buy any property to be sure the costs are reasonable for your area.

2. Have your heating and air-conditioning units serviced regularly so that they operate at maximum efficiency.

3. Keep thermostats set at the "Goldilocks" temperature, which means not too hot and not too cold. (Some communities mandate minimum day and night temperatures during cold months.)

Interior painting

Interior painting is a frequent expense of property ownership. One way to save money is to pick one color of paint for all your units and use it on all future paint jobs. Besides never having to worry about whether paint matches again, in many cases it will allow you to just do touch-up painting when you have a turnover.

You usually can find lots of competing companies and handymen looking for painting work. You can either use professionals or, again, trim costs by hiring a handyman. The key point here is to check references for speed and quality of workmanship. A quick-and-cheap job will not save any money if your carpets are stained with paint and the windows all need to be cleaned of over-spray.

Carpet and floor covering

Carpet, if it is of decent quality, should last three years or more. The best way to help your carpet last is frequent and proper cleaning. If your tenants aren't in the habit of paying to get their carpet cleaned, you should do it yearly and tack on the cost with their annual rent increase. They get something for the increase, and you add some life to the carpet.

You should pick carpet for your units just like paint. Pick one color and one brand and stick with it. Make sure it's a brand and color that won't be discontinued in a few years when you need it. If a unit has a bad stain, you usually can cut the stain out and patch it with some of the extra carpet you have lying around. If the stain is in a unit for which you don't have any extra carpet, take a piece from a closet to make the repair or take a 3' × 3' section from in front of the front door. You can always replace

 Bright Idea

Be sure to tell your painters whether you will be putting in new carpet after they paint. If so, their preparation time and labor costs will be cut down considerably.

Bright Idea

If you only need carpet in one or two rooms, consider buying used carpet. You sometimes can locate used carpet by talking to a carpet installer and telling him what you are looking for. Odds are, he would be more than happy to make a buck by selling you something he otherwise would throw away.

the closet with a remnant from any carpet store. The piece in front of the door can be replaced with vinyl, which will look fine. The idea is to make the repair and save having to replace the entire carpet because of one or two stains. You will find that it isn't unusual for bedroom carpet to last much longer than other areas of the unit. By sticking with one style of carpet, you might be able to get by with cleaning the bedroom carpet and just replacing the area that sees more foot traffic.

Like carpet, vinyl and linoleum can take a beating, especially in the kitchen. The usual problem is a tear or hole caused by a tenant dragging a refrigerator or stove across the floor. If the overall condition of the vinyl is decent, your handyman should be able to repair a tear by taking a small piece of existing vinyl from underneath the refrigerator or stove. This can be replaced with a 12" × 12" square that can be purchased at any hardware or home improvement center. Don't worry if it is not an exact match because the stove or refrigerator will be covering it.

Master-metered properties

Some properties are master-metered. This means there is only one utility meter for all the units, and, unfortunately, the landlord is the guy who gets stuck paying the bill. You usually find master-metered properties in areas where the buildings are older, and most are made up of smaller units containing singles and one bedrooms. To a novice investor, these buildings look attractive at first because the price compared to the income looks good. Once you factor in the added costs of the utilities, however, any initial attraction may quickly fade.

Watch Out!

The big problem with master-metered buildings is that tenants in these build-ings have no incentive to turn off any of the utilities. This is because you are paying the bill and they are not. We say, don't disregard master-metered buildings outright. Rather, analyze potential purchases thoroughly before buying to make sure you can still make the profit you desire.

There are a few things you can do to cut costs on master-metered buildings. First, explore the feasibility of changing the metering so that the tenants pay their utility bills instead of you. This will require you to get some bids and then do an analysis to see whether it is worth the expense. Many older properties are in need of a wiring upgrade, and doing this at the same time might not add that much more to the price of just changing the metering. Gas, on the other hand, might be more costly to sep-arate. Its value and feasibility will depend on the location of the stoves and heaters in the units.

Another method to cut costs on a master-metered building is to install energy-saving light fixtures and appliances to each and every apartment. Long-life, low-voltage lights can save sig-nificantly on the electric bill. Installing modern stoves and heaters also can save on gas usage while improving the appear-ance of your units. Many utility companies offer rebate pro-grams to encourage these upgrades. Some will even assist in the cost of upgraded insulation, which will help cut down the cost of heating.

Finally, do what you can to tack the prorated costs of utilities on to your rents. By advertising your master-metered units as "utilities included," tenants will understand why their units cost a bit more.

High-cost capital expenses

Capital expenses are costs that cannot be written off in full in the year you spend the money. The IRS says that these are items that have a useful life of more than one year or that increase the value of the property. Some examples include

- Carpeting
- A new stove or refrigerator
- New plumbing or a new roof
- A structural addition to the building
- New asphalt on the driveway

When you purchase your property, you should make an assessment of all capital expenses and start working on cost estimates for replacements. By doing this from the get-go, you can start setting some money aside each month so that you will be able to take the cost of the item out of operations rather than out of your pocket. It wouldn't hurt to put some of that money in a money market account or even a certificate of deposit. Just make sure you keep some money in reserve for emergencies.

The following capital expense budget is for our four-unit example at 333 Richmond Street. We have estimated the time for the expense in months to make it easier to calculate the monthly amount you should put aside from the cash flow.

Item	Months Until Replacement	Total Cost	Monthly Reserve
Carpet unit #1	12	$400	$33
Carpet unit #3	24	$700	$29
Paint exterior	48	$1,500	$31
Replace roof	60	+ $3,000	+ $50
Total		$5,600	$143

By budgeting for capital expenditures and setting aside money each month, you will be able to pay for the expense as planned without feeling as if you'd been pickpocketed every time a capital expense comes along. Remember, this is an ongoing process, so you will need to revisit your budget every year or so to add and delete items.

Moneysaver

As long as you stay within legal limits, don't be shy about asking tenants for a sizable security deposit. If they take care of the unit, they probably will get all, or a good portion, of it back. If they do any serious damage, you'll have the money to make it rent-ready for the next tenant.

The major disadvantage of larger capital items is that the IRS says you must write off the expense over time, even though you spend the money in one lump sum. A new roof, for instance, might require a depreciation schedule that goes beyond the period you will be holding the property. For that reason, many investors prefer to repair major items in stages rather than doing them all at once. If you can divide your roof into four sections, for example, you might be better off repairing each section separately and expensing the cost in the year you do the work. This also might save on permit fees because many cities don't require a permit for a mere repair, but they would if you put on a whole new roof.

If you are purchasing a property as a fixer-upper project, you will be doing the same kind of budget. The difference is that you will be including the costs in your initial capital requirements rather than in your future capital budget. Most properties will need some kind of capital budget unless they are new or recently upgraded. At a minimum, you should be setting aside money for floor and window coverings because they are the most frequently changed items.

Handling tenant turnovers

The last and least desirable, yet ongoing, expense of a property is the turnover. Unfortunately, turnovers come with very short notice, usually 30 days or less. What's worse is that tenants could care less if you had earmarked their rent money for something else or had a vacation planned for the very weekend they give notice. When it comes time to move on, they do.

The key to making turnovers as emotionally and financially tolerable as possible is having a plan in place before they happen. To that end, you should develop a turnover budget for each apartment or each size of apartment in your property. By having this budget and cost breakdown ahead of time, you will know what items to order and which subcontractors are needed the minute someone gives notice. The budget might look like this:

Turnover budget—2 bedroom, 800 square feet

Carpet	75 yards	$600
Vinyl	125 square feet	$125
Carpet cleaning		$60
Painting	Off white #6800	$225
Blinds	7 windows	$105
General cleaning		$75
Accessories and misc.		+ $50
Total		$1,240

Crunching the numbers and handling the expenses of your soon-to-be-burgeoning real estate empire is not the most fun you will have, but it is a necessary evil. By intelligently managing your expenses, you will ensure that your profits exceed your headaches, which, after all, is the name of the game.

Just the facts

- Insist on seeing all income and expense statements before you buy.
- Any bookkeeping system you choose should correspond with IRS tax forms to make filing your taxes easier.
- Use impound accounts to help save for property taxes and insurance payments.
- A good handyman is essential to a successful real estate operation.
- You must budget in advance for capital expenses and turnovers.

GET THE SCOOP ON...
What "curb appeal" is and why you must have it ■
How to manage the common areas of your
building ■ The truth behind security systems ■
Why you need a resident manager ■ The best
way to structure a manager's salary ■ Getting the
most out of professional property management ■
How to dramatically increase your profits by
doing an interior upgrade

The Big Picture of Management

Once you become an income property owner, you are the owner and CEO of your own small business. Sure, it feels great to puff up your chest and tell everyone you know that you're now a landlord and owner of your own private money-maker. Unless it's raw land, however, you have to work at it just like any other business. As a real estate investor, the business you chose is the renting of apartments. Your goal now is to keep the units full and to get the highest rent per square foot possible.

Curb appeal

The most important sales tool you have as a property owner is your building's "curb appeal." Curb appeal is how inviting your building looks from the street. It's been said that the clothes make the man. Well, the same holds true for your rental property. The first impression from the street will be the one to which potential tenants respond. If your building doesn't show well when prospects drive up, the odds are good that they will probably just keep on going.

To get the best tenants and command the highest rent, you want to have a sharp-looking building. In fact, when a prospective tenant drives up, you want him to think, "Wow, this is where I want to live!" In fact, this is an area of owning property where you should put yourself in the position of a prospective tenant. As you drive up to your building, ask yourself, "Would I live here?" It's not that you need to make your rental property as nice as your own home, but, for a rental, you do want it to be one of the more attractive buildings in the neighborhood.

An identity all your own

The first thing a prospect will see when he drives up is the front elevation of your property. The front elevation is the view as you approach the building. It is a combination of the paint, landscaping, and identity of your property. These aspects combine to create a theme for your building.

Most large and successful apartment complexes have an identity or theme all their own. This begins with having a sign out front with the name of the property on it. This kind of attention to detail can work for large and small units alike. Consider having a nice wooden sign made up with a catchy name for your building etched into it. If your building is on Richmond Street and the landscaping is something you are especially proud of, why not name it "Richmond Gardens?" This special touch will help create the kind of identity people like in a place they call home.

 Bright Idea

When placing ads to fill your vacancies, make sure they are factual and list the most positive aspects of your rental. Also be sure to say how much the unit's rent is. This will help reduce calls from people who can't afford your apartment.

Moneysaver

Make sure to landscape with low-maintenance plants that are hearty. Having shrubbery that won't die easily will help keep your hard-earned money where it belongs—in your pocket.

Hearty plants and a mowed lawn

Landscaping is an important aspect of the curb appeal of your property. There is nothing appealing or attractive about a drab lawn surrounding a square-shaped building. You don't need to spend a fortune on landscaping, however, to spruce up your investment. Simply buying some low-maintenance plants and shrubs will make your property stand out from your neighbors.

A good way to plan a project like this is to drive around and look at buildings and homes that have landscaping you like. If you take photos of the ones that catch your eye, you can later review them with the experts at your local home-improvement center. Seek out their help so you can come up with a plan for your property that will be affordable and attractive. Another option is to contact the owner or resident manager of the buildings you like and ask who did the landscaping. Most owners would probably be happy to help out.

Automatic sprinklers and outdoor lighting

Paying to have an automated sprinkler system installed upon taking ownership would be well worth the initial extra expense. In fact, it will pay for itself the first time your manager goes on vacation and your landscaping lives to tell about it. Most people set their sprinkler systems to water very early in the morning so as to avoid running it during the heat of the day. This saves water and, thus, saves you money. For that reason, make sure you, or your gardener or manager periodically do a test run on the system to make sure it is running properly.

Another nice addition to the outside of your building is a low-voltage lighting system. These are usually reasonably priced and will add a lot of class to the curb appeal of your property in the evenings. This is important because many prospective tenants see your property for the first time at night, after they get off work. You'll see that this touch really makes a property stand out from the competition. This lighting also can reduce the potential for crime and lawsuits, making it an even smarter investment.

A fresh coat of paint

The exterior paint of your building also is key to making a great first impression. Your building's color choice can either date it or make it. Once again, while driving around, look at color combinations that stand out on properties similar to yours. Take pictures and keep track of the addresses in case you want to try to match the colors for your own property. A word of caution, however: Before you order 50–100 gallons of paint, get a pint of the color (or colors) you plan to use and try it out on an inconspicuous wall to see how it will actually look. Just as new clothes often look better on the mannequin in the store, new paint sometimes looks completely different on your building.

A good paint job should last for many years, but the sun and the elements do take their toll, even after just a few years. Therefore, it would be wise to put a couple of extra gallons of your paint aside, or at least save the paint code when you paint. This way you will be able to freshen up your property on a regular basis. Finally, check to see whether there are any zoning restrictions on exterior colors. Some towns and historical districts have strict regulations.

 Bright Idea

Make a point of driving around the neighborhood and seeing how your competition takes care of their properties. Are they doing a better job than you are? If so, they will attract the good tenants and the high rents you desire.

The front entrance and lobby

Because the front entrance and lobby are such high traffic areas, you should always put in some extra effort to make sure they are kept clean. In fact, for a few extra dollars your gardener or manager would probably be happy to take on this job. Consider putting a couple of pieces of furniture, a few silk plants, and some pictures in the lobby area. You also can carpet or tile this entrance to enhance its appeal. Your current tenants, as well as any potential new ones, will surely appreciate it. Again, tending to details like these will pay off with more money for you on the bottom line.

The common areas

Another area that needs regular maintenance is the common area of a property. Even in smaller buildings, areas that aren't rented still need attention. One of the most visited areas that often goes unattended is the laundry room. This area should be kept locked (with keys for your tenants) and well lit. Your tenants need to feel safe if they have to do laundry in the evening. Keeping the laundry room clean also is important. Health and legal concerns could arise if your laundry room isn't kept up.

If your laundry machines are provided by an outside laundry contractor, which is very common, make sure they regularly service them and keep the exteriors clean. Have them post a sign in the laundry room so that the tenants know how to get in touch with them if something goes wrong with a machine. This information also should be spelled out in your rental agreement

 Watch Out!

Beware of tenants who monopolize the laundry machines. You don't want to lose good tenants because they consistently have a problem finding an empty washer or dryer.

so that the tenants know you are not responsible for the laundry machines.

Your laundry room should have a trashcan and, if there is enough room, a table so that your tenants can fold their clothes. If you have a table, you'll want a couple of inexpensive folding chairs, too; otherwise, people will sit on the table, which might break or collapse under them. It's also important to have non-slip floor covering because water leaks are common in laundry rooms. You don't want a tenant with an armload of laundry to slip and fall because the floor is wet. A wet floor in a laundry room is a lawsuit waiting to happen.

As for trash areas, they often get dirty and litter strewn if not attended to regularly. Because these areas often are out of the way, you should make sure they are well lit and secure. You also should consider having a window that peers into this area so that tenants can see if a stranger is in there before they go in. Recycling bins should be clearly marked.

Parking concerns

Parking areas are another location that often gets overlooked. The way you maintain this area depends on whether you have open parking, garages, carports, or a subterranean parking structure. Regardless, the first thing to do is to paint numbers on the spots and assign them to your tenants. You should do this even if you have open parking. Nothing starts feuds quicker in a building than someone who monopolizes all the parking. Assigning spots will help eliminate any potential conflicts.

> 66 As a landlord, I insist on no car washing in the parking area. I know it sounds like a harsh rule, but to allow it just costs too much. I haven't met a tenant yet who hasn't left the water on and the hose out. 99
>
> —Lori S., landlord

Any extra parking spaces can be used for two things:

1. They should be made available to tenants who need more parking (for an extra monthly fee, of course).

2. You should have spots available for guest parking. If there aren't any rules governing guest parking in your area, one guest space for every four units is a good rule of thumb to live by.

Your parking area should have a sign that says you have the legal right to remove any non-tenant cars from tenant spots. Your tenants will appreciate this. Most cities require posting a sign that cites the corresponding vehicle code and a phone number to call if a car is towed.

Parking rules should be spelled out in your rental agreements and also be posted in the parking area. They might include

- Only park in designated areas.

- Guest parking in assigned areas only.

- No storage in assigned parking spots.

- No storage of flammable or dangerous materials.

- No car washing in parking area.

- No auto repairs or oil changing in parking area.

Driveways and parking surfaces should be properly maintained and serviced. Your tenants see these areas every day, and they are part of the overall appearance of your building. If you fix small cracks and holes as they occur, it will save you a major expense later on. Your best tenant with the nice car might just move out because of the holes in the pavement and the dingy driveway you didn't maintain.

Security gates and entrance systems

In recent years, more and more parking areas have some type of security gate or system. In addition to the cost of the gates and the equipment that runs them, you have codes, cards, or clickers to worry about. At best, they keep out the guests that would normally park in the spots marked "No Parking." In truth, these systems do little to discourage car break-ins or car thefts, but they do give potential tenants a sense of security. Nevertheless, even if your building has these systems, it is not wise to advertise and induce people to rent your units because you have "secure parking." If your tenants suffer a loss and convince a court that they rented your unit because of the secure parking, you could be held legally liable.

The same thinking that goes into advertising a building as having security gates also applies to advertising security entrance systems. When you advertise an amenity such as a security entry system as a way of inducing a tenant to rent your property, it can easily create additional legal liability for you if those systems fail. Often enough, they do fail, and it is the tenants who cause the failures. They forget their keys, they lose their clickers, or they have to make several trips with packages, so they prop the security door open and somehow harm the system. Regardless of how it happens, it happens. Unfortunately, you need an expensive specialist to do the repairs. Conventional wisdom says that a lawsuit resulting from a failed security system could be costly, so be careful.

Locks and keys

Many tenants make extra keys for their apartments and take old keys with them when they move. It would be a disaster if a former tenant gained unlawful entry to a current tenant's unit. For this reason, after every tenant moves out you must either change the locks or, at the very least, make sure you rekey each unit.

 Bright Idea

It is best if tenants are home when repair work is done. This way, they can communicate the problem they have and can keep an eye on their belongings. If the tenants cannot be home, it is imperative that someone trustworthy stay with the repair contractor at all times while he is completing his work.

It is not advisable to leave extra sets of keys with a manager unless you know him extremely well. Even then, there is some risk involved because an intruder could break into the manager's apartment, take the keys, and have access to all the other units. Instead, if you keep all extra sets of keys, you probably won't have to worry about your manager ever being accused of taking anything from any of your tenants.

Maintenance and repairmen

Many maintenance and repair people will need access to your units. It is important for you to use reputable companies that are bonded and/or insured. Never give a key to a repair contractor to use unsupervised. A situation like this simply has too great a potential to create liability for both of you when the tenant starts to complain about missing jewelry, money, CDs, or television sets. If at all possible, let the tenant and contractors set the appointment for repair themselves, and let them know that it is their responsibility to be home to supervise the repair work.

Window security

Security for your windows also is important. If the windows in your units have any type of locks, you must make sure they are always working properly. In some urban areas, security window bars are common. These bars can indeed keep intruders out, but if not maintained properly, they also can make it nearly impossible to escape in the case of a fire or another emergency. For that reason, window bars, especially in bedrooms, all should be equipped with working quick-release mechanisms. Furthermore, check the building codes to make sure your window bars meet current safety and legal standards. Again, your potential legal liability for these items is enormous if they fail.

 Bright Idea

Keep trees and bushes trimmed and away from ground-floor windows. They can inadvertently offer an intruder a place to hide when trying to open a window.

Security summary

Security is a major issue for most tenants, and it should be for you as well. There are two major points to remember regarding security:

1. If you advertise that your building is a "secure building" (either in print-ads or in what you say), although it becomes part of the inducement for people to rent your units, it might also become part of your contract and can create a lot of additional liability on your part.

2. It is imperative that you quickly repair any security-related items that are broken including door locks, security doors, window locks, window bars, and security gates. Delays in making these repairs can leave you and your tenants wide open to potential trouble.

Your management team

Unless you're Superman, you probably will need the help of others to manage your properties. In the beginning, you most likely will use the services of a superintendent or a modified resident manager. This person is a tenant who helps out on occasion. From there, you might go with a paid resident manager. Eventually, you might even want to turn your buildings over to a professional property management company.

Manage the first one yourself

As we've said time and time again, we strongly advise that you manage your first property yourself. This experience will be invaluable to you. The most important skill you will learn from managing the first one yourself is the ability to understand and communicate with your customers effectively. It is very easy to forget that tenants are customers. Without them, you could not make any money in this business. The more absent you are from contact with them, the less you understand them. A side benefit of doing the management yourself is that you will probably end up with a list of decent subcontractors that you can have future management utilize. At a minimum, you will know what most common maintenance items cost, so you can audit the fees that your management company's vendors charge.

A resident manager or superintendent

The duties of a resident manager can vary greatly. Large apartment complexes have full-time resident managers who get a rent-free apartment and a salary for managing the property. Some are even professionally trained and are usually in high demand. Your first resident manager probably won't need these kinds of credentials.

Most buildings, even small ones (two to four units), can use a resident manager. (Note: Many cities and states have rules that require you to have a resident manager for a certain number of units. Check with your local city or county government to find out the rules in your area.) This person will serve as your eyes and ears when you're not there, which is most of the time. He should phone you if there is a problem and can show the apartments to potential new tenants when there is a vacancy. For this level of assistance, you should give him slightly reduced rent and an additional flat fee if he assists you in renting a unit. A situation like this is good for you and is good for him, too.

As a rule of thumb, the resident-management fee you are going to pay should be about 5 percent of the gross income of the property. On our example property at 333 Richmond Street, the income is $550 per apartment for a monthly total of $2,200. You wouldn't pay someone to manage themselves, so the fee would be 5 percent of the rent on the remaining three units, which is $82.50 per month ($1,650 × .05 = $82.50). You could structure the deal so that you give the individual a rent reduction

---

 Watch Out!

It is risky to allow your resident manager to collect rent in cash. Not only is it tempting, but cash on hand also poses a giant safety risk.

of $50 every month and then an additional fee of about 10 percent of the cost of any rental he helped with. This would give him an additional $55 ($550 × .10 = $55.00) on top of his monthly $50 rent reduction. Though he made $105 this month, ($50 rent reduction plus $55 for helping to rent a vacant unit), there will be other months when there won't be any rentals to help with, so he'll only get the $50 rent reduction. In the end, your manager will end up averaging around the $82.50 proposed target per month.

For this small level of management, you won't need a big list of rules for your manager to follow. He should call if he knows of a problem, should look out for the building, and occasionally will help out renting a vacant unit.

An involved resident manager

When you own larger properties (say, 10 or more units), it will probably become necessary to have a more involved resident manager. In these larger properties, the manager can perform more duties for you, so a more organized system of directing his efforts is necessary. You should create a list of tasks for the resident manager to accomplish each month. This should be in writing and should be signed by both you and your manager. It is important for the compensation to be spelled out for the work you expect. As a general rule, it is best to have a small basic salary with duties listed for that amount. Offer an additional flat fee on top of the salary for any other tasks you want completed.

It helps to express all the tasks in terms of hours and to use an hourly wage to arrive at the flat fee for the task. The reason for this is that, from a practical standpoint, most of the salary on smaller property just goes to a reduction in what the manager pays in rent. If you only give a flat fee, the person gets used to paying this lower rent and has no incentive to do a good job on the various other things that should get done around the building. By separating the various tasks, the implication is that someone else can do them if the manager decides he's not up to doing the job.

With any management job such as this, you have to start with a budget and then assign the work and the hourly wage based on that budget. Let's assume you have a 20-unit building, and the units rent for $600 each. This means a monthly gross of $11,400 ($600 × 19 units = $11,400) not counting the manager's apartment. Using the rule of thumb of 5 percent, the management fee should be $570 per month ($11,400 × .05 = $570). Remember, you should assign a reasonable hourly wage for duties you want the manager to accomplish. If we assume an hourly wage of $8.50, this equates to about 67 hours per month ($570 ÷ $8.50 = 67).

> 66 Having my superinten-dent do extra work around the building gives him more money and keeps him in the building. As it's 'his' building, he tends to take more pride in his work and costs me less than an outside person would. 99
>
> —Matthew K., investor

The following is an example of the kind of tasks you might expect from your manager:

Management duties

Collect rent from tenants	3 hours
Bring rent to owner	1 hour
Be available for tenants	30 hours
General cleaning of grounds	7 hours
Clean decks and laundry area	8 hours
General maintenance	18 hours
Touch up painting	
Light gardening	
Minor repairs	
Total hours	67 hours

Watch Out!

Having a property manager might create a situation requiring you to carry workman's compensation insurance. Be sure to check with your insurance agent on this issue and, above all, protect yourself.

Now the manager has some guidelines as to the amount of time expected for the salary you are paying. In reality, he probably won't be putting in nearly this much time on all these tasks, but this type of list will serve as a reminder of just how much he is receiving for this job as compared to a regular job. If you find that cleanup isn't getting done or that the manager is complaining about doing the repairs you requested, you can hire someone else to do the work and adjust the salary accordingly.

Managing the big buildings

When you graduate to any building much larger than 20 units, you certainly will have to fine-tune your management control system. At this high level of investing, you should have written policy manuals, reporting systems, and formalized meetings to review the operation of the property. We don't have space in this book to properly cover this level of management, but we have recommended several books in Appendix C that should be helpful.

Professional property management

Most owners, at some point in their investment careers, decide to turn their properties over to professional property management companies. You might choose to do this to spend more time with your family, because the demands of your regular job have increased, or maybe you just want "out." Whatever the reason, there are a number of realities about professional property management companies of which you need to be aware.

The most important reality is this: You probably will never find a company that will do as good a job as you did. It is not that they don't want to do a good job or that they don't have the capability of doing the job. The fact is simply that you couldn't afford to pay them to work your properties as you would. We say this with the assumption that you have worked your way into management. You bought that first three- or four-unit building years ago and now have five properties totaling 65 units. You have done it all and can do it all, but now you just want to kick back for a while.

Remember that the management company is in business to make a profit. You will be paying a fee based on the scheduled rent of your property. This typically is 5 to 7 percent of your gross rents, though it might be higher in some areas. For this fee, the company has to pay its office staff to do your accounting, pay its field staff to oversee the property, and make a profit.

> 66 The best property manager I ever had was a married couple. He was handy and worked during the day. She was a stay-at-home mother who didn't mind looking after things at the building while her husband was away. 99
>
> —Neil C., investor

There are a couple of things you can do to get the biggest bang for your buck. First, don't pick a company because they have a fancy office or an attractive brochure stating how good they are. What you really want from management are three specific things:

1. Units rented at the market rates

2. As little vacancy as possible

3. Expenses controlled and on budget

Ask around before you pick a company. Your trusted real estate agent should be able to make some good suggestions. No doubt though, the absolute best source for finding a reliable management company will be to personally interview some of the management companies who manage buildings in the area

Watch Out!

Do not get owner referrals from the management companies themselves. They no doubt will pick the ones who will give them the most favorable review.

around your properties. Most management companies put signs on the properties they manage, so you should easily be able to find a few local companies that way. Additionally, try to get the names and numbers of some of the owners of properties managed by the companies you are considering, and then go talk to them. Your local title company may be able to help track these owners down. It will take some extra work to hunt down the owners using this method, but by seeking out other owners, you will get the most unbiased opinion of each company you are considering.

After you have narrowed the field down to a couple of choices, make an appointment and go talk to the person in charge of new business. Once you have listened to the sales pitch, you will want to focus in on the philosophy of management to which the company adheres. Ask some specific questions so that you know how much effort will be devoted to hands-on management. These questions should include

- What is their management fee?
- How do they set rental rates?
- Are there any extra charges for showing rentals or going to court on evictions?
- What kind of advertising do they do for vacancies?
- What is the typical cost of cleaning a vacant unit?
- How long does it usually take to make a vacant unit rent ready?
- What are their business hours?
- Who covers rental calls on the weekends?
- What types of reports will they give you?

- When are the reports mailed each month?
- What is their policy on slow or nonpaying tenants?
- What kind of training does their staff have?
- Do the owner and/or manager own property themselves?
- Does anyone check up on the repair work done by the contractors they use?
- What dollar amount of expense needs owner approval?
- Is the repair approval amount negotiable?
- Is there a problem if you regularly visit your property to check on their performance?

After you have interviewed the managers of these companies as well as the other owners that use them, a prime candidate should emerge. Make sure you feel comfortable with the person who runs the operation. You both should share a common philosophy of management. Note: The more time you personally spend with your property management team and the more positive feedback you give them for a job well done, the more personal attention they will give your property.

After you have picked a company and are getting ready to turn your building over to management, you should then go over the operation of your property the way it has been running for you. The historical data will give the new manager a target to work toward. During this transition, you should expect some of your expenses to increase because of the contractors the company uses, but you should discuss this with the person in charge and budget accordingly. Now is when you should be setting some profit goals so that the company knows you expect them to earn your business. Their years of experience should show up on your bottom line.

Managing the manager

We say that "managing the managers" is the key to keeping your empire running smoothly. It's pretty easy to turn your property over to management and then sit back and wait for the checks to roll in. Josh Billings, a nineteenth-century American humorist and real estate agent, said it best when he coined the phrase, "the squeaky wheel gets the grease." When it comes to property management, this couldn't be truer.

For the first three months, you should probably personally meet with the management team once a month in order to make sure the transition to professional management goes off without a hitch. After that, you should meet quarterly to discuss the performance of the properties and to review any current problems, potential problems, or changes in the foreseeable future. At least one meeting per year should include a trip out to the property with the head of the company to review the overall condition.

These meetings will be extra work for the management company and the staff, so keep this in mind: Don't waste their time. Have an agenda, review what you need to, and let them go back to work. Remember, management is a thankless job. Don't forget to let them know when they are doing a good job.

Upgrading the interiors

At some point in the life cycle of your property you will need to upgrade the interior of your units. Although the existing fixtures might still work properly, they probably look tired and worn. Maybe the toilet and the bathtub have each seen better days. What's more, you realize that another coat of paint would be about as effective as an adhesive bandage on a major head wound. If this is the position you find yourself in, yes, it's probably time for an interior upgrade.

Don't fret; rental properties always get in this condition quicker than owner-occupied, single-family homes do. This is because the people who live in those rental units don't have an ownership interest, and, unfortunately, most apartment owners are in such a hurry to fill their vacancies that they tend to do the minimum when fixing up units between tenants. When you begin to notice that you are unable to attract the high-end rents your competitors are getting, it is time to assess your building and determine whether an upgrade to the units is in order. It probably is. This is when you should do another "would I live there?" test on your property.

As an example, let's assume you currently are averaging $.80 per square foot on your apartments, and you have noticed that similar properties in better condition are regularly getting $.95 per square foot. Your four units average 800 square feet each and your building is in an area where the capitalization rates are 8.5 percent. By upgrading, you will be able to increase your rents to match those of your competition. Even though this will increase your annual expenses some, it still gives you a net increase of $.10 per square foot. The potential profit from an upgrade looks like this:

New rental rate	$.95 per square foot
Existing rate	– $.80 per square foot
Expense increase	– $.05
Potential increase	$.10 per square foot

Unit size	800 square feet
# of units	× 4
Total footage	3,200

Total footage	3,200
Increased rent	× $.10
Monthly increase	$320

Yearly increase	$3,840

Remember, with the capitalization method, we divide the net income by the capitalization rate to estimate value. If we apply this formula to our increased income, we get an estimate of the new value as follows:

$$\frac{\text{Increase rent } \$3,840}{\text{Capitalization rate .085}} = \$45,176$$

As you can see, $45,176 in value appreciation and $3,840 in annual cash flow are both sizable increases that might make an interior upgrade worth your efforts. Note: This kind of a rehab effort must start with diligent research on your part. You first must visit the properties commanding the higher rent per square foot and see what they have that you don't. This will give you the overall feel of these properties so that you can assess whether you, too, will be able to command similar rent.

Unlike a home remodel, it usually isn't practical to add rooms or bathrooms to a rental property. Instead, you should look at the finish of the apartments from the walls out. If it's necessary and financially feasible, you might consider removing everything in your units down to the drywall and begin your upgrade project from that point.

The following list covers items to rehab from the least expensive to the most expensive:

Interior Rehab Checklist

- Floor and window coverings
- Wall and ceiling finish
- Electrical outlets and switches
- Moldings and trim wood
- Closet and interior doors and hardware
- Front and rear doors and hardware
- Kitchen and bathroom plumbing fixtures
- Bathroom vanity or sink, medicine cabinet, and toilet
- Bathtub and/or shower
- Kitchen appliances

- Kitchen cabinets and layout
- Heating and/or air-conditioning system

Floors and window coverings

Floor and window coverings are ongoing maintenance items, but in the case of a rehab project, they need to be redone with an eye to the overall look you are trying to achieve. It's relatively painless to change drapes to mini-blinds or to put in new linoleum on the kitchen floor. Thankfully, these kinds of additions aren't too expensive and can make a huge difference.

Walls and ceiling finish

The walls and ceilings of your units are a good place to start a property makeover. You will find that the paint, trim, and moldings all suffer because of tenant turnovers followed by many quick repainting jobs over the years. This phase of a makeover usually includes some updating of the look of these finishes. Older moldings might need to be removed for a cleaner, simpler finish. The ceilings might have the old-style "cottage cheese," but a plain flat finish is now the preferred look.

This doesn't have to be too costly because a handyman-level contractor usually can do this type of work. It is preferable to remove all the trim molding even if only some of it will be replaced because the paint buildup really shows in these areas. You might need some special help with the ceilings because some of the older cottage cheese finishes have asbestos in them and need a special contractor for removal. After the preparation work is complete, your normal painting contractor can give you the new finish you desire.

 Moneysaver

It pays to do your homework before you start on a project of this magnitude. A major upgrade might increase your property's value and cash flow, but you might find through your research that an upgrade actually would not be worth the time, effort, and expense.

Bright Idea

Go ahead and change any worn-out or damaged outlets or switches once you repaint. This way, you won't have to return to the unit to fix a dead outlet when your tenant moves in and begins to complain.

In older buildings, years of painting oil-based paint over calcimine results in a permanently peeling ceiling. The only solution is to scrape down to the plaster or to drywall over the ceiling. Drywall is quicker and less painful.

Electrical outlets and switches

If you go to the trouble of refinishing the walls, it is advisable to put in new electrical outlets, switches, and face plates as well. Nothing looks worse on a newly painted wall than an electrical outlet that has an old, painted cover plate. You also should replace and update the light fixtures. Most major home improvement centers have great selections of lighting at very reasonable prices. Make sure you save the brand name and style information of your new fixtures for future reference.

New doors

The doors of apartments seem to suffer greater abuse than those in most homes. This is because numerous coats of paint and lock changes over the years naturally take their toll. Remember that the first thing a prospective tenant sees is the front door of your vacant unit. If the door looks clean, your new prospect will see right away that you are the kind of landlord that takes pride in his rentals. This might just lay the groundwork for him wanting to rent from you. Remember, these front doors also are an integral part of the overall appearance of the exterior of your property. It ruins the effect of the thousands of dollars you spent to paint and landscape the exterior if you have a conglomeration of new and old exterior doors with mismatched knobs and hardware. You also might add brass kick plates to keep down scuffmarks from shoes holding the doors open.

Bathroom upgrades

Bathroom upgrades can provide a significant improvement in the look of your unit. What's great is that they don't have to cost as much as you might think. The simplest upgrade is a new medicine cabinet and light fixture. If there is a shower in the bathtub, a new shower enclosure is nice, too. You also should install low-flow showerheads. They're cheap, easy to install, and will save you money on the water bill.

The next upgrades might be to replace the sink, vanity, and toilet. These items can cost a bit, so shop wisely. Because they are all necessary items, however, they usually are worth the expense.

Many older apartments still have their original toilets. Although they might work fine, they don't have the efficiency of modern, water-saving units. Most of your water and sewer costs come from the use of the toilets in your building. Therefore, the new low-flush toilets now available will provide a permanent savings once installed.

The final item in the bathroom, and potentially the most costly to upgrade, is the tub or shower. You should know that it is usually a major expense to remove an ugly, old, cast-iron or plastic tub unit and install a new one. For this reason, we generally do not recommend doing this kind of upgrade. Luckily, a coating process is available that can give your old tub the appearance of a new one at a substantially lower price. This process is not permanent, but it should last years and can be touched up as needed to keep the new look. Ask your local home improvement expert for guidance. Note that these coatings can also be used on the tile walls.

 Moneysaver

Many cities offer rebate programs that reduce the cost of new low-flush toilets for your units. This savings, combined with cheaper water bills, makes this upgrade well worth it.

A beautiful new kitchen

Upgrading a kitchen usually costs a bundle. A common problem with older kitchens is that they are located in separate rooms and have doors closing them off from the rest of the apartment. In some areas, a more open kitchen is desired. The idea is that a breakfast bar–type opening to the living area adds an open and homey feel. If this can be done without any major structural modifications by just opening up a wall, it probably is worth the effort, as your unit will be able to command a higher rent.

Kitchen cabinets, counters, sinks, and stoves

It usually is not cost-effective to put new cabinets in the kitchen. Assuming the kitchen has a workable layout, there are two options you should consider. The least expensive, but most labor intensive, option is to take all the cabinet doors off, take the drawers out, and do a very thorough job sanding them and the base cabinets. You then can get your painter to prime and paint the cabinets and drawers. This takes a lot of time and effort, but the finished product should look great.

The other option is to install new cabinet doors and drawer fronts and just refinish the base cabinets. This costs more, but you can achieve the most up-to-date style this way. You can get prices for the doors and drawer fronts at most large home-improvement centers and local cabinet shops. In either case, wait until the cabinets are finished to install the new hardware.

If you are updating the cabinets, it probably is a good time to repair or replace the counters, too. If the counters are made of Formica, they can be replaced or resurfaced with a process similar to the one used on bathtubs. Your bids will determine which process you decide on. If the counters are made of tile, it can be more costly to do an upgrade. One way to save is to have new tile put directly over the old tile. This can be done by using a special additive with mastic-type glue designed for setting tile on tile.

Moneysaver

When replacing faucets, it usually is best to also replace the supply lines and the angle stops. This will save you money in the long run.

Along with the new counters and cabinets, it might be time to install a new sink and faucet. If you are not tearing out the countertop, however, it might not be practical to replace the sink. Instead, consider using the same refinishing system recommended for the bathtub. As with the bathroom coating, you can probably also coat the tile at this point for a fresh look. You then can replace the faucet, and everything will look new again for a reasonable price. Chances are, if you need to freshen up the kitchen with this coating process, you will probably also have to do the bathroom as well. Try to negotiate a better price for doing multiple rooms at the same time.

The last items in the kitchen are the stove and vent fan. If you have the old freestanding-style stoves in your units, you might consider upgrading to the built-in or slide-in type. They will give your kitchen a great look and should give you years of trouble-free service. You can sell the existing stoves, and this might pay a good portion of the cost of the new ones. If you have vent hoods over the stoves, go ahead and change these to match the color of the new stoves.

Summary of your interior upgrade

For the most part, if you even did a fraction of all the work previously mentioned, you now have a "new" apartment. This will attract the best tenants who are willing to pay premium rents for a great place to live. Keep in mind, however, that your expensive interior upgrade will all have been for naught if you have yet to do any upgrades outside. Tenants who will pay premium rents for upgraded units will not even stop to see them if the exterior

Bright Idea

It is wise to do your exterior upgrade first and then upgrade the interiors one at a time as tenants move out.

of your building does not grab their attention from the street. Remember, curb appeal!

You should test the market one unit at a time to help determine the correct rent for your upgraded apartments. You might find that the market rent is actually higher for your units than your original rent survey indicated. If you get a lot of interest in the units and more than the usual number of interested applicants, your rent might be on the low side. If this happens, you can raise the rent some on the next upgraded unit to again test the interest level. It is not unusual for there to be a large pent-up demand for nicer apartments in markets that have been stagnant for several years. Unless there is a wave of new construction in the area, however, this demand is not usually seen.

Just the facts

- Your property's curb appeal must grab a potential tenant's attention from the street.

- Landscaping doesn't have to cost a bundle to achieve your desired effect.

- To limit your liability, make sure your tenants adhere to the rules of your common areas and parking facilities.

- To avoid manager complacency, structure financial incentives into his contract.

- Staying in touch with your professional property management team will help to ensure that they do a good job for you.

- Do some market research to make sure an interior upgrade is worth the expense.

Facing Your Fears

PART VII

So What's Stopping You?

The first thought that creeps into people's minds when they consider investing is, "The entire market is going to collapse the day I make my move." If this mirrors your thinking, know that you're in good company. In fact, that very idea has crossed the mind of every investor (including the authors) who has ever risked a nickel at anything.

It would be a terrible shame, however, if your fear kept you from doing what you know could change your life. The fact of the matter is there usually is as much risk from inaction as there is from action. With the uncertainty of the stock market, let alone the minimal help that Social Security and your company pension plan will bring, not acting will probably keep you stuck in the 9-to-5 rat race forever. For that reason, this last chapter is dedicated to addressing the most common fears about investing in real estate. Our goal is to help you get over the hump, if, in fact, there still is one to get over.

Fear of negative cash flow

As you know, negative cash flow exists when your income can't cover your expenses. That's a problem no one wants to have. Here are three good techniques used to combat negative cash flow with your investment properties:

1. Apply the right formula to determine how much you can afford to pay for a property and still stay positive.

2. Convert money normally used to purchase equity into money to offset any initial negative cash flow.

3. Manage a negative building into profitability.

Let's examine these techniques one at a time.

The break-even formula

As you learned in Chapter 3, "Elements of Return," cash flow is directly related to the percentage of your down payment in relation to the cost of the property. By utilizing a bit of advanced math, it is possible to predetermine the maximum that you can pay for a property in a given area and still break even. Don't worry; these calculations aren't that tough, provided that you take them one step at a time. We'll use the following abbreviations in these equations:

> 66 "If you always do what you've always done, you'll always get what you always got." 99
>
> —A wise man

G.M. = Average gross rent multiplier in your area

I = Current market interest rate

N.I.P = Net income percentage

D.P.P. = Down payment percentage

The first thing to determine is your net income. Your net income is determined by subtracting your gross expenses from your gross income, as follows:

Gross income – Gross expenses = Net income

Moneysaver

Think about any negative cash flow from your real estate investments as the equivalent of the money you invest in life insurance and retirement packages. It is a savings plan for the future.

Then, you need to figure out your net income percentage (N.I.P.). This is achieved by dividing your net income by your gross income, like this:

$$\frac{\text{Net income}}{\text{Gross income}} = \text{N.I.P}$$

Once you know your net income percentage (N.I.P.), plug that number into the following formula to find out your down payment percentage (D.P.P.):

$$\text{D.P.P.} = 1 - \left(\frac{\text{N.I.P.}}{\text{G.M.} \times \text{I}}\right)$$

As an example, let's say your net income percentage is 75 percent. Let's also suppose that the average gross rent multiplier (G.M.) in your area is 9 times gross, and the current market interest rate (I) is 10 percent. Plug these numbers in as follows:

$$1 - \left(\frac{.75}{9 \times .1}\right) = .17$$

As you can see, to avoid going negative, your down payment must be at least 17 percent of the purchase price. Therefore, to determine how much you can afford, apply this formula:

$$\frac{\text{Available down payment}}{\text{D.P.P.}} = \text{Maximum purchase price}$$

Let's say that given these parameters, you have $35,000 to invest and your goal is to avoid any negative cash flow; your maximum purchase price can be determined as follows:

$$\frac{\$35{,}000 \text{ available down payment}}{.17 \text{ D.P.P.}} = \$205{,}882 \text{ maximum purchase price}$$

As illustrated, with a down payment of $35,000, a building costing no more than about $205,000 should keep you in the black. Make sure you plug in your own variables so as to get results that match your own situation.

Again, this math is a bit complicated, but it can be mastered as long as you take it one step at a time. If you do, you can reasonably determine how much building you can afford and can thereby minimize having to dip into your pocket to pay expenses. We say "minimize" because increased vacancy, reduction in market rent, or unanticipated expenses in the future could affect you negatively. Of course, increased occupancy or rents and lower expenses will be to your advantage.

Use cash to offset the negative

A second technique is sometimes used to manage cash flow. In this example, we'll assume you have found a property that is priced higher than you can finance using the break-even formula in the preceding section. You believe that with better management you can increase your gross income and turn the negative cash flow situation around. In this example, let's assume that the owner of this property wants out. After a bit of negotiation, he has agreed to carry the loan and accept a 10 percent down payment of just $25,000, which is $10,000 less than the $35,000 you set aside for your purchase. This will allow you to purchase the property and keep a sizable reserve in your bank account. The facts are as follows:

 Moneysaver

For the most part, our tax laws—both state and federal—compensate us for negative cash flows. We are returned for every dollar lost a percent of that dollar equal to our combined state and federal top tax bracket levels.

Price	$250,000
Down payment	$25,000
Gross income	$25,000
Expenses	$6,000
Loan	$225,000
Loan payment at 10% interest only	$22,500 per year

Operating summary

Income	$25,000
Expenses	– $6,000
Loan payments	– $22,500
Net negative cash flow	– $3,500

As you can see, the negative cash flow is $3,500 per year. This comes to about $292 per month ($3,500 ÷ 12 = $291.66). Remember that your cash investment is $10,000 less than you originally had budgeted ($35,000 to invest less $25,000 down payment = $10,000). The idea is to use some of these cash reserves to offset the negative until you can turn the building around. You will need to do some careful property management to justify raising rents. Whether you need to re-landscape and paint the building, fix all the outstanding deferred mainte-nance, or even turn over your entire tenant base, your bottom line in this scenario depends on getting the building up to par so that you can charge market rent.

The kinds of buildings that have the possibility of increasing your income with careful management are ones that have absentee owners or buildings that have been in the same hands for many years. For these owners, their real estate is secondary to the rest of their lives. When the property they own performs adequately, they tend to ignore it as an investment. They don't raise rents or make any changes for fear they will need to get more involved in the day-to-day operations. In these instances, tenants with low rents hesitate to bother the owner, and owners keep the rents low so that they won't be bothered.

Watch Out!

This technique should be reserved for properties that show strong evidence that you can generate a positive cash flow within a year. Properties that are "management fixer-uppers" with rents well below market usually are the ones that would fit this bill.

Manage your property to riches

The most effective defense against negative cash flow is the ability to recognize a potentially good business opportunity, to negotiate its purchase under reasonable terms, and to manage it into profitability. This is the method most frequently overlooked by beginning investors, yet it is the method of choice for investors who have been around awhile.

The following are some characteristics of a property that will allow you to buy it for a good price and then turn any negative into a positive fairly quickly:

- Lower-than-market rents: You find a building where the price looks very good but the rents are low. Negotiate the price based upon the lower rents and then raise the rents to market rate. Once your rents are up any negative cash flow may very well disappear. What's more, now that you've raised your rents, the value of your building has gone up as well.

- Excessive operating expenses: Many owners, especially absentee owners, fail to control their operating expenses. By locating owners whose expenses appear too high, you might be able to negotiate a significant price reduction. Once you take over, follow the guidelines laid out in Chapter 14, "Managing the Expenses," to lower costs and increase your cash flow and the property's value.

- Debt service costlier than market: Many owners put their buildings on the market because the cost of their financing is too high. For whatever reason, they are unable or unwilling to refinance their debt, so selling seems to be the only alternative. With your down payment and good credit, you can rescue them. Your reward should be the purchase of a building at a substantial reduction in price. What was once a property that was in the red should soon be able to become a positive cash cow.

Fear that this isn't the "right time" to invest

So you don't think this is the right time to invest, huh? Maybe the economy is floundering? Perhaps it's an election year? What if interest rates are on the rise? What about terrorism? Actually, a close observation of the last 50 years would reveal that not one of those years passed without potential real estate investors feeling that it would be advantageous to wait for better times. This illustrates, however, a significant misconception about real estate investing. Remember, this isn't the stock market. It's not a game of chance where

> 66 The low rents on the last building we bought allowed us to get a good buy, but it also gave us negative cash flow in the beginning. We did some minor upgrades and then raised the rents a bit. We haven't been negative since. 99
>
> —Sydney and Mara S., investors

you have to speculate as to whether it's the right time to get in or out. In fact, as far as real estate goes, the only unprofitable investments in the last 50 years were the ones that never closed escrow.

The truth is that profiting from real estate investing has little to do with the economic climate at the time you buy. Of course, the economy surely should be examined with any investment you make, but you must understand that it is not the main factor in determining whether you will succeed in real estate. Remember, success, as a real estate investor, requires you to look at this investment over the long haul. Therefore, thinking that it is advantageous to wait to buy for one reason or another does nothing more than delay your success.

Let's blow up the belief that there is a mystical "better time" to buy out there. We will see how an average property you purchase might perform over an extended period of time using the following facts:

Purchase price: $100,000

Down payment: $10,000 (10%)

Annual income: $10,000

Annual expenses: $2,500 (25% of gross income)

Now let's examine value appreciation in a couple of ways:

1. If the property goes up in value a modest 3.5 percent in one year, it increases $3,500. That is a 35 percent return on your down payment. One question: Where are you going to find an investment vehicle that will pay you 35 percent on your money?

2. If your expenses increase 5 percent because of inflation and you raise your rents only 7 percent to help compensate, you would have an operating expense increase of $125 per year and an income increase of $700 per year. This would give you a $5,757 increase in net income per year. Again, where are you going to find an investment that will do that for you?

A universal truth when it comes to making life-changing decisions is that something invariably comes up to delay acting on them. Maybe it's your fluctuating stock market portfolio, the new brakes you need to put on your car, or just a hunch that the timing isn't right. Whatever it may be, by allowing this mystical "something" to dictate your major choices, you could get stuck in the rat race for good. The Beatles' great John Lennon understood this concept well when he wrote the lyric, "Life is what happens to you while you're busy making other plans." We say, get started investing now. If you're like most people, you work much too hard not to have a fruitful future waiting for you at the finish line.

To that end, we believe that the soundest way to circumvent the notion that tomorrow will be a better time to invest than today is to

1. Develop a small investment plan with attainable goals.

2. Absorb a reasonable amount of knowledge about real estate investing.

And, most important,

3. Get started by buying your first property.

Fear of losing your money

By now, you probably realize that real estate is the answer, but you've still got one nagging fear that won't go away—you're afraid of losing your money. This is because this investment will probably represent the biggest financial move of your life. Tapping into your savings and investing the fruits of years of hard work is nothing if not unnerving, even under the best of circumstances. This fear usually comes from two things:

1. A lack of a plan of attack

2. A lack of knowledge about the product in which you are investing

We believe that having a well-thought-out business plan will give you the direction you need to run your real estate business

 Moneysaver

Never volunteer to put more money down than the seller or the bank requires. Instead, put down the minimum amount of money necessary, and then let the bank finance the rest of the property for you. The great leverage you will have created will allow you to earn a much higher percentage return on your investment.

effectively (see Chapter 9, "Building an Investment Plan"). As for your education, there are many sources from which to learn about real estate investing including

- Practical property-management seminars offered by your local apartment owners association (see Appendix B, "National Apartment Owners Association Locales—Listed by State").

- Lots of great books on the subject (see Appendix C, "Recommended Reading List").

- Community college courses taught by teachers with real-world experience.

- Weekend and evening seminars given by authors and lecturers. Along with the chance to purchase their books and tapes, these individuals usually have plenty of good information and ideas to share.

You might ask, "How can I be sure I won't lose all my money?" Perhaps an accurate, yet flippant answer would be to make sure you don't invest in the stock market. As for real estate, the best way to protect your investment is to make sure you buy your property at fair market value. Remember that *fair market value* is defined as "the price a reasonable buyer would pay a reasonable seller for a property that has been on the market for a reasonable period of time." Besides doing your own analysis of fair market value on a prospective purchase, you should also insist on obtaining an expert appraisal from a real estate professional. Two common sources for appraisals are

1. **Investment real estate agents:** Appraisals from agents who specialize in investment property generally are free and are a good way to learn about value in general.

2. **Professional property appraisers:** These appraisals cost a bit of money, but they are worth the expense for the piece of mind they will bring.

The good news is that when it comes time to actually buy a property, any conventional lender will require a professional appraisal be done before they lend you even one thin dime. Thankfully, if the building doesn't appraise for the agreed-upon purchase price, you usually will be able to walk away completely unscathed. As the late Los Angeles Lakers announcer, Chick Hearn, used to say, "No harm, no foul."

The bottom line is that most investments have some risk. When you begin to think about venturing into a new world of investing, having some concerns is normal. The key is to do enough study and research that you feel comfortable with the investments before you buy. By having an appraisal done, you are tapping into the mind of an expert. This will further increase your comfort level for a particular property.

Fear of tenant and management hassles

Many people balk at investing in rental property because they are afraid of the headaches that come with property management. In general, the smaller buildings (two to four units) that we have touted here tend to have fewer management hassles than larger ones. At the most, you'll have just a few small buildings to worry about. In time, you'll be able to manage them with your eyes closed.

But, maybe you're not sold yet. If so, the clear solution is to hire professional property management to do the job. There are plenty of reputable companies out there and, for a small fee, they will manage your building for you. If this is your solution, make sure you do your due diligence when hiring them. Your goal should be to hire a management company who is committed to keeping your expenses down and your units rented for at least market rate. Anything less should be unacceptable.

Remember, however, by hiring someone other than yourself, you will be giving away some of your profits for a job you could easily do. Maybe, more importantly, by hiring management you are giving the reigns of control of your investment over to a third party. As mentioned, they'll do a fine job (just as they will with the 1,000 other units they manage), but it will pale in comparison to what you could do if you were looking after your own building.

If, however, you discover that it's against your fiscal religion to pay for property management, and managing tenants is the one hurdle that is keeping you from investing in real estate, you might want to consider a completely different route—that is,

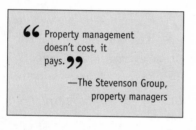

66 Property management doesn't cost, it pays. **99**

—The Stevenson Group, property managers

investing in commercial and industrial buildings. What's great is that these properties frequently rent on a triple-net basis. Remember that a triple-net lease means the tenants are responsible for all operating expenses and the upkeep of the property. During the term of the lease, the tenant would run the building as if it were his own. Additionally, your interaction with the tenants would be significantly reduced as compared to an investment in residential real estate.

Fear of bad and low-income areas

One of the truly great mistakes made, especially by beginning investors, is thinking in terms of "pride of ownership" rather than "profit of ownership." In truth, just as many substantial fortunes have been made in low-income areas as in high-end areas and usually for a much smaller initial investment.

When talking to beginning investors about the kind and location of property they would like to buy, the answer they give is almost always the "best property" in the "best location" with the "best tenants." It rarely is articulated in this concise a fashion, but boiled down, that's what they want. Furthermore:

- By best property, they mean a property they would be willing to live in or better.

- By best location, they mean something comparable to their own neighborhood or better.

- By best tenants, they mean themselves or better.

In theory, these goals are well and good. Unfortunately, you probably couldn't afford to repurchase your own home let alone buy units in your neighborhood today. You might be surprised to learn that the best property in the best location only rarely makes the best investment. For starters:

- You will pay a premium for such a property.

- The seller will want the best terms for himself or herself.

- The economics of operation will be considerably less attractive.

On the other hand, lesser buildings located in a less desirable location often will have just the reverse effect:

- Prices will be favorable.

- Terms will be negotiable.

- The operating costs of the building will be within reason.

- Lower down-payment options often are available (better leverage).

- Sellers sometimes will carry some of the financing at good terms.

- It is usually the area that is least affected by recession.

Unfortunately, when most investors think of property in less desirable neighborhoods, the word "slum" creeps into their thoughts. They think it's going to be a hassle managing "those kinds of tenants." Actually, nothing could be further from the

 Bright Idea

If it's positive cash flow you're looking for, low-income areas will provide you with plenty of it. Though these areas require considerably more hands-on management, you will always get more building for your buck than you can in upscale neighborhoods.

Bright Idea

One sensible approach is to make your fortune in less prestigious properties, and then trade your equities into more desirable properties for your retirement years. You'll probably own the Taj Mahal one day, just not yet.

truth. They might not be as financially fortunate as others, but they work hard to raise a family and would like the nicer things in life if they could afford them. The truth is that tenants in these areas usually really appreciate all the little things you might do to make their home nicer. Conversely, the tenants in the best areas expect it and then some.

Though we're not advocating that you buy in the worst neighborhood in town, we are suggesting that you find an average area in between the best and the worst. This is where the money is made. Working-class areas seem to be the least affected during recessionary periods. One reason is that these tenants seem to be the last to lose their jobs, and if they do, government safety nets such as welfare and Section 8 programs are available to help with housing.

Fear of rocking the boat

Most people never think much about their retirement until it is staring them in the face. This is because, during their most productive years, their lives are very comfortable. So comfortable, in fact, that there doesn't appear to be any need to worry about retirement. Any money that would be spent on investments would take away from enjoying the current pleasures in life. As they say, "Why rock the boat?"

The problem is that, as we grow older, our financial burdens often get heavier. For one thing, we are less able to perform for ourselves those things necessary for our daily existence, and we need to begin to purchase such services. More and more people are taking on the responsibility of caring for aging parents. The costs of this kind of care can be staggering. And finally, it is not unheard of for parents to have the additional burden of financially helping their children as the children begin to build lives and careers of their own.

Before you convince yourself that you are financially comfortable now, you'd better be sure your net worth today plus all projected retirement income will meet your retirement needs. The earlier in your career you face this issue, the better your chances are for an enjoyable retirement. To do this, you need to find out what you need to preserve your current lifestyle.

> ❝I wasn't sure what I'd need to fund the kind of retirement I wanted. I was lucky. A friend recommended a financial planner who was able to help. He charged me for his time rather than a commission on what he could sell me.❞
>
> —Bill B., computer specialist

We'll refer to this level of income as the minimum-security level. What we're talking about here is a level of income for you and your family that is independent of your efforts. It will be a combination of Social Security, any retirement plans, and other investments you may have. Be aware that experts all agree that pre-retirees will have to generate 100 percent of their pre-retirement income in retirement to maintain their current lifestyle.

Several factors should be considered when defining your minimum security level. Two of the most important are

1. Present and future material needs for you and your family

2. Present and projected economic conditions such as inflation, recession, the cost of capital, and the potential effects of these on your retirement

Once you have a good idea of your minimum security level, you need to determine whether you'll have enough assets at retirement to sustain it. If not, you should begin investing now in a plan that will guarantee this level of security as soon as possible. Investing until that level is reached is the key to a secure retirement.

As you analyze your finances, remember that we are talking about a level of income that just maintains your current lifestyle.

> **66** The hardest part of climbing the ladder to success is getting through the crowd at the bottom. **99**
> —Anonymous

This means you can pay your bills, feed the family, and take one or two vacations a year, but that's about it. When you were working, you spent 5 days a week and 49 or 50 weeks a year at your job. Now you won't have to go to work, but you won't have any money to do anything else either. That's why it's called the "minimum" security level.

If you want to truly enjoy all that free time, you'd better decide how you want to spend your retirement years and what it's going to cost. Then you'd better take a hard look at what you're going to have to do to amass enough assets to fund this retirement. If you do this early enough in your life and get the boat rocking, you might truly be able to enjoy your retirement.

Fearing fear itself

The hardest part of anything new is just getting started. That's because human beings are great at making excuses. We've heard every excuse there is for why someone shouldn't invest, whether it's the shaky economy, credit card debt, or the new baby that's due in June. Whatever the reason, many people who could be financially set today are instead cheating themselves out of what could be a better life.

With all due respect to David Letterman's *The Late Show,* here are the top 10 excuses we have heard for not investing in real estate:

10. They are waiting for a better time to invest.

 9. They are waiting for interest rates to drop.

8. They have to pay off their credit card debts first.

7. They believe managing the property will be too hard.

6. They insist buying a house first is more important.

5. They had a brother-in-law who lost a bundle this way.

4. They think the economy isn't right.

3. They think any negative cash flow will swallow them whole.

2. They are waiting for a "good deal" to land in their lap.

And the number one reason people wait is

1. They don't truly recognize the urgency in creating a fruitful future for themselves now.

In reality, the most valid reason anyone could have for not moving forward is that they just don't understand what this game is all about. Fair enough. If that's what's stopping you, we applaud you for putting the brakes on. Experience has shown that, if you proceed without adequate knowledge, the results could be disastrous.

If, at this point, you find yourself still struggling, here is what we suggest:

1. Reread this book (but slower this time).

2. Read lots of other books on this subject.

3. Find someone who understands the value in real estate investing and get them to explain it to you.

Do what you have to do to get this knowledge, but get it one way or another. Someone is collecting rent on all those small apartment buildings in your town. It could be you.

 Moneysaver

Ask your investment real estate agent to give you data on how property has appreciated in your area during the last 20 years. Compare this information to that of other investments and the return they provided. See for yourself whether real estate investing would be in your best interest.

The plan of attack

Merriam-Webster's dictionary defines an entrepreneur as "a person who organizes and manages a business undertaking, assuming the risk for the sake of profit."

We'd venture to say that there hasn't been a successful entrepreneur yet who hasn't stumbled a bit along the way. The key is that they've dusted themselves off, stepped out of their comfort zone, and kept working at something they have come to believe in. That is the real ticket to success. You might make some mistakes along the way, but real estate is a forgiving investment. By applying what you've learned here, any mistakes you might make should be easily overcome.

Let's review the game plan we've laid out together:

1. **Learn:** Your best guarantee of success is to never quit educating yourself about this business. There are enough books, classes, and seminars on the subject to keep you in school until the day you decide to turn your business over to the next generation. Some will teach you a lot and some only a little, but all education stimulates you to keep thinking deeper about your business.

2. **Research:** Along with learning about real estate in general, you need to learn about your specific real estate market and the way it performs in your area. Your goals must be to become an expert on what property has done in the past and what it is doing today. By doing diligent research, you will ensure that you are choosing the best properties to reach your goals.

3. **Plan:** Planning is the key to being successful in any business. Real estate is no exception. When you have a plan for your future, you create the road map toward financial security. Investing without that plan is like taking a trip to Twig without a map. The probability of success in either case is remote. Without a plan, you're never quite sure which properties are right for you. Without a map, you wouldn't even know where Twig was (pssst... Minnesota).

4. **Invest:** Now it's time to pick that first property and make a purchase. You have educated yourself on what and where to buy, and you have identified the kind of property you need to satisfy your investment plan goals. You will next use due diligence to make sure the property you have found meets all your criteria.

5. **Manage:** Once you have acquired your property, you take over as the manager. Your long-term plans will be put aside, and you will now be involved in the day-to-day operational goals for your business. You will work to increase your income, to keep the expenses under control, and to meet profit expectations. In time, you will be able to move on to bigger and better buildings.

Adieu, adieu

In this, the second edition of *The Unofficial Guide to Real Estate Investing,* we have attempted to give you as much of the inside scoop on real estate investing as possible. We believe that, if you apply the principles we've laid out here with a concerted effort to keep educating yourself, great success will follow. Our hope is that we have motivated you to take control of your destiny. It's time for you to take some risks, and it's time for you to reap the rewards.

This is the place where we would normally wish you good luck, but at this point we know you don't need it. Instead, we wish you good fortune.

Just the facts

- Effective management is the savvy investor's solution to negative cash flow. The idea is to increase your income, lower your expenses, and improve your financing costs.
- Lack of adequate knowledge is the real reason people hesitate to invest in anything.
- Real estate can produce a profit in both good and bad times.

- If the day-to-day hassles of property ownership are keeping you from investing, turn your properties over to a professional property management company.

- Less affluent economic areas can offer greater potential for profit.

- Without proper planning, a comfortable retirement might be out of the question.

Glossary

acceleration clause   A clause in a loan that requires the loan to be paid off in the event of an occurrence, such as the unauthorized transfer of title.

accommodator   A neutral third party that assists in completing a delayed exchange. The accommodator usually is a corporate entity.

active investor   An IRS classification for a real estate investor who materially participates in running a property.

adjustable-rate mortgage (ARM)   A loan in which the future interest rate might change, with that change determined by an index of rates. The frequency and amount of change are limited by the mortgage contract.

adjusted cost basis   For the purpose of computing capital gains or losses, this refers to the original purchase price, plus closing costs paid at the time of purchase, plus the cost value of improvements done while the property was held, less all depreciation claimed.

adjusted gross income   The income from a piece of property after any adjustments are made for other income or rental losses.

adjusted sale price   The price of a piece of property after deducting the costs of sale.

agent   One who represents another, called the principal, in dealing with third persons.

all-inclusive loan   This is a loan that incorporates several loans. The borrower makes one payment on the all-inclusive loan, and the person receiving that payment pays on the underlying financing.

amortization   The repayment terms of a loan—including the required principal and interest—based on the interest rate and the period of time allowed to pay down, or amortize, the loan to zero.

annual depreciation allowance   The deduction you can take on your income tax against earnings to recapture the cost of the structures on your property.

annual expenses   All the costs you must pay to operate your property.

annual percentage rate (APR)   A term used in the Truth in Lending Act. It represents the total cost of credit—including interest, discount points, origination fees, and loan broker commission—as a percentage of the amount financed.

appraisal   The process of estimating the current market value of a property.

appreciation   Increase in value due to any cause.

"as is"   When you buy a property "as is," the seller is not making any warranties or guarantees about its condition.

assumption   A loan feature providing for the borrower to allow a future buyer to take over payments on the loan as well as responsibility for repayment.

average return on equity (AROE)   Each year that you own a property, you can calculate the return on the equity for that year. If you add these up for several years and divide by the number of years, you get the average.

balloon mortgage   A mortgage that has one large payment due at the end of the loan.

balloon payment   The outstanding balance due at the maturity of a mortgage or loan.

bank repossessions   Properties that have been taken by the lender because of the owner's failure to meet the terms and conditions of the loan.

basis   The cost of the building on your property, plus improvements and fixtures, that can be depreciated but not claimed as deductions. This is calculated as original cost plus capital improvements less depreciation.

Board of Realtors   An association of Realtors in a given town or district.

boot   An IRS term for taxable proceeds from a sale other than cash.

building cost tables   Tables that show the current cost to build structures in various parts of the United States.

buyer's agent   The agent who locates the buyer and brings an offer to the seller.

cap   A limit on the amount of increase a lender can impose under the terms of an adjustable-rate mortgage. The annual cap specifies the maximum annual increase, and the lifetime cap specifies the overall increase the lender is allowed to pass on to the borrower.

capital expense   The outlay to purchase any asset with a useful life of more than one year. (The tax treatment for such an expenditure allows the asset to be "capitalized," which means that its cost is deducted over its useful life according to the applicable depreciation method rather than an expense in the current period.)

capital gains   The profit you make on an investment.

capitalization of income   A valuation method achieved by dividing the net income of a property by the capitalization rate of that kind of property.

capitalization rate   The percentage return you get by dividing the net income from a property by the price of a property.

cash flow   The amount of money received from rental income each month less the amount paid out in mortgage payments, the purchase of capital assets, and the payment of any operating expenses. Cash flow is not the same as profit because it includes nondeductible payments.

cash-on-cash return   The cash profit from an investment divided by the cash invested to buy the investment.

chain of title   A history of all titles to a piece of real estate, beginning with the original transfer from government to private ownership and ending with the latest document transferring title.

clear title   A title held without disputes concerning ownership or liens against the property. All liens are agreed to, identified, and not in dispute.

closing   Takes place when the buyer takes possession of the property and the seller gets the proceeds from the sale.

co-insurance   A clause in an insurance policy that says the property owner will assume some of the liability for any loss.

collected rent   The amount of rental income actually collected.

commercial loans   Any loan not classified as a residential loan, usually on five units or more.

commercial property   Nonresidential property operated for business use.

commission   An agent's compensation or fee for negotiating a real estate or loan transaction, usually a percentage of the transaction amount.

common area   Space not used and occupied exclusively by tenants such as lobbies, corridors, and stairways. In a condominium, the property in which a unit owner has an undivided interest.

comparables (comps) Properties that are similar to the property being considered or appraised.

comparative analysis A method of appraisal in which selling prices of similar properties are used as the basis for arriving at the value estimate. This also is known as the market data approach.

compound interest Interest paid on the original principal and also on the accrued interest.

compound interest algorithm A mathematical formula used to calculate the percentage of return when the profits from an investment are reinvested over a given period of time.

condominium A form of property ownership that combines absolute ownership of an apartment-like unit and joint ownership of areas used in common with others.

condominium association A condominium's governing body to which every unit owner automatically belongs.

constructive receipt An IRS term that means the IRS will tax you as though you had received monies even though you might not have been in physical possession of them during that tax period.

consumer price index A figure constructed monthly by the U.S. Bureau of Labor Statistics that weighs products by their importance and compares prices to those of a selected base year, expressing current prices as a percentage of prices in that base year.

contingencies Terms in a contract that qualify the agreement by stating that, for the deal to go forward, one side or the other agrees to meet certain conditions. Typical contingencies include completion of inspections and qualifying for financing.

contract for deed A method of financing a property. It is similar to an all-inclusive trust deed or a mortgage.

conventional loan A loan not underwritten by a government agency.

cost basis Your basis for calculating the capital gain on a property you own.

damages Financial compensation awarded to a person who was injured by another.

debt coverage The comparison between the net income of a property and the loan payments on the property.

debt service The total of the monthly payments on a property.

deduction An expense of property ownership that can be written off against income for tax purposes.

deferred maintenance Ordinary maintenance that is not performed and that negatively affects a property's use and value.

delayed exchange An IRS-approved technique for completing an exchange of equity to postpone taxes. Also called a "Starker" exchange.

demand appreciation Appreciation in value related to an increase in the desire to possess the property.

Department of Veterans Affairs The federal government agency that administers GI or VA loans, previously known as the Veterans Administration.

depreciable improvements The value of the structures on a property that the IRS allows you to depreciate.

depreciated value The value that remains after deducting the depreciation from the cost base for a property.

depreciation As an appraisal term, this means loss of value due to any cause.

depreciation allowance The dollar amount the IRS allows you to deduct each year from the earnings from a property.

down-leg property The lower priced property in a tax-deferred exchange.

dual agency A situation in which one agent represents both sides in a transaction.

due diligence The effort made to study and research a property and all the components of a purchase before you make the final decision to purchase.

earned increment of value That part of the increase in a property's value attributed to the efforts of the owner.

easements A right to use the land of another for a specific purpose.

encumbrance Anything that burdens or limits the title to a property such as a lien, easement, or restriction of any kind.

energy-saving blanket An insulating pad placed around an appliance such as a water heater.

equity The portion of real estate you own. In the case of a property bought for $200,000 with a $133,000 mortgage owing, the equity is the difference, or $67,000.

equity growth from appreciation The increase in a property's value because of the effects of inflation.

equity growth from loan reduction The increase in the owner's equity in a property from the payoff of the financing.

escrow The process of completing contractually required steps (such as obtaining financing, completing inspections, and paying and transferring funds) and of checking and clearing the title to the property to ensure that all liens have been identified and are satisfied before closing.

estoppel certifications Agreements usually signed by the tenants of a property outlining the terms of their tenancy.

fair market value The price a reasonable buyer will pay a reasonable seller for a property that has been on the market for a reasonable period of time.

Federal Housing Administration (FHA)   An agency created by the National Housing Act of 1934 to provide a home-financing system through federal mortgage insurance.

fiduciary   A relationship founded in trust and legally requiring loyalty, full disclosure, full accounting, and the application of skill, care, and diligence.

fixed expenses   The regular recurring costs required in holding a property, such as taxes and insurance.

fixed-rate loan   A loan in which the interest rate will not change during the contract period as a matter of contract.

fixer-upper   A property requiring repairs, either structural or cosmetic, to gain its full potential market value.

foreclosure   A court action initiated by the mortgagee for the purpose of having the court order the debtor's real estate sold to pay the mortgage.

fully amortized   Refers to a loan that is completely paid off when all the payments are made.

GI loan   A guaranteed loan available to veterans under a federal government program administered by the Department of Veterans Affairs. It also is called a VA loan.

good-faith deposit   A deposit presented by the proposed buyer at the time an offer is made. If the buyer's offer is accepted and the contract is later breached, the good faith deposit may be forfeited.

gross lease   An agreement in which the tenant pays an agreed-upon rent and the owner pays all the expenses associated with operating the property.

gross rent multiplier   A factor used for appraising income-producing property. The multiplier times the gross income gives an approximate property value.

guaranteed replacement clause   A clause in an insurance policy whereby the policy will pay to replace a damaged property regardless of changes in valuation or the cost of the replacement.

hard money loans Loans made by nonconventional lenders. They usually have high interest and high fees.

highest and best use The use of a property for the most profitable, efficient, and appropriate purpose, given the zoning and other restrictions placed on the land.

impound account A trust account in which funds are held, usually by a lender, for the payment of property taxes and insurance premiums required to protect the lender's security. These amounts usually are collected with the note payment.

improvements Any structures or additions to a piece of raw land.

index One of the components used to calculate the interest rate on an adjustable-rate loan.

in-fill project A construction project in an area where most of the land already is developed with structures.

inflation An economic condition occurring when the money supply increases in relation to goods. It is associated with rising wages and costs and decreasing purchasing power.

inflationary appreciation This refers to the value of a product increasing due to inflation taking place in the economy.

installment note The name of the note carried by the seller of a property that gives the seller special tax benefits.

installment sale The sale of a property in which the seller carries an installment note.

interest-only loan A loan for which no amortization is required and the entire principal balance is due at maturity.

invest To commit money or capital in a business to earn a financial return. The outlay of money for income or profit.

land sales contract Another name for a conditional sales contract. The buyer takes possession. The seller retains the title until all conditions are met.

landlord The owner of real estate who rents property to another.

leverage The use of borrowed money to purchase an investment that realizes enough income to cover the expense of the financing with the excess accruing to the purchaser.

liability The penalty for failure to act in a manner as prescribed by law.

lien An encumbrance on a property for the payment of a debt or obligation.

linear regression analysis A mathematical formula for calculating the best-fitting line through a series of points on a graph or chart.

liquidated damages A definite sum of money to be paid under a contract in the event of a breach of the contract.

listing A contract authorizing a broker to sell, buy, or lease real property on behalf of another.

management fixer-upper A property with management problems that need to be corrected.

margin The number added to the index of a loan to get the final interest rate of the loan.

market analysis The process of placing a property in a specific market and then evaluating it by those market standards.

master-metered properties Properties that only have one meter for the utilities.

Modified Accelerated Cost Recovery System (MACRS) The IRS system for determining the depreciation schedule for capital items.

mortgage A contract that makes a specific property the security for payment of a debt.

mortgage over basis When the amount of the loan on a property exceeds the cost basis of the property.

mortgage relief   When a taxpayer sells a property for which the mortgage (loan) balance exceeds the cost base.

Multiple Listing Service   An association of real estate agents and appraisers that pools listings, shares commissions on a specified basis, and provides data for agents and appraisers in preparing market evaluations and appraisals of real property.

"neg-am" loans   Loans in which you have the option to pay a lower payment than is needed to pay all the interest due.

negative amortization   This takes place when the payments on an adjustable loan are not sufficient to pay all the interest due. In this case, the loan increases by the amount of the unpaid interest.

negative cash flow   The condition in which payments are greater than receipts.

"no-neg" loans   Loans in which the payment will always pay all the interest due on the loan.

nonrecourse loan   Loans, usually long-term mortgages, for which no partner, limited or general, assumes personal liability. In most cases, the debt is secured by the property itself.

offer   The proposed terms of a contract in real estate. An offer is put forward and must be accepted by the other side before a contract can exist.

operating expenses   Periodic expenditures necessary to maintain a property and to continue the production of effective gross income.

opinion of value letter   A letter that expresses an opinion of value but that is not a complete appraisal.

package policy   An insurance policy that covers more than one type of loss.

passive investor   An IRS term that refers to someone who is limited in the deductions that can be claimed against earnings.

point   One percent of the loan amount; an additional charge added on by a lender as a fee assessed for getting the loan. Points also are called loan fees.

positive cash flow   A situation in which cash receipts are greater than cash payments.

preliminary title report   A report by a title company that gives all the basic title information, usually given at the opening of an escrow.

prepayment penalty   A clause in a note that provides for a monetary penalty in the event of an early payoff of the note.

private mortgage insurance (PMI)   Insurance to protect lenders from loss on a loan. This usually is required when the loan-to-value ratio is over 80 percent.

property management   A service profession in which someone other than the owner supervises a property's operation according to the owner's objectives.

raw land   A parcel of land or acreage not zoned for any specific purpose or a parcel of land that is zoned but that lacks basic services and, thus, is not yet buildable.

Realtor   A trademark name of the National Association of Realtors (NAR). Members using this title agree to conduct themselves according to a Realtors' Code of Ethics, and they are subject to the rules of the association. Some jurisdictions make a distinction between Realtors (who must be licensed as real estate brokers) and Realtor-Associates (who hold sales licenses). Others designate all their members as Realtors.

recordation   A system by which documents concerning title and other legal matters are collected in one convenient, public place, commonly the county recorder's office. Documents properly recorded constitute constructive notice of the contents of the documents.

recovery period   Under depreciation rules, the number of years over which depreciation is claimed.

rent   Money paid (or sometimes services rendered) for use and occupation of a property.

rent control   Laws enacted on a city-by-city basis that dictate the amount of rent landlords can charge tenants.

rent survey   A survey done to find out what other owners are charging for rent in a given area.

rental agreement   An agreement between a landlord and a tenant that sets forth the terms of a tenancy.

reproduction cost   The cost to rebuild a property today.

resident manager   An agent of the owner of a building who is employed on a salary to manage the property in which the manager resides.

residential loans   A loan on a residence or residential units up to and including four units.

RESPA   The Real Estate Settlement Procedures Act, a federal law that ensures that buyers and sellers in certain federally related residential real estate deals receive full disclosure of all settlement costs so that they can shop around for settlement services.

return on equity (ROE)   A percentage of return calculated by dividing annual net income by equity.

return on investment (ROI)   Interest or profit from an investment.

Schedule C   The schedule used to report income and expenses from an investment property for tax purposes.

scheduled rent   The current rent scheduled for all the units in a building.

seasoned financing   Any loan that is more than one year old.

second position   A loan recorded after another loan.

Section 8   The federal government's principal medium for housing assistance. It was authorized by the Housing and Community Development Act of 1974, which provides for new construction and rehabilitation.

seller's agent   The agent who enters into a listing contract with a seller, agreeing to find a buyer and to represent that seller's interest in negotiating a contract.

short sale   When someone sells a property for less than what is owed on the property.

slumlord   A slang term used to describe the owner of a building in which overcrowding and deterioration are evident.

specific performance   A doctrine of contract law by which a party can be compelled by the court to perform as agreed.

speculating   To enter into a transaction or venture in which the profits are conjectural or subject to chance; to buy or sell with the hope of profiting through fluctuations in price.

Starker exchange   A type of tax-deferred exchange that got its name from the court case with the same name. Also called a delayed exchange.

straight note   A note with only one payment at which time the amount of the loan and the interest are paid.

tax benefits   The tax savings from property ownership.

tax shelter   An investment with paper losses that can be used to lower one's otherwise taxable income. In other words, the tax loss from the tax-shelter investment is a write-off against regular salary or other income, therefore "sheltering" that income.

tax-deferred exchange (1031 tax-deferred exchange)   A method of deferring capital gains by exchanging real property for other like-kind property.

tenant   A person who pays rent to occupy or gain possession of real estate.

three-party exchange   A tax-deferred exchange that involves three different parties.

title company   A company that specializes in establishing the title to real property including identification of all existing liens on the property. The title company issues a title insurance policy ensuring that all liens have been disclosed at the time of closing.

title insurance policy   A special form of insurance issued by a title company to insure the buyer against any undiscovered liens on the property. The coverage is paid by a single premium during escrow, and it remains in force as long as the buyer owns the property.

title opinion   An analysis of the chain of title of a property in a state where the property owner keeps all the original deeds.

title report   A report that discloses all matters of public record that affect a piece of property.

transfer disclosure statement   A form filled out by the seller of a property to disclose any knowledge the seller has about the property.

triple-net lease   A type of lease in which the tenant not only pays rent but also might pay for property taxes, insurance, and property maintenance.

turnover   When one tenant moves out of a property and another moves in. This usually means no loss of rent.

unearned increment of value   An increase in the value of property not brought about by the owner, due primarily to the operation of social forces, such as an increase in population.

up-leg property   The higher priced property in a tax-deferred exchange.

U.S. Department of Housing and Urban Development (HUD)   A government agency established in 1965 to provide federal assistance in planning, developing, and managing public housing.

useful life   For tax purposes, this is the period of time over which you must depreciate a property. As a general concept, this is the period of time that a property is expected to be functional.

utility   A public service such as gas, water, or electricity.

vacancy rate   The average percentage of units vacant in a given market area.

value   The worth or usefulness of a good or service expressed in terms of a specific sum of money.

value appreciation   An increase in the value of a property due to any cause.

variable expenses   Expenses on a property that tend to be different each month or pay period.

Veterans Administration (VA)   *See* Department of Veterans Affairs.

zoning   Any restriction on the use of real property within a given area.

National Apartment Association Locales— Listed by State

Alabama

Alabama Apartment Association
2806 Artie Street, Suite 3
Huntsville, AL 35805
Phone: (800) 318-8785
Fax: (256) 539-6311

Apartment Association of the Tennessee Valley, Inc.
2608 Artie Street
Huntsville, AL 35805
Phone: (256) 539-2998
Fax: (256) 539-6311

Birmingham Apartment Association
1553 Deer Valley Drive
Birmingham, AL 35226
Phone: (205) 989-5785
Fax: (205) 426-7919
Web site: www.birminghamapartmentassociation.com

Mobile Bay Area Apartment Association
255 St. Francis Street
Mobile, AL 36602

Phone: (334) 626-7142
Fax: (334) 666-4220

Montgomery Apartment Association
P.O. Box 11493
Mobile, AL 36111
Phone: (334) 213-7307
Fax: (334) 260-0665

Alaska

National Apartment Association
201 North Union Street, Suite 200
Alexandria, VA 22314
Phone: (703) 518-6141

Arizona

National Apartment Association
201 North Union Street, Suite 200
Alexandria, VA 22314
Phone: (703) 518-6141

Arkansas

Arkansas Apartment Association
P.O. Box 250273
Little Rock, AR 72225
Phone: (501) 664-8300
Fax: (501) 664-0927
Web site: www.arapartments.com

Arkansas Multi-Family Housing Association
P.O. Box 250313
Little Rock, AR 72225
Phone: (501) 312-3055
Fax: (501) 604-2678
Web site: www.arapartments.com

Northwest Arkansas Apartment Association
1916 South 9th Street, #143
Rogers, AR 72758-6370
Phone: (479) 621-8236
Fax: (479) 621-8239
Web site: www.nwaaa.biz

California

National Apartment Association
201 North Union Street, Suite 200
Alexandria, VA 22314
Phone: (703) 518-6141

Colorado

Apartment Association of Colorado Springs
888 Garden of the Gods Road, Suite 103
Colorado Springs, CO 80907
Phone: (719) 264-9195
Fax: (719) 264-9198
Web site: www.aacshq.org

Apartment Association of Metro Denver
650 South Cherry Street, #635
Denver, CO 80246
Phone: (303) 329-3300
Fax: (303) 329-0403
Web site: www.aamdhq.org

Boulder County Apartment Association
P.O. Box 17606
Boulder, CO 80308
Phone: (303) 449-9048
Fax: (303) 449-7028

CAA-Fort Collins Chapter
P.O. Box 1075
Fort Collins, CO 80522
Phone: (970) 223-0545
Fax: (970) 223-4541
Web site: www.fortcollins-rentals.net

Colorado Apartment Association
650 South Cherry Street, #635
Denver, CO 80246
Phone: (303) 329-3300
Fax: (303) 329-0403

Pueblo Apartment Association
P.O. Box 987
Pueblo, CO 81002
Phone: (719) 584-2121
Fax: (719) 584-2204

Weld County Apartment Association
P.O. Box 1418
Greeley, CO 80632
Phone: (970) 352-1608
Fax: (970) 353-0325

Connecticut

Connecticut Apartment Association
41 Crossroads Plaza, #141
West Hartford, CT 06117
Phone: (203) 554-2822
Fax: (860) 953-9719
Web site: www.ctaahq.org

Delaware

Delaware Apartment Association
799 Montclair Drive, #4
Claymont, DE 19703-3625
Phone: (302) 798-0635
Fax: (302) 798-1726

District of Columbia

Apartment & Office Building Association (AOBA)
1050 17th Street NW, #300
Washington, DC 20036
Phone: (202) 296-3390
Fax: (202) 296-3399

Florida

Apartment Association of Greater Orlando
340 North Maitland Avenue
Maitland, FL 32751
Phone: (407) 644-0539
Fax: (407) 644-6288
Web site: www.aago.org

Bay Area Apartment Association
4509 George Road
Tampa, FL 33634
Phone: (813) 882-0222
Fax: (813) 884-0326

Bay County Multi-Housing Association
P.O. Box 16686
Panama City, FL 32406
Phone: (850) 763-5522

Capital City Apartment Association
431 Waverly Road
Tallahassee, FL 32312
Phone: (850) 531-0628
Fax: (850) 531-0628

Florida Apartment Association
1133 West Morse Boulevard, Suite 201
Winter Park, FL 32789
Phone: (407) 647-8839
Fax: (407) 629-2502
Web site: www.fl-apartments.org

Gainesville Apartment Association
P.O. Box 140926
Gainesville, FL 32614
Phone: (352) 335-1800
Fax: (352) 335-1800

Jacksonville Apartment Association
3047-1 St. Johns Bluff Road South
Jacksonville, FL 32246
Phone: (904) 997-1890
Fax: (904) 997-1891

Naples Area Apartment Association
P.O. Box 990028
Naples, FL 34116
Phone: (941) 455-6663
Fax: (941) 455-9567

South East Florida Apartment Association
1650 South Dixie Highway, Suite 500
Boca Raton, FL 33432
Phone: (561) 447-0696

Fax: (561) 395-8557
Web site: www.sefaa.com

Southwest Florida Apartment Association
P.O. Box 61933
Fort Myers, FL 33907
Phone: (941) 338-6055
Fax: (941) 275-0504

Space Coast Apartment Association
c/o SCPM
1617 Cooling Avenue
Melbourne, FL 32935
Phone: (321) 757-9609
Fax: (321) 757-9597

Tri-City Apartment Association
4509 George Road
Tampa, FL 33634
Phone: (800) 276-1927
Fax: (813) 884-0326

Georgia

Athens Apartment Association
P.O. Box 7086
Athens, Georgia 30604
Phone: (706) 549-8888
Fax: (706) 549-3304

Atlanta Apartment Association
8601 Dunwoody Place, #318
Atlanta, GA 30350
Phone: (770) 518-4248
Fax: (770) 518-4373
Web site: www.atl-apt.org

C.S.R.A. Apartment Association
P.O. Box 211325
Martinez, GA 30917-1325
Phone: (706) 868-9567
Fax: (706) 866-4949

Columbus Apartment Association
P.O. Box 8986
Columbus, GA 31909
Phone: (706) 653-2024
Fax: (706) 653-2203

Georgia Apartment Association
8601 Dunwoody Place, Suite 318
Atlanta, GA 30350
Phone: (770) 518-4248
Fax: (770) 518-4373
Web site: www.ga-apt.org

Mid Georgia Apartment Association
P.O. Box 18184
Macon, GA 31209
Phone: (478) 994-8773
Fax: (478) 994-8774

North Georgia Apartment Association
P.O. Box 200535
Cartersville, GA 30120
Phone: (770) 386-2921
Fax: (770) 386-1937

Savannah Apartment Association
P.O. Box 13247
Savannah, GA 31416
Phone: (912) 920-3207

Fax: (912) 920-3207
Web site: www.savaptassoc.org

Hawaii
National Apartment Association
201 North Union Street, Suite 200
Alexandria, VA 22314
Phone: (703) 518-6141

Idaho
Idaho Rental Owners & Managers Association
P.O. Box 15393
Boise, ID 83715-5393
Phone: (208) 336-9449
Fax: (208) 336-5559

Illinois
Chicagoland Apartment Association
4825 North Scott, Suite 119
Schiller Park, IL 60176
Phone: (847) 678-5717
Fax: (847) 678-5731
Web site: www.caapts.org

Illinois Apartment Association
4825 North Scott, Suite 119
Schiller Park, IL 60176
Phone: (847) 678-5717
Fax: (847) 678-5731

Indiana
Apartment Association of East Central Indiana
P.O. Box 1129
Muncie, IN 47308-1129
Phone: (765) 288-2492
Fax: (765) 286-7349
Web site: www.rentmuncie.com

Apartment Association of Fort Wayne/NE Indiana
6155 Stoney Creek Drive
Fort Wayne, IN 46825
Phone: (260) 482-2916
Fax: (260) 482-5187
Web site: www.apartmentsfortwayne.com

Apartment Association of Indiana
9202 North Meridian, Suite 250
Indianapolis, IN 46260
Phone: (317) 816-8900
Fax: (317) 816-8911
Web site: www.aptassociationindiana.org

Apartment Association of Southern Indiana, Inc.
P.O. Box 5526
Evansville, IN 47716-5526
Phone: (812) 473-0917
Fax: (812) 473-6401
Web site: www.aaosi.com

Apartment Association of Terre Haute
839 East Jackson Street
Sullivan, IN 47882
Phone: (812) 268-5518

Clinton County Property Managers
859 Walsh Avenue
Frankfort, IN 46041
Phone: (765) 659-5485
Fax: (765) 659-5878

Howard County Apartment Association
3334 Dixon Lane
Kokomo, IN 46902

Phone: (317) 455-0250
Fax: (317) 453-5990

Monroe County Apartment Association
P.O. Box 202
Bloomington, IN 47402
Phone: (812) 332-7363
Fax: (812) 339-0138
Web site: www.mcaaonline.org

Northern Indiana Apartment Council
9202 North Meridian, Suite 200
Indianapolis, IN 46260
Phone: (317) 571-5600
Fax: (317) 571-5603

Riverbend Apartment Association
19886 Miller Road
South Bend, IN 46614
Phone: (219) 289-7785

Tippecanoe Apartment Association
983 South Creasy Lane
Lafayette, IN 47905
Phone: (765) 464-3800

Iowa
National Apartment Association
201 North Union Street, Suite 200
Alexandria, VA 22314
Phone: (703) 518-6141

Kansas

Apartment Association of Greater Wichita
949 South Glendale, #400
Wichita, KS 67218
Phone: (316) 682-3508
Fax: (316) 684-4080

Apartment Association of Kansas City
11338 Shawnee Mission Parkway
Shawnee Mission, MO 66203
Phone: (913) 248-0355
Fax: (913) 248-0882

Apartment Association of Topeka
P. O. Box 3845
Topeka, KS 66604
Phone: (785) 273-1392
Fax: (785) 273-3319
Web site: www.ACTopeka.org

Kansas (State) Apartment Association
949 South Glendale-Parklane, #400
Wichita, KS 67218
Phone: (316) 682-3508
Fax: (316) 684-4080

Kentucky

Greater Cincinnati & Northern Kentucky Apartment Association
525 West 5th Street, Suite 233
Covington, KY 41011
Phone: (859) 581-5990
Fax: (859) 581-5993
Web site: www.gcnkaa.org

Greater Lexington Apartment Association
210 Malabu Drive, #7
Lexington, KY 40502
Phone: (859) 278-6540
Fax: (859) 277-9187
Web site: www.lexaptassoc.com

Louisville Apartment Association
7400 South Park Place, #1
Louisville, KY 40222
Phone: (502) 426-6140
Fax: (502) 426-2148
Web site: www.laaky.com

Louisiana

Acadiana Apartment Association
P.O. Box 53741
Lafayette, LA 70505
Phone: (337) 235-6080
Fax: (337) 235-6029

Apartment Association of Greater New Orleans
3017 Harvard Avenue, #201
Metairie, LA 70006
Phone: (504) 888-2492
Fax: (504) 888-2601
Web site: www.aagno.com

Apartment Association of Louisiana
515 South College Road, #210
Lafayette, LA 70503
Phone: (337) 237-3773
Fax: (337) 235-6029

Baton Rouge Apartment Association
1933 Wooddale Boulevard, #K-1
Baton Rouge, LA 70806-1514
Phone: (225) 923-2808
Fax: (225) 927-8159
Web site: www.braa.com

Houma-Thibodaux Apartment Association
425 West Tunnel Boulevard
Houma, LA 70360
Phone: (985) 879-2772
Fax: (985) 879-2726
Web site: www.houmathibodauxapts.com

Northeast Louisiana Apartment Association
P.O. Box 8461
Monroe, LA 71211
Phone: (318) 322-9927
Fax: (318) 322-9931

Shreveport-Bossier Apartment Association
P.O. Box 5938
Shreveport, LA 71135-5938
Phone: (318) 677-4229
Fax: (318) 868-5845

Southwest Louisiana Apartment Association
P.O. Box 6534
Lake Charles, LA 70606
Phone: (337) 477-2851
Fax: (337) 478-1148

Maine

National Apartment Association
201 North Union Street, Suite 200

Alexandria, VA 22314
Phone: (703) 518-6141

Maryland
Apartment & Office Building Association (AOBA)
1050 17th Street NW, #300
Washington, DC 20036
Phone: (202) 296-3390
Fax: (202) 296-3399

Massachusetts
Greater Boston Real Estate Board
11 Beacon Street, 1st Floor
Boston, MA 02108
Phone: (617) 668-8282
Fax: (617) 338-2600
Web site: www.gbreb.com

Michigan
Detroit Metropolitan Apartment Association
26899 Northwestern Highway, Suite 120
Southfield, MI 48034-8419
Phone: (248) 799-9151
Fax: (248) 799-5497

Property Management Association of Eastern Michigan
P.O. Box 884
Grand Blanc, MI 48439
Phone: (810) 513-5073

Property Management Association of Michigan
2757 44th Street, #104
Wyoming, MI 49509-4192
Phone: (616) 970-0399
Fax: (616) 257-0398
Web site: www.pmamhq.com

Property Management Association of Mid-Michigan
P.O. Box 27011
Lansing, MI 48909-7011
Phone: (517) 485-1917
Fax: (517) 647-7451
Web site: www.pmamm.com

Property Management Association of West Michigan
2757 44th Street, #306
Wyoming, MI 49509
Phone: (616) 531-5243
Fax: (616) 257-0398
Web site: www.pmawm.com

Washtenaw Area Apartment Association
179 Little Lake Drive
Ann Arbor, MI 48103
Phone: (743) 663-1200
Fax: (743) 996-1008
Web site: www.mlive.com/apartments/aaaaa/

Minnesota
National Apartment Association
201 North Union Street, Suite 200
Alexandria, VA 22314
Phone: (703) 518-6141

Mississippi
National Apartment Association
201 North Union Street, Suite 200
Alexandria, VA 22314
Phone: (703) 518-6141

Missouri

Apartment Association of Kansas City
11338 Shawnee Mission Parkway
Shawnee Mission, MO 66203
Phone: (913) 248-0355
Fax: (913) 248-0882

Columbia Apartment Association
P.O. Box 1504
Columbia, MO 65205
Phone: (573) 815-1150
Fax: (573) 815-7573

Mid-Missouri Apartment Association
820 Southwest Boulevard
Jefferson City, MO 65109
Phone: (573) 636-3168
Fax: (573) 636-3705

Mid Missouri Rental Properties Association
P.O. Box 977
Rolla, MO 64501
Phone: (573) 364-1985
Fax: (573) 364-5836

Missouri Apartment Association
P.O. Box 480187
Kansas City, MO 64148
Phone: (888) 859-5192
Fax: (816) 941-3296
Web site: www.moapts.org

Saint Louis Apartment Association
12777 Olive Boulevard, #B
St. Louis, MO 63141
Phone: (314) 205-8844
Fax: (314) 205-1410
Web site: www.slaa.org

Southwest Missouri Rental Housing Association
P.O. Box 1801
Joplin, MO 64802
Phone: (417) 437-3839
Fax: (417) 6782-5212
Web site: www.swmorent.com

Springfield Apartment & Housing Association
P.O. Box 10945
Springfield, MO 65808
Phone: (417) 883-4942
Fax: (417) 886-3685
Web site: www.springfieldhousing.net

Montana

National Apartment Association
201 North Union Street, Suite 200
Alexandria, VA 22314
Phone: (703) 518-6141

Nebraska

Apartment Association of Greater Omaha
P.O. Box 540705
Omaha, NE 68154
Phone: (402) 968-8360
Fax: (402) 965-3372
Web site: www.aagomaha.org

Nevada

Northern Nevada Apartment Association
1 East First Street, Suite 1105
Reno, NV 89501
Phone: (775) 322-6622
Fax: (775) 322-9860
Web site: www.nnaa.info

New Hampshire

New Hampshire Multi-Family Housing Association
P.O. Box 321
Manchester, NH 03105
Phone: (603) 668-8282
Fax: (6030 647-6133

New Jersey

New Jersey Apartment Association
197 Route 18 South, #230
East Brunswick, NJ 08816
Phone: (732) 247-6661
Fax: (732) 247-6669
Web site: www.njaa.com

New Mexico

Apartment Association of New Mexico
6755 Academy Road NE, Suite B
Albuquerque, NM 87109-3345
Phone: (505) 822-1114
Fax: (505) 822-8557
Web site: www.aanm.com

New York

Apartment Council of Western New York
142 Bauman Road
Williamsville, NY 14221
Phone: (716) 633-0959
Fax: (716) 631-0899
Web site: www.acwny.com

North Carolina

Apartment Association of North Carolina
2101 Rexford Road, #330-E
Charlotte, NC 28211
Phone: (704) 334-9511
Fax: (704) 333-4221

Charlotte Apartment Association
2101 Rexford Road, #330-E
Charlotte, NC 28211
Phone: (704) 344-9511
Fax: (704) 333-4221
Web site: www.charlotteapartmentassn.org

Cumberland County Apartment Association
P.O. Box 9417
Fayetteville, NC 28311
Phone: (910) 829-1843
Fax: (910) 822-0510

Greater Asheville Area Apartment Association
P.O. Box 846
Asheville, NC 28802
Phone: (828) 277-7290
Fax: (828) 277-7293

Greenville Area Property Managers
P.O. Box 275
Greenville, NC 27835-0275
Phone: (252) 758-1921
Fax: (252) 355-4973

Triad Apartment Association
3407-E West Wendover Avenue
Greensboro, NC 27407
Phone: (336) 294-4428
Fax: (336) 294-4481
Web site: www.taa.bz

Triangle Apartment Association
3739 National Drive, #202
Raleigh, NC 27612
Phone: (919) 782-1165
Fax: (919) 782-1169
Web site: www.triangleaptassn.org

Wilmington Apartment Association
P.O. Box 3413
Wilmington, NC 28403
Phone: (910) 799-8580
Fax: (910) 452-2650

North Dakota
Bismarck-Mandan Apartment Association
P.O. Box 1793
Bismarck, ND 58502-1793
Phone: (701) 255-7396
Fax: (701) 222-0103
Web site: www.bisman-apts.com

FM Apartment Association
P.O. Box 11342
Fargo, ND 58107-2025
Phone: (218) 233-6245
Fax: (218) 233-6245

North Dakota Apartment Association
P.O. Box 2317
Bismarck, ND 58502
Phone: (701) 221-2751
Fax: (701) 224-9824

Ohio

Columbus Apartment Association
1225 Dublin Road
Columbus, OH 43215
Phone: (614) 488-2115
Fax: (614) 488-8526
Web site: www.columbusapts.org

Greater Cincinnati & Northern Kentucky Apartment
Association
525 West 5th Street, Suite 233
Covington, KY 41011
Phone: (859) 581-5990
Fax: (859) 581-5993
Web site: www.gcnkaa.org

Greater Dayton Apartment Association
2555 South Dixie Drive, #100
Dayton, OH 45409-1532
Phone: (937) 293-1170
Fax: (937) 293-1180
Web site: www.gdaa.org

Ohio Apartment Association
1225 Dublin Road
Columbus, OH 43215
Phone: (614) 294-4222
Fax: (614) 421-6887

Oklahoma

Apartment Association of Central Oklahoma
3750 West Main Street, #112
Norman, OK 73072
Phone: (405) 701-1710
Fax: (405) 701-1719

Oklahoma Multi Housing Association
718 Northwest 17th Street
Oklahoma City, OK 73103
Phone: (405) 840-9855
Fax: (405) 840-9838

Stillwater Apartment Association
P.O. Box 882
Stillwater, OK 74076
Phone: (405) 372-8862
Fax: (405) 372-8862

Tulsa Apartment Association
6855 South Canton
Tulsa, OK 74136-3405
Phone: (918) 747-6217
Fax: (918) 747-6244
Web site: www.taaonline.org

Oregon

National Apartment Association
201 North Union Street, Suite 200
Alexandria, VA 22314
Phone: (703) 518-6141

Pennsylvania

Apartment Association of Central Pennsylvania
644 Allenview Drive
Mechanicsburg, PA 17055-6181
Phone: (717) 691-8984
Fax: (717) 691-8984

Apartment Association of Greater Philadelphia
One Bala Plaza, Suite 515
Bala Cynwyd, PA 19004
Phone: (610) 664-1800
Fax: (610) 664-4481
Web site: www.aapg.com

Rhode Island

National Apartment Association
201 North Union Street, Suite 200
Alexandria, VA 22314
Phone: (703) 518-6141

South Carolina

Apartment Association of Greater Columbia
P.O. Box 7515
Columbia, SC 29202
Phone: (803) 252-5032
Fax: (803) 252-0589

Charleston Apartment Association
P.O. Box 1763

Columbia, SC 29202
Phone: (843) 722-7585
Fax: (803) 252-0589

Myrtle Beach Apartment Association
P.O. Box 2752
Myrtle Beach, SC 29588
Phone: (843) 293-7256
Fax: (843) 293-9001

South Carolina Apartment Association
P.O. Box 7515
Columbia, SC 29202
Phone: (803) 252-5032
Fax: (803) 252-0589

Upper State Apartment Association
535 North Pleasantburg Drive, #202
Greenville, SC 29607
Phone: (864) 242-0200
Fax: (864) 233-2807

South Dakota

Black Hills Area Multi-Housing Association
P.O. Box 434
Rapid City, SD 57709
Phone: (605) 336-7756
Fax: (605) 330-0500

South Dakota Multi-Housing Association
812 South Minnesota Avenue
Sioux Falls, SD 57104
Phone: (605) 336-7756
Fax: (605) 336-7756

Tennessee

Apartment Association of Greater Knoxville
5410 Homberg Drive, #17-A
Knoxville, TN 37919
Phone: (865) 588-8961
Fax: (865) 588-7905
Web site: www.akag.org

Chattanooga Apartment Association
P.O. Box 4367
Chattanooga, TN 37405
Phone: (423) 876-8121
Fax: (423) 877-9846

Greater Nashville Apartment Association
810 Royal Parkway Drive, Suite 110
Nashville, TN 37214
Phone: (615) 883-9941
Fax: (615) 883-1922

Tennessee Apartment Association
810 Royal Parkway Drive, Suite 110
Nashville, TN 37214
Phone: (615) 883-9941
Fax: (615) 883-1922

Tri-City Apartment Association
P.O. Box 981
Johnson City, TN 37605
Phone: (423) 926-4156
Fax: (423) 926-5530

Texas

Apartment Association of Central Texas
1920 North Main, #102

Belton, TX 76513
Phone: (254) 939-5655
Fax: (254) 939-6664

Apartment Association of Greater Dallas
4230 LBJ Freeway, #140
Dallas, TX 75244-5804
Phone: (972) 385-9091
Fax: (972) 385-9412
Web site: www.aagdallas.com

Apartment Association of SE Texas
985 IH-10 North
Beaumont, TX 77706
Phone: (409) 899-4455
Fax: (409) 899-1507
Web site: www.setxaa.org

Apartment Association of Tarrant County, Inc.
6350 Baker Boulevard
Fort Worth, TX 76118
Phone: (817) 284-1121
Fax: (817) 284-2054

Apartment Association of the Panhandle
5601 Enterprise Circle, Suite D
Amarillo, TX 79106-4631
Phone: (806) 355-6391
Fax: (806) 355-0451

Apartment Association of the Permian Basin
P.O. Box 12392
Odessa, TX 79768
Phone: (915) 333-7133
Fax: (915) 332-2209

Austin Apartment Association
4107 Medical Parkway, #100
Austin, TX 78756
Phone: (512) 323-0990
Fax: (512) 323-2979
Web site: www.austinaptassoc.com

Big County Apartment Association
P.O. Box 7045
Abilene, TX 79608
Phone: (915) 695-7431
Fax: (915) 659-3489
Web site: www.bigcountryapartments.com

Bryan-College Station Apartment Association
1808 Barak Lane
Bryan, TX 77802-3448
Phone: (979) 260-9842
Fax: (979) 260-2894
Web site: www.bcsaa.com

Corpus Christi Apartment Association
4630 Corona Drive, #35
Corpus Christi, TX 78411-4315
Phone: (361) 852-4226
Fax: (361) 852-0763
Web site: www.ccapts.org

Corsicana Apartment Association
1025 North 24th Street
Corsicana, TX 75110
Phone: (903) 874-7165
Fax: (903) 872-8267
Web site: www.CorsicanaApartments.org

El Paso Apartment Association
1155 Larry Mahan, #H-2
El Paso, TX 79925
Phone: (915) 598-0800
Fax: (915) 598-1881
Web site: www.epaa.org

Galveston County Apartment Association
P.O. Box 3934
Galveston, TX 77552
Phone: (409) 762-8339
Fax: (409) 762-6345

Greater Longview Apartment Association
2127 Gilmer Road
Longview, TX 75604
Phone: (903) 759-3966
Fax: (903) 759-5516

Heart of Texas Apartment Association
P.O. Box 8250
Waco, TX 76714
Phone: (254) 776-5451
Fax: (254) 776-5877

Houston Apartment Association
10815 Fallstone Road
Houston, TX 77099-3496
Phone: (281) 933-2224
Fax: (281) 933-8412
Web site: www.haaonline.org

Lubbock Apartment Association
4227 85th Street
Lubbock, TX 79423
Phone: (806) 794-2037
Fax: (806) 794-9597
Web site: www.lubbockapartments.com

Midland Apartment Association
P.O. Box 9534
Midland, TX 79708
Phone: (915) 699-5265
Fax: (915) 694-0707
Web site: www.rentmidland.com

North Texas Rental Properties Association
2403 9th Street
Wichita Falls, TX 76301
Phone: (940) 322-7667
Fax: (940) 723-0896

Piney Woods Apartment Association
P.O. Box 631280
Nacogdoches, TX 75963-1280
Phone: (936) 560-2211
Fax: (936) 569-1883

Rio Grande Valley Apartment Association
902 East Tyler, Suite C
Harlingen, TX 78551-3299
Phone: (956) 428-5072
Fax: (956) 412-6192
Web site: www.rgvaa.org

San Angelo Apartment Association, Inc.
P.O. Box 3282

San Angelo, TX 76902
Phone: (915) 942-1332
Fax: (915) 942-6529

San Antonio Apartment Association
4204 Gardendale, #200
San Antonio, TX 78229
Phone: (210) 692-7797
Fax: (210) 692-7277
Web site: www.saaaonline.org

Texarkana Apartment Association
P.O. Box 1378
Texarkana, TX 75504-1378
Phone: (903) 793-7533
Fax: (903) 791-0923

Texas Apartment Association
606 West 12th Street
Austin, TX 78701
Phone: (512) 479-6252
Fax: (512) 479-6291

Tyler Apartment Association
1600 Rice Road
Tyler, TX 75703
Phone: (903) 581-0082
Fax: (903) 561-3463
Web site: www.taa.org

Victoria Apartment Association
P.O. Box 7192
Victoria, TX 77902
Phone: (361) 578-2954
Fax: (361) 578-0671

Utah

National Apartment Association
201 North Union Street, Suite 200
Alexandria, VA 22314
Phone: (703) 518-6141

Vermont

National Apartment Association
201 North Union Street, Suite 200
Alexandria, VA 22314
Phone: (703) 518-6141

Virginia

Apartment & Office Building Association (AOBA)
1050 17th Street Northwest, #300
Washington, DC 20036
Phone: (202) 296-3390
Fax: (202) 296-3399
Web site: www.aoba-metro.org

Blue Ridge Apartment Council PMB 230
977 Seminole Trail
Charlottesville, VA 22901-2824
Phone: (804) 977-3033
Fax: (804) 979-4826
Web site: www.brac.com

Fredericksburg Area Multihousing Association
P.O. Box 1495
Midlothian, VA 23113
Phone: (804) 273-0845
Fax: (804) 747-8465

New River Valley Apartment Council
301 Hunt Club Road, #6800

Blacksburg, VA 24060
Phone: (540) 951-1221
Fax: (540) 951-9302

Roanoke Valley Apartment Association
1650 Lancing Drive, #55
Roanoke, VA 24153
Phone: (540) 389-0209
Fax: (540) 389-4495
Web site: www.apt-guide.com/rvaa

Valley Landlords Association
640 Maple Avenue
Waynesboro, VA 22980
Phone: (540) 943-3555
Fax: (540) 943-3555

Virginia Apartment & Management Association
8611 Mayland Drive
Richmond, VA 23294
Phone: (804) 288-2899
Fax: (804) 288-4022
Web site: www.vamaonline.org

Washington
National Apartment Association
201 North Union Street, Suite 200
Alexandria, VA 22314
Phone: (703) 518-6141

West Virginia
National Apartment Association
201 North Union Street, Suite 200
Alexandria, VA 22314
Phone: (703) 518-6141

Wisconsin

Apartment Owners & Managers Association of Milwaukee
701 North Plankinton Avenue, Suite 207
Milwaukee, WI 53203
Phone: (414) 278-7557
Fax: (414) 271-6126

Wausau Area Apartment Association
P.O. Box 723
Wausau, WI 54402-0723
Phone: (715) 359-1500
Fax: (715) 355-0028
Web site: www.apartmentassociationonline.com

Wyoming

National Apartment Association
201 North Union Street, Suite 200
Alexandria, VA 22314
Phone: (703) 518-6141

Recommended Reading List

Investing

Allen, Robert G., *Multiple Streams of Income*. John
Wiley & Sons, Hoboken, New Jersey, 2000.

Bronchick, William and Robert Dahlstrom, *Flipping
Properties: Generate Instant Cash Properties in Real
Estate*. Dearborn Trade Publishing, Chicago,
Illinois, 2001.

Conti, Peter and David Finkel, *Making Big Money
Investing in Real Estate: Without Tenants, Banks,
or Rehab Projects*. Dearborn Trade Publishing,
Chicago, Illinois, 2002.

Kiyosaki, Robert and Dolf de Roos, *Real Estate
Riches: How to Become Rich Using Your Banker's
Money*. Warner Books, New York, New York,
2001.

Kiyosaki, Robert and Sharon L. Lechter, *Cash Flow
Quadrant: Rich Dad's Guide to Financial Freedom*.
Warner Books, New York, New York, 2000.

Kiyosaki, Robert and Sharon L. Lechter, *Rich Dad,
Poor Dad: What the Rich Teach Their Kids About
Money That the Poor and Middle Class Do Not!*
Warner Books, New York, New York, 2000.

McClean, Andrew and Gary W. Eldrid, *Investing in
Real Estate*, 3rd ed. John Wiley & Sons,
Hoboken, New Jersey, 2001.

Strauss, Spencer and Martin Stone, *Secure Your Financial Future Investing in Real Estate.* Dearborn Trade Publishing, Chicago, Illinois, 2003.

Vollucci, Eugene E. and Gene Vollucci, *How to Buy and Sell Apartment Buildings.* John Wiley & Sons, Hoboken, New Jersey, 1993.

Landlording

Edwards, Brian F. and Casey Edwards, *Complete Idiot's Guide to Being a Smart Landlord.* Alpha Books, New York, New York, 2000.

Griswold, Robert S., *Property Management For Dummies.* John Wiley & Sons, Hoboken, New Jersey, 2001.

Patton, David and Leigh Robinson, *Landlording: A Handy Manual for Scrupulous Landlords and Landladies Who Do It Themselves,* 9th ed. Express Publishing, Newbury, Berkshire, United Kingdom, 2001.

Perry, Greg M., *Managing Rental Properties for Maximum Profit.* Prima Publishing, Roseville, California, 2000.

Strauss, Steven D., *Ask a Lawyer: Landlord and Tenant.* W.W. Norton & Co., New York, New York, 1998.

Sample Real Estate Investment Plan

Property
333 Richmond Street

Prepared for
The Unofficial Guide to Real Estate Investing,
Second Edition

Prepared by
Spencer Strauss & Martin Stone

BUCKINGHAM INVESTMENTS
333 Richmond St. Suite 10
El Segundo, CA 90245
PHONE: 310-322-8343
FAX: 310-322-4050

www.buckinghaminvestments.com
Spencer Strauss: spence@spencerstrauss.com
Martin Stone: gr8profit@aol.com

Appendix D

Contents of the Plan

Financial Goals for the Plan

Real Estate Investment Plan Summary

Property Financial Parameters

Tabular Presentation of Market Value, Gross Equity, and
Annual Liquidated Income by Year

Tabular Presentation of Cash Account, Tax Account, and Net
of the Two Accounts by Year

Year-by-Year Financial Details of the Plan

Financial Goals for the Plan

1. Final gross equity position in the property of $431,000.00

2. Potential of an annual installment sale income of
    $40,300.00

3. Hedge against inflation during the entire period of the
    plan

4. Minimize negative cash flows during the entire period of
    the plan

5. Schedule operating expenses for professional property
    management

Real Estate Investment Plan
Summary

This 10-year real estate investment
plan was prepared for

The Unofficial Guide to Real Estate Investing, Second Edition

The plan maintains a 30-percent average leveraged return to achieve a final gross equity position of $518,797.00 in 9 years. During the last year of the plan, an installment sale is made. The cash down payment received from the sale is only that amount of money required to pay federal and state taxes due and to bring the cash and tax accounts to positive balances. The balance of the sale price is loaned to the buyer and is evidenced by a note, secured by a trust deed, bearing interest at 10 percent.

After the installment sale, the investor will have $49,395.00 in annual interest income from the note and cash account balance. The plan assumes the following:

1. A 5 percent annual value appreciation rate,

2. A 3 percent annual increase in income
   collected, and

3. A 2 percent annual increase in operating expense costs.

PROPERTY FINANCIAL PARAMETERS

Purchase Price	$220,000.00	Equity	$30,000.00
Monthly Income	$2,200.00	Monthly Expenses	$660.00
Account Balance	$0.00		
1st Td & Note		**2nd Td & Note**	
Loan Amount	$190,000.00	Loan Amount	$0.00
Interest Rate	9.00%	Interest Rate	0.00%
Years of Loan	30.00	Years of Loan	0.00
Monthly Payment	$1,450.00	Monthly Payment	$0.00
V.A. Rate	5.00%	Income Increase	3.50%
Vacancy Rate	2.50%	Expense Increase	2.50%
Land Value	$66,000.00	Depreciable Imp.	$154,000.00
Annual Operating Expenses:			
Property Taxes	$2,640.00	Insurance Costs	$380.00
Licenses	$98.00	Utilities	$1,372.00
Management	$1,372.00	Maintenance	$1,029.00

Real Estate Investment Plan

	Market Value, Gross Equity, and Annual Liquidated Income		
Year	**Market Value**	**Gross Equity**	**Income***
2003	$220,000.00	$30,000.00	$3,000.00
2004	$231,000.00	$41,300.00	$4,172.00
2005	$242,550.00	$53,177.00	$5,472.00
2006	$584,520.00	$58,452.00	$5,845.00
2007	$613,746.00	$91,126.00	$8,506.00
2008	$644,433.00	$125,572.00	$11,524.00
2009	$1,260,483.00	$126,048.00	$12,605.00
2010	$1,323,507.00	$196,508.00	$18,342.00
2011	$1,389,682.00	$270,788.00	$24,852.00
2012	$1,459,166.00	$349,107.00	$32,171.00
2013	$1,532,124.00	$431,694.00	$40,339.00

* The annual liquidated income is computed as follows: The property is sold using an installment sale, any cash in the cash account is added to the equity account, and finally, we assume you carry the balance at 10 percent interest.

The data in this analysis is approximate, should only be used with a Buckingham Investments agent, and is not a guarantee or warranty of investment return.

Real Estate Investment Plan

	Cash Account, Tax Account, and Net of the Two Accounts		
Year	**Cash Account**	**Tax Account**	**Net**
2003	$0.00	$0.00	$0.00
2004	$420.00	$1,415.00	$1,835.00
2005	$1,543.00	$2,619.00	$4,162.00
2006	$0.00	$0.00	$0.00
2007	−$6,070.00	$5,075.00	−$995.00
2008	−$10,328.00	$9,535.00	−$793.00
2009	$0.00	$0.00	$0.00
2010	−$13,089.00	$9,500.00	−$3,589.00
2011	−$22,271.00	$19,000.00	−$3,271.00
2012	−$27,395.00	$28,500.00	$1,105.00
2013	−$28,306.00	$35,276.00	$6,970.00

The data in this analysis is approximate, should only be used with a Buckingham Investments agent, and is not a guarantee or warranty of investment return.

YEAR OF THE PLAN IS 2003

Market Value	$220,000.00	Equity	$30,000.00
Cash Account	$0.00	Tax Account	$0.00

During-the-Year Values

Income	$26,400.00	Expenses	$7,920.00
Cash Flow	$420.00	Tax Rebates	$1,415.00
Amortization	$300.00	Appreciation	$11,000.00
Roe	44	Delta Roe	30

End-of-the-Year Values

Market Value	$231,000.00	Equity	$41,300.00
Cash Account	$420.00	Tax Account	$1,415.00

YEAR OF THE PLAN IS 2004

Market Value	$231,000.00	Equity	$41,300.00
Cash Account	$420.00	Tax Account	$1,415.00

During-the-Year Values

Income	$26,400.00	Expenses	$7,920.00
Cash Flow	$1,123.00	Tax Rebates	$1,204.00
Amortization	$327.00	Appreciation	$11,550.00
Roe	34	Delta Roe	14

End-of-the-Year Values

Market Value	$242,550.00	Equity	$53,177.00
Cash Account	$1,543.00	Tax Account	$2,619.00

YEAR OF THE PLAN IS 2005

Market Value	$242,550.00	Equity	$53,177.00
Cash Account	$1,543.00	Tax Account	$2,619.00

During-the-Year Values

Income	$27,324.00	Expenses	$8,118.00
Cash Flow	$1,852.00	Tax Rebates	$983.00
Amortization	$356.00	Appreciation	$12,128.00
Roe	29	Delta Roe	9

End-of-the-Year Values

Market Value	$584,520.00	Equity	$58,452.00
Cash Account	$0.00	Tax Account	$0.00

Tax Deferred Exchange Occurred in the
Last Quarter Of 2005

Trade Out Of:

Market Value = $254,678.00

Total Loans = $189,017.00 [Leverage: 74%]

Total Equity = $65,661.00

Accounts = $0.00

::

Total "Out-of-Pocket" Exchange Transaction
Cost = $14,206.00

::

Total Equity = $58,452.00

Accounts = $0.00

Market Value = $584,520.00

Total Loans = $526,068.00 [Leverage: 86%]

Trade Into: Exchange Property

[Costs: Sell – 3.0% Buy – 1.0%]

[Gm – 8.50 Va Rate – 5.00%]

[Loans: 86.4% First At 9.0%]

YEAR OF THE PLAN IS 2006

Market Value	$584,520.00	Equity	$58,452.00
Cash Account	$0.00	Tax Account	$0.00

During-the-Year Values

Income	$68,767.00	Expenses	$24,068.00
Cash Flow	−$6,070.00	Tax Rebates	$5,075.00
Amortization	$3,448.00	Appreciation	$29,226.00
Roe	54	Delta Roe	6

End-of-the-Year Values

Market Value	$613,746.00	Equity	$91,126.00
Cash Account	−$6,070.00	Tax Account	$5,075.00

YEAR OF THE PLAN IS 2007

Market Value	$613,746.00	Equity	$91,126.00
Cash Account	−$6,070.00	Tax Account	$5,075.00

During-the-Year Values

Income	$71,174.00	Expenses	$24,670.00
Cash Flow	−$4,258.00	Tax Rebates	$4,460.00
Amortization	$3,758.00	Appreciation	$30,687.00
Roe	38	Delta Roe	13

End-of-the-Year Values

Market Value	$644,433.00	Equity	$125,572.00
Cash Account	−$10,328.00	Tax Account	$9,535.00

YEAR OF THE PLAN IS 2008

Market Value	$644,433.00	Equity	$125,572.00
Cash Account	−$10,328.00	Tax Account	$9,535.00

During-the-Year Values

Income	$73,665.00	Expenses	$25,287.00
Cash Flow	−$2,376.00	Tax Rebates	$3,816.00
Amortization	$4,097.00	Appreciation	$32,222.00
Roe	30	Delta Roe	2

End-of-the-Year Values

Market Value	$1,260,483.00	Equity	$126,048.00
Cash Account	$0.00	Tax Account	$0.00

Tax Deferred Exchange Occurred in the
Last Quarter of 2008

Trade Out Of:

Market Value = $676,654.00

Total Loans = $514,764.00 [Leverage: 76%]

Total Equity = $161,890.00

Accounts = $ 0.00

::

Total "Out-of-Pocket" Exchange Transaction
Cost = $36,489.00

::

Total Equity = $126,048.00

Accounts = $0.00

Market Value = $1,260,483.00

Total Loans = $1,134,434.00 [Leverage: 86%]

Trade Into: Exchange Property

[Costs: Sell – 3.0% Buy – 1.0%]
[Gm – 8.50 Va Rate – 5.00%]

[Loans: 86.4% First At 9.0%]

YEAR OF THE PLAN IS 2009

Market Value	$1,260,483.00	Equity	$126,048.00
Cash Account	$0.00	Tax Account	$0.00
During-the-Year Values			
Income	$148,292.00	Expenses	$51,902.00
Cash Flow	−$13,089.00	Tax Rebates	$9,500.00
Amortization	$7,436.00	Appreciation	$63,024.00
Roe	53	Delta Roe	2
End-of-the-Year Values			
Market Value	$1,323,507.00	Equity	$196,508.00
Cash Account	−$13,089.00	Tax Account	$9,500.00

YEAR OF THE PLAN IS 2010

Market Value	$1,323,507.00	Equity	$196,508.00
Cash Account	−$13,089.00	Tax Account	$9,500.00
During-the-Year Values			
Income	$153,482.00	Expenses	$53,200.00
Cash Flow	−$9,182.00	Tax Rebates	$9,500.00
Amortization	$8,105.00	Appreciation	$66,175.00
Roe	38	Delta Roe	5
End-of-the-Year Values			
Market Value	$1,389,682.00	Equity	$270,788.00
Cash Account	−$22,271.00	Tax Account	$19,000.00

YEAR OF THE PLAN IS 2011

Market Value	$1,389,682.00	Equity	$270,788.00
Cash Account	−$22,271.00	Tax Account	$19,000.00
During-the-Year Values			
Income	$158,854.00	Expenses	$54,530.00
Cash Flow	−$5,124.00	Tax Rebates	$9,500.00
Amortization	$8,834.00	Appreciation	$69,484.00
Roe	31	Delta Roe	4
End-of-the-Year Values			
Market Value	$1,459,166.00	Equity	$349,107.00
Cash Account	−$27,395.00	Tax Account	$28,500.00

YEAR OF THE PLAN IS 2012

Market Value	$1,459,166.00	Equity	$349,107.00
Cash Account	-$27,395.00	Tax Account	$28,500.00

During-the-Year Values

Income	$164,414.00	Expenses	$55,893.00
Cash Flow	-$911.00	Tax Rebates	$6,776.00
Amortization	$9,629.00	Appreciation	$72,958.00
Roe	25	Delta Roe	4

End-of-the-Year Values

Market Value	$1,532,124.00	Equity	$431,694.00
Cash Account	-$28,306.00	Tax Account	$35,276.00

YEAR OF THE PLAN IS 2013

Market Value	$1,532,124.00	Equity	$431,694.00
Cash Account	-$28,306.00	Tax Account	$35,276.00

During-the-Year Values

Income	$170,169.00	Expenses	$57,290.00
Cash Flow	$3,464.00	Tax Rebates	$5,256.00
Amortization	$10,496.00	Appreciation	$76,606.00
Roe	22	Delta Roe	3

End-of-the-Year Values

Market Value	$1,608,731.00	Equity	$518,797.00
Cash Account	-$24,842.00	Tax Account	$40,532.00

This analysis was generated by a Buckingham Investments Analysis Automated System.

It is to be understood that the computerized systems employed by Buckingham Investments are simulations only. As such, they are *what if* not *what is*.

The calculations used in the systems are accurate as to representing the true financial mechanisms that most investments in real property undergo. Therefore, the systems are quite accurate when the assumptions concerning the future values of certain significant parameters used in the systems also are accurate. Your participation in selecting these parameters is solicited and welcomed.

The significant parameters for which future values are predicted or assumed are

1. Value appreciation rate
2. Rate of increase of rental income
3. Rate of increase of operating expenses
4. Vacancy rate
5. Loan interest rate increases
6. Competent level of property management
7. General assumptions such as your longevity, health, and the continuance of a stable political and economical order

You have considerable control over some of these parameters. Others are at the mercy of external forces.

Of course, continual updating of any analyses using the systems will guarantee greater accuracy.

When using the analyses generated by the systems as a plan, two major benefits accrue:

1. The plan is a measure of what you should do.
2. The plan is a measure as to how well your financial intentions are being executed.

The data in any analysis generated is approximate, should only be used with a Buckingham Investments representative, and is not a guarantee or warranty of return on investment.

It is distributed with the understanding that it is for planning purposes only.

Inspection Report

INSPECTION REPORT

PROPERTY ADDRESS:

333 Richmond Street   El Segundo, CA

EXCLUSIVELY FOR:

The Unofficial Guide to Real Estate Investing – Second Edition

MARK 1
& SON

HOME INSPECTORS

1621 Loma Drive   Hermosa Beach, CA 90254
310-318-5634

PURPOSE OF THE INSPECTION

This inspection report is intended to describe the general conditions of the property mentioned herein, as seen on the date the inspection was performed. The inspection *is not* to be considered exhaustive, but general in nature. **The inspection is focused on the visible and accessible portions of 5 specific areas: 1. Roof; 2. Structural; 3. Electrical system; 4. Plumbing system; 5. Heating/Air conditioning system.** The extent of the inspection of each area is explained throughout the report. Although other subjects are covered, the opinions given for these items are based on a random sampling of each covered item (i.e. doors, windows, valves, faucets, electrical outlets, switches, etc.). Opinions may be made on items excluded from the inspection. These opinions are given in good faith and are solely intended to make the report more complete. Said opinions may be inexact and are only an indication that there may or may not be a problem. These opinions do not represent a waiver of the exclusions (see "Exclusions" below).

This inspection is not designed or intended to supersede any required disclosures. We will not assume any responsibility of disclosures required by others including but not limited to seller disclosures as outlined in California Civil Code 1102.5, (II), (B), or (C), and any others. Said disclosures are beyond our control or knowledge. This inspection is not intended to satisfy, preclude, or take the place of said disclosures. Nor does this inspection serve to satisfy, preclude, or remove the responsibility of those required to make disclosures.

SCOPE OF THE INSPECTION

The scope of this inspection is limited to a visual inspection of areas of the premises which are exposed and readily accessible. Any area which is not exposed to view, inaccessible or concealed because of soil, fill, foliage, walls, wall coverings, floors, floor coverings, ceilings, furnishings, belongings or any other thing, is not included in this inspection. Furthermore, this inspection does not include any destructive testing or dismantling of equipment, systems or exposed surfaces. All items covered within this inspection are operated normally, as is possible by the inspector, however, the overall effectiveness of these items is excluded (e.g. cleaning ability of dishwashers, flushing ability of toilets, heating/cooling capacity and efficiency overall or at each furnace/air-conditioning distribution point, etc...)

EXCLUSIONS

This inspection does not extend to chemical analysis or visual recognition of any condition relating to products liability or environmental hazards of any nature, nor does it mention, test or inspect for sound (decibel) levels. In addition and not limited to, the following are specifically **excluded** from this report: Asbestos-containing or contaminated materials (unless by special addendum to this Agreement), radon, lead, wood rot or wood destroying organisms and pests and/or related damaged from same; household pests; geological or soil conditions (including but not limited to area drainage); underground or concealed pipes; electrical lines and connections; sewer lines and/or septic tanks; roofing paper below rock, tiles or shingles; portable appliances; vacuum cleaner systems; the automatic functions of built-in appliances; low voltage wiring; TV cables and antennas; alarm, intercom or music systems; radiant heating pipes or wires; humidifiers; elevators; fountains; retaining walls; sprinklers; water softening or purifying systems; shower pans; furnace and/or air conditioning gas fired fireboxes or heat exchangers; solar systems; common areas in planned developments.

CODE RELIANCE

Because of the complicated nature of and variations in all building codes and because these codes are constantly changing, no assurance is given that the subject premises or its systems are built or maintained in accordance with the requirements of said codes.

NOT AN INSURANCE POLICY, WARRANTY OR GUARANTEE

This report does not insure nor is it intended to insure against the items covered in the Inspection. Insurance policies covering certain items, however, are available from various companies licensed by the State to provide such service.

No warranties, representations or guarantees, expressed or implied are intended or given on the future operating ability of any items covered.

LIMIT OF LIABILITY

For additional information regarding the purpose and limitations of the inspection please read the INSPECTION AGREEMENT. This agreement is a contract and limits our liability. If you have any questions concerning the INSPECTION AGREEMENT or the results of the inspection contained herein, we encourage you to contact us immediately.

> **NOTE: IT IS THE RESPONSIBILITY OF THE CLIENT TO READ THIS REPORT IN ITS ENTIRETY. FAILURE OF THE CLIENT TO READ AND UNDERSTAND THE ENTIRE REPORT RELIEVES MARK 1 OF _ALL_ LIABILITY. IF THERE ARE ANY QUESTIONS REGARDING ANY PART OF THIS REPORT THE CLIENT SHOULD CALL MARK 1 HOME INSPECTORS IMMEDIATELY AT (310) 318-5634.**

PREFACE

Page 1 of 11   *GENERAL DATA / ACTION LIST*

General Data
Information provided in this report is to the best of our knowledge. We are unable to determine or recreate the actual conditions from the past or their effects unless physical evidence is observed by the inspector.

Condominiums / Townhomes
We inspect the interior only, we do not inspect the exterior of any association maintained or controlled common areas of private or public planned developments. The client should seek from others, all information of common areas or association maintained areas and understand all rules and bylaws, including the previous or current status of the common areas; physical and financial.

Action List
This space is reserved for the client or others to list items of concern to the client throughout the report to serve as a summary or "action list" of items to be serviced and/or repaired.

PAGE 2 of 11   *EXTERIOR*

Stucco
It is normal to find minor stucco cracking. Cracking is caused by a number of things including normal aging, vibration, expansion and contraction, earth movement , settling etc.. Continued observation of the stucco and its condition is advisable. It is wise to keep such cracks grouted to prevent moisture from penetrating and undermining the material, especially on walls directly exposed to wind and rain.

Vents
Vent screens should be kept in place to prevent unwanted creatures from entering sub area or attic. Vents should be kept clear to allow proper ventilation.

Trim
The conditions of all wood including the wood trim will be covered by the termite report. Proper paint seal and caulking should be considered normal maintenance to all wood on the exterior.

Chimney
Our inspection of the chimney and fireplace(s) is a surface inspection only. We *do not* use any device to determine condition. Cracking and deterioration may be present and not visible or evident to the inspector. For complete and full in-depth evaluation we strongly urge full inspection by a licensed chimney specialist. We advise the installation of spark arrestors where they are not present, as well as keeping the inside flue area well swept to prevent fire hazards.

Utility shut-off
It is wise to communicate to all occupants of the premises, the locations of all utility shut-offs. Accordingly, it is also advisable to have a plan, in the event of emergency to shut off necessary utilities. We suggest a wrench be attached to the gas meter to facilitate immediate shut off of the gas system in the event of earthquake or other disaster.
NOTE: It is recommended that a main shut off be present and readily accessible for all utilities. For those utilities that have no main shut off, we recommend that one be installed.

We DO NOT report on the presence of any earthquake shut-off apparatus on gas meters as may be required by specific municipalities or otherwise. Separate certifications should be obtained for proof of compliances. Further information is available at The Gas Company.

Preface continued...

PAGE 3 of 11 STRUCTURAL / ROOF

Foundation
We can only comment on portions of the foundation readily accessible and visible, as the whole of this report is considered "general" in nature and we can only comment on the general condition of the foundation to the extent that we are able to observe it. **Note:** Homes or structures built on hillsides or known expansive soil areas or areas known to experience movement of any kind should be evaluated by a structural engineer or soil specialist.

Bolting
In this Report, the structure is considered "bolted" if one (1) bolt is located and observed in either the house or matching garage. We *do not* suggest that the bolting is sufficient or adequate in any way. We only refer to the fact that bolting does exist if we observe one bolt. For further evaluation of the adequacy of the bolting system or for a retro-fit of a non-bolted structure we recommend a licensed specialist be contacted for further consultation.

Floor System
Out-of-level flooring is common in older properties. This is usually caused by a variety reasons such as normal earth settling, earth movement, expansion and contraction etc. Out-of-level floors can be re-leveled in most cases. It is advised that if you experience a significant change in levels of the floors that a licensed specialist be contacted to evaluate the cause. It is recommended that the ability of water collection close to the foundation be minimized, especially around hillside properties and properties within expansive soil areas.

Roof
If there is no evidence of active leakage it is assumed that the roof does not leak, however, a roof may begin leaking at any given time. It is our endeavor to make an accurate assessment of the current condition based on the visible character of the roof. Unless documented proof of repair exists, evidence of leakage must be considered a potentially active leak. It is recommended that an ongoing maintenance schedule be kept during the life of the roof to prevent future leakage. We *do not* walk on any roof unless there is ready access. In the absence of ready access roofs are observed from the perimeter.

We can comment only on the portions of the roof system that are readily visible. This report *is not* a roof certification. For roof certification a licensed roofing contractor should be consulted.

PAGE 4 of 11 ELECTRICAL SYSTEM

Service
In most cases, maintenance of the lines that run from the power pole to the weather head are the responsibility of the local power company. It is advisable to notify the power company if wires are old, damaged or show wear and if branches and/or foliage obstruct the path to the pole.

Panel(s)
We do not remove the back plate(s) or dismantle any breaker or fuse panels which may exist. If fuse box panel(s) still exist we recommend that they be upgraded to breaker panel(s).

NOTE, If moisture or rust is discovered inside of the breaker panel, it may indicate a need to reseal at the weather head or where the lines enter the property.

We recommend that all circuits are labeled to indicate their function.

System
We can only report on what we are able to see. Wiring and connections may vary and may be obstructed from view by walls, insulation, framing, personal belongings etc., and may be inaccessible during a general inspection. Wire splices, open junction boxes, damaged wire, worn wire, knob and tube wire, or any other sub-standard condition will be reported only if viewed. For a complete evaluation and exhaustive report of the electrical system, an evaluation by a licensed electrician is advised. **IN ALL CASES WE RECOMMEND THE IMMEDIATE UPGRADE OF ANY GLASS FUSE SYSTEM TO A BREAKER SYSTEM AND UPGRADE AND REMOVAL OF ANY _KNOB AND TUBE WIRING._**

Plugs and Switches
We test a representative sampling of the wall switches and receptacles, We *do not* test all plugs and receptacles.

NOTE: We recommend that old, worn switches and ungrounded or two (2) pronged plugs be upgraded.

It is recommended that Ground Fault Interrupter (GFI) receptacles be installed at all outdoor outlets and on outlets in wet areas such as laundry, garage, bathrooms and kitchen counter areas. Consult a licensed electrician for local codes and requirements. GFIs should be tested monthly to ensure they are functioning.

Preface continued...

PAGE 5 of 11 PLUMBING SYSTEM

Plumbing system
We can only comment on what we are able to see. We cannot report on what we cannot see due to pipes being underground, inside walls, in inaccessible areas, personal obstructions or otherwise.

Water lines
Galvanized water pipe rusts and corrodes from the inside out causing loss of water pressure. When corrosion and rust, becomes visible to the eye, it means that the pipe has no metal remaining at that spot on the pipe. Eventually the pipe begins leaking and will ultimately break. It is common to replace galvanized pipe with copper pipe that has a life expectancy of sixty (60) plus years. This can sometimes be done in two stages; (1) replace horizontal pipes and (2) replace vertical pipes later as needed.

Waste lines
During our inspection we make every effort to run as much water down the drains as necessary to detect any leaks, clogs or backup potential. We cannot detect root intervention problems or broken drain lines unless reasonable evidence is found at the time of the inspection. Any area where wet soil or other moisture exists may indicate the existence of water line seepage or drain line seepage underground. Accordingly, immediate steps should be taken to prevent further plumbing problems or structural settling.

Vent lines
We *do not* inspect drain vents for blockage.

Toilets
Toilets should be checked frequently to be sure they are tightly fastened to the floor. Loose toilets can leak at their base below the visible floor line and cause damage to floors and walls and ceilings below. Some areas require "low flow" toilets to be installed, check with your broker/ agent or the building department in the area for further information.

Water treatment systems
We *do not* inspect or test water treatment systems.

PAGE 6 of 11 WATER HEATERS / HEATING & AIR CONDITIONING

Water heater(s)
The average life expectancy of a water heater is from eight (8) to twelve (12) years. Draining the water heater and allowing settlement build-up to be drained off can extend life expectancy.

Safety codes require the water heater to be properly strapped for earthquake safety. A licensed contractor should be used to strap any water heater which is not properly strapped.

Pressure Relief Valves and accompanying drain pipe should be installed on each water heater. We do not test the Pressure Relief Valve.

Venting should be intact and extend above the roof line. We do not test for vent leaks or blockage, or for carbon monoxide leaks.

Water heater(s) in a utility area, such as Laundry room, garage etc., or any other interior water heating unit(s) should be raised at least eighteen (18) inches off the floor to prevent potential combustion of flammable liquid spills by pilot lights. It is recommended that whenever possible, water heater(s) be moved from living space out to the exterior.

Heating unit(s)
Our inspection includes running the unit(s) when possible. We do not dismantle the unit(s). As a secondary inspection, we strongly urge the full inspection by The Gas Company prior to the close of escrow. This inspection is usually free and will uncover potential problems with areas of the unit that we do not inspect, such as heat exchangers and fire boxes. We do not inspect for proper ventilation, ventilation blockage or leaks, or carbon monoxide leaks.

If there is no proof of a recent service call performed on the heating unit within the last two (2) years, it is recommended that a full service of the unit(s) be performed by a licensed contractor prior to the close of the escrow.

It is common for older homes and buildings to have duct work and exhaust pipes that contain asbestos material. In this report we define the suspicious materials as *"asbestos-like"* material o determine that asbestos content does exist a lab analysis of the suspicious material is required.

Preface continued...

Air conditioning
Our inspection is limited to turning on the unit and determining that it runs. In all cases we recommend that a routine service call be performed to determine the condition and to check for adequate Freon levels. Running an air conditioner with a low level of Freon can severely damage the unit. We *do not* check Freon levels.

PAGE 7 of 11   KITCHEN(s)

Appliances
We will run the appliances whenever possible. We *do not* dismantle or represent that any unit runs properly. We simply determine that the unit is operational. We will report any obvious abnormalities.

Vents / fans
We recommend that all ovens and stoves be properly vented, preferably by a charcoal filter or exhaust fan to prevent unventilated cooking areas.

Garbage disposals
Many times garbage disposals will dry out and become stuck if not used. A tool exists that will assist in freeing the unit. In the event there is no power at the unit it may be restored by pressing the reset button on the bottom of the unit.

Occasionally, due to debris clogging the drain line water will flow out of the air vent which is usually located on top of the sink which is supposed to drain down into the garbage disposal. This can be corrected by removing the rubber hose on the unit and cleaning out debris caused from prematurely turning off the disposal unit prior to debris being washed away.

We *do not* dispose of food etc., to test the unit.

Trash compactor
We *do not* compact trash to test the unit.

Oven / stove / microwave
We *do not* cook on the units or test temperature accuracy. We simply report whether or not they operate.

Note: We do not inspect refrigerators, intercom systems, built-in blenders or can openers.

PAGE 8 of 11   BATHROOM(s)

Grout
Grout between tile joints should be maintained on a regular basis. Poor grout allows water to seep between tile and walls and can allow water to seep into wood framing and flooring.

Caulking
Caulking should be maintained on a regular basis. It is important to caulk at the joints between tub/shower and flooring to prevent water from seeping underneath to wood framing and to lower levels. It is also important to maintain caulking around shower enclosures to prevent leaking while the shower is in use.

Whirlpools
We will fill the whirlpool and test the motor, blower, and air adjustments if able. We will view the motor if readily accessible. We do not inspect adequacy of the motor or amount of air that it produces, sanitary quality, hook-ups or location of the unit. If we are unable to fill the unit with water, get the unit to hold water, locate the switches or controls, we cannot make no report on the functional capability of the unit.

Flooring / Walls
It is not uncommon to have water blisters on walls around tubs, showers, floors at tubs or showers, or floors around toilets. If blisters or soft spots are discovered, it is advisable to have a termite inspection to determine severity of any wood damage, to stop the source of any running water, and repair any damage. Linoleum flooring should be kept well sealed around toilets, tubs and showers to prevent water from seeping underneath. The termite company is responsible to report floor and wall damage or dry rot in bathrooms.

Shower pans
We are not able to report on the quality of installation or adequacy of a shower pan. See termite report.

PAGE 9 of 11   ROOMS

Floors
We *do not* remove any floor coverings to view floors below.

Preface continued...

Doors

We test doors randomly. Exterior doors should be solid core doors. Sliding glass doors should have tempered safety glass which is indicated by a small etched label in the corner of the glass. The absence of a label would indicate that the glass is NOT likely to be tempered safety glass.

Windows

We test windows randomly. We *do not* test all windows. In older homes which have wooden double hung windows, the sash cords can become detached. Sash cords attach to counter balance weights which are inside the window unit and function as the means to hold the window up after it is raised. When the sash cords become detached the window will not stay up. Routine repair by a handy person can remedy this situation. Wooden windows can also become stuck due to normal aging, excessive painting, swelling due to moisture etc.. It is advisable to make sure all windows are kept in operational condition. It is advisable to keep the exterior of the windows well sealed with caulk to maintain a weather seal. Wooden windows eventually become old and deteriorated and are typically upgraded to a newer type of window.

Fireplaces

Significant cracks in the firebox should be kept grouted and the flue should be kept clean. We *do not* light the fireplace.

PAGE 10 of 11 BEDROOM(s) / LAUNDRY ROOM

Acoustic ceilings

Some acoustic ceilings contain small traces of asbestos material. To determine if the acoustic material contains asbestos material a sample must be taken for analysis by a laboratory. Upon request, and by special addendum to the Inspection Agreement, we will extract sample(s) and obtain a certified lab analysis and report.

NOTE: See "Doors", "Windows", and "Flooring" information above.

Laundry room

We *do not* run or inspect washer/dryer units. We inspect visible connections only.

Garage floor

Hair-line cracks are considered normal on garage floors as well as on side walks, patios and driveways. Severe cracking or buckling can be caused by expansive soil conditions and/or settling due to excessive water collection or tree/foliage roots. A licensed contractor can perform remedies in most cases.

PAGE 11 of 11 GARAGE / ATTIC / GROUNDS

Garage doors

We will inspect the garage door(s) provided we have access and if it is unlocked. Safety springs should be installed if not present.

Garage door openers

We will test the garage door opener(s) provided we have access. All garage door openers should be equipped with a "safety reverse" mechanism to prevent injury to people or animals. If there is no safety reverse one should be installed. Consult a licensed contractor or a garage door opener dealer for further information.

Fire door

A fire door separates utility area or garage from the living quarters. The fire door should have a "1 hour" rating. If the door is not marked we cannot determine a "1 hour" rating.

Attic access

Each attic area should have ready access. Full view of rafter and joists is limited in many cases due to limited accessibility and/or attic insulation. We do not crawl through the entire attic area so as to prevent peril to the inspector and to prevent damage to the structure. When attic insulation is present we observe the attic from the opening only.

Attic and side wall insulation

The majority of older properties do not contain attic or side wall insulation. For those that do, we report on the type of insulation if visible to the inspector. Attic insulation should not block attic venting.

Fencing and retaining walls

We inspect visible fences and walls. Leaning of fences and walls can be caused by any number of events. Any severe leaning should be repaired. Consult your broker to determine what property owner controls jurisdiction.

Sprinklers

We test sprinklers upon request. We will not test sprinkler systems that are on a timer system. In general sprinkler heads are easily broken and require constant maintenance. We *do not* test timers. When possible consult the seller regarding the function of the sprinkler system.

INSPECTION AGREEMENT
THIS AGREEMENT LIMITS OUR LIABILITY - PLEASE READ IT   Page 1 of 3

Mark 1 Home Inspectors ("Mark 1") has been retained by *THE UNOFFICIAL GUIDE TO REAL ESTATE INVESTING* ("Client") to conduct a limited visual inspection ("Inspection") of the property located at:

333 RICHMOND ST. EL SEGUNDO, CA ("Property")

Mark 1 will provide a written inspection report of the present general condition of visible portions of buildings on the Property ("Report").

A. SCOPE OF THE INSPECTION

1. Effective Date

Mark 1 will perform a limited visual inspection to identify the general features and major deficiencies of the Property AS THEY EXIST AS OF THE DATE AND TIME OF INSPECTION. Client acknowledges that conditions may change after the Inspection. Mark 1 makes no representations as to the future condition of any items included within the Inspection.

2. Inaccessible Items

The Inspection is a visual inspection of those areas of the premises which are exposed to view. Any area which is not exposed to view or is otherwise concealed or inaccessible for any reason, including but not limitated to soil, fill, walls, wall coverings, floors, floor coverings, ceilings, furnishings or belongings, is not included in the Inspection. Furthermore, the Inspection does not include any destructive testing or dismantling or removal of any equipment, systems or exposed surfaces, including access panels, face plates and doors. All items covered in this Inspection are operated normally, however, the overall effectiveness of these items is excluded (e.g. cleansing ability of dishwashers, flushing ability of toilets, heating/cooling capacity at each distribution point etc.).

3. Items Included

The Inspection will include an investigation of the general condition of the roof, plumbing, electrical and mechanical systems of the Property. See Report form that follows.

4. Testing Procedure

The conclusions in the Report for these items are based on a random sampling of each item covered (i.e., doors, windows, valves, faucets, electrical outlets, switches, etc.).

B. DISCLAIMER OF WARRANTIES

THIS INSPECTION DOES NOT CONSTITUTE A WARRANTY OF MERCHANTABILITY OR FITNESS FOR A PARTICULAR PURPOSE, AN INSURANCE POLICY, OR A GUARANTEE OF ANY KIND, ALL OF WHICH ARE EXPRESSLY DENIED.

The Inspection is not designed to supersede any disclosures required by law, including disclosures made by the Seller of the Property pursuant to Section 1102.6 of the California Civil Code.

C. EXCLUSIONS

1. Specific Exclusions

The following items are specifically excluded from this Inspection whether or not they are concealed: Asbestos-containing materials (unless by special addendum to this Agreement) or environmental hazards of any nature, including any mold mildew (which is beyond the scope of this inspection), sound or noise transmission, wood rot or wood destroying organisms and pests and/or related damage from same; household pests; geological or soil conditions, including area drainage; underground pipes or concealed or out of the way, hard to see pipes and wires; electrical lines; sewer lines and/or septic tanks; sprinklers and landscape illumination systems; roofing paper below rock, tiles or shingles, clay or concrete tiles; inspection of portable or moveable appliances and built-in refrigerators or freezers; low voltage wiring; alarm systems or intercom and entertainment systems; the condition of radiant heating pipes or wires; solar systems; water or energy conservation items; requirements of provisions for the handicapped; elevators; fountains; retaining walls; water softening or purifying systems; shower pans; gas fired appliance fire boxes; or, common areas in planned developments. **Mark 1 cannot report on the condition of concealed or inaccessible portions of the Property. NOTE: The primary cause of mold and mildew is excessive moisture. It should be assumed by the client that mold and mildew may exist within the subject property. The client is responsible to hire an expert to determine it's actual presence and remedy if necessary.**

Specific Exclusions, continued...   **Inspection Agreement - Page 2 of 3**

Opinions are occasionally given on items which are excluded from the Inspection. The making of these comments is not a waiver of the exclusion. These opinions are given for the sole purpose of making a more complete Report, they may be inexact and are only an indication that there may or may not be a problem.

Again, Mark 1 DOES NOT inspect for MOLD OR MILDEW . It is beyond the scope of this inspection. Client is responsible for hiring a mold and mildew expert to determine it's presence and related health risks as an additional inspection..

2. Code Compliance and Title Matters
Because of the complicated nature and variations in all applicable governmental laws and regulations including but not limited to, local building and zoning codes, Mark 1 does not represent or warrant that the subject building or its systems are built or maintained in accordance with requirements of any laws or regulations. Mark 1 will not investigate or report on any easements, conditions of title or any conditions that may exist relating to any legal and/or public records.

D. ARBITRATION AND ATTORNEY'S FEES

All claims, disputes and other matters in question arising out of, or relating to this Agreement, the Inspection or the Report, or the breach thereof, shall be decided by arbitration in accordance with the Rules of the American Arbitration Association then obtaining. This agreement to arbitrate shall be specifically enforceable under the prevailing arbitration law. Notice of demand for arbitration shall be filed in writing with the other party to this Agreement and with the American Arbitration Association. The parties shall mutually select an arbitrator that is familiar with the professional home inspection industry. If the parties cannot mutually agree upon the selection of an arbitrator within one (1) month from the filing of the notice of demand for arbitration, then either party may petition the Superior Court of the county in which the property is located for appointment of a Neutral Arbitrator pursuant to California Code of Civil Procedure 1281.6. The award rendered by the arbitrator shall be final and non-appealable, and judgment may be entered upon it in accordance with applicable law in any court having jurisdiction thereof. All claims which are related to or dependent upon each other shall be heard by the same arbitrator or arbitrators, even though the parties are not the same, unless a specific contract provision prohibits such consolidation. Upon the motion of either party hereto or any other party whose interest or responsibility may be material to the dispute between Client and Mark 1, a court of competent jurisdiction may order the joinder or consolidation of any other party whose interest or responsibility may be material to the dispute between Client and Mark 1 or of any other action involving common questions of law or fact. During the course of said arbitration, the parties hereto shall have the right to conduct discovery in accordance with the provisions of California Code of Civil Procedure Sections 1283.05 and 1283.1. Any arbitration shall take place in Los Angeles County, California. The prevailing party in the arbitration or any proceeding or action arising out or relating to this Agreement shall cover all attorney's fees, costs, and expenses from the other party. Mark 1 or its designated agents shall be allowed to reinspect the Property prior to the earlier of (i) any arbitration or legal proceeding relating to or arising from this Agreement, or (ii) the alteration or repair of any item under dispute.

E. DISPUTES

Client understands and agrees that any claim for failure to accurately report the visually discernible conditions at the subject "property", as limited herein above, shall be made in writing and reported to the inspector within (10) ten business days of discovery. Client further agrees that, with the exception of emergency conditions, Client or Client's agents, employees or independent contractors, will make no alterations, modifications or repairs to the claimed discrepancy prior to a reinspection by the inspector. Client understands and agrees that any failure to notify the inspector as stated above shall constitute a waiver of any and all claims for said failure to accurately report the condition in question.

F. FEES AND LIQUIDATION DAMAGES

It is understood and agreed by and between the parties hereto that the INSPECTOR/INSPECTION COMPANY is not an insurer, that the payment for the subject inspection is based solely on the value of the service provided by INSPECTOR/INSPECTION COMPANY in the performance of the limited visual inspection and production of a written

Fees and Liquidation Damages, continued... **Inspection Agreement - Page 3 of 3**

inspection report as described herein, that it is impracticable and extremely difficult to fix the actual damages, if any, which may result from a failure to perform such services, and in case of failure to perform such services and a resulting loss, the INSPECTOR/Mark1's liability hereunder shall be limited and fixed in an amount equal to the inspection fee paid multiplied by two (2), or to the sum of five hundred dollars ($500), whichever sum shall be less, as liquidated damages, and not as a penalty, and this liability shall be exclusive.

No legal action or proceeding of any kind, including those sounding in tort or contract, can be commenced against INSPECTOR/Mark1, or its officers, agents or employees more than one (1) year after the date of the subject inspection. Time is expressly of the essence herein. This time period is shorter than otherwise provided by law.

The Client agrees that the fee for this Limited Inspection will be $_____. Client acknowledges that a Comprehensive Inspection of the Property without a limit on liability is available for a fee of $1500. Client specifically requests this Limited Inspection and not a Comprehensive Inspection.

F. NOT TRANSFERABLE

Client acknowledges that this Inspection not transferable and is intended for use by the Client only and may not be relied upon by any third party including but not limited to prospective lenders, real estate agents or brokers, buyers, sellers or others.

G. RETENTION OF DOCUMENTS

Mark 1 shall not be required to retain any materials pertaining to the Inspection after six (6) months from the date of the Inspection.

H. ENTIRE AGREEMENT / NON SIGNATURE

This Agreement contains the entire agreement between the parties and supersedes any other agreement, written or oral, relating to the Inspection. Mark 1 has made no representations regarding this Inspection, Report or this Agreement, except those specifically stated in this Agreement. In the event this Inspection Agreement is unsigned by the Client, reading of this Inspection Report and its use constitutes acceptance of all the terms and conditions of this Inspection Agreement and Report unless contested immediately by the Client within 24 hours of the Inspection. Accordingly, contesting this report does not change, waive, or alter any provision in this Agreement or Report and does not release Client from liability of the cost of the Inspection fee.

I. SEVERABILITY

Nothing contained herein shall be construed as to require the commission of any act contrary to the law, and wherever there is any conflict between any provision contained herein and any present or future statute, law, ordinance or regulation, the latter shall prevail, but the provision of this Agreement which is affected shall be curtailed and limited only to the extent necessary to bring it within the requirements of the law.

I have read and fully understand and agree to all the above terms and conditions set forth in this Inspection Agreement.

Client's signature _____ Dated: _____

Inspector's signature _____ Dated: _5-4-03_

ADDENDUM:

Client's Initials to addendum _____

☒ Inspection Report delivered to Agent/Broker.

GENERAL DATA / ACTION LIST   PAGE 1

REPORT # _____

GENERAL DATA

Date _____ 5-4 _____ 200 3 _____ Time of day _____ 9 : 30 (AM) PM

Current weather conditions _____ CLEAR _____ Most recent rain was approximately 2 WEEKS ago

Other known factors_____ ☐ None

Type of property: ☐ Single family ☐ Duplex ☐ Tri-plex ☒ 4-unit ☐ 2 on lot ☐ Other _____

Current status: ☒ Occupied ☐ Vacant   Electricity: ☒ On ☐ Off   Water: ☒ On ☐ Off   Gas: ☒ On ☐ Off

Approximate age of structure: 20 years old   Additions: ☐ Yes ☒ No ☐ Could not determine

Present during inspection: ☒ Buyer ☒ Buyer's agent ☒ Seller ☒ Seller's agent ☒ Other SELLER'S MANAGER

Remarks: _____

_____

NOTE: All utilities must be on at the time of the inspection, if not,

we cannot determine the functional capability of that utility.

ACTION LIST

This space is for client/agent use.

NOTE: See "Preface" and read paragraph " Page 1 of 11 - General data / Action List" for further information, explanation and limitations.

EXTERIOR   PAGE 2

A-Construction: ☒ Stucco : ☐ Minor cracking ☐ Excessive cracking ☒ Color coat separation *ON NORTH + EAST WALL NEAR GROUND*

☐ Siding : ☐ Wood ☐ Wood shingle ☐ Aluminum ☐ Vinyl ☐ Asbestos-like shingle
☐ Composition lap ☐ Other _____
☐ Intact ☐ Loose/broken/missing pieces ☐ Dry rot (See termite report)

☐ Brick : ☐ Minor cracking ☐ Excessive cracking ☐ Repair / maintenance suggested

☐ Mold / mildew : ☐ Minor ☐ Excessive

☒ Foliage overgrowth noted ☒ Pruning suggested

B-Ventilation : Attic vents : ☒ Eave vents ☐ Gable vents ☐ Top vents ☐ Side vents ☐ Turbines
☒ Screens present ☒ Screens missing *1 IN REAR* ☐ Screens rusting out ☐ Other _____

Foundation vents : ☒ Present ☐ N/A on slab ☒ Screens present ☒ Screens missing *1 - IN REAR*
☐ Screens rusted / damaged

C-Trim : ☒ Eaves open ☐ Eaves covered ☒ Wood ☐ Aluminum ☒ Needs scrapping / painting *ON SOUTH SIDE*

Fascia Boards : ☐ Complete ☐ Incomplete ☐ Damaged ☐ Dry rot (see termite report)

Note: See termite report for condition of all wood

D-Guttering : ☒ Galvanized ☐ Plastic ☐ Other ☐ Partial only ☐ None ☒ (Full of debris) ☐ Rust noted

Downspouts : ☒ Complete ☐ Incomplete ☐ None ☒ System appears over-all functional

E-Chimney(s) : Chimney #1: Location *WEST SIDE* ☒ Brick ☐ Metal ☐ Stucco ☐ Block

FOR CHIMNEY #3 + #4 SEE BELOW

Spark arrestor present : ☐ Yes ☒ No ☒ Needed

Chimney #2: Location *EAST SIDE* ☒ Brick ☐ Metal ☐ Stucco ☐ Block

ALL DAMPERS FUNCTIONAL

Spark arrestor present : ☐ Yes ☒ No ☒ Needed   ☒ *NO GAS JETS IN FIREPLACES*

☐ Cracks : ☐ #1 ☐ #2   Separations : ☐ #1 ☐ #2
☐ Caulk seal (at wall) needed: ☐ #1 ☐ #2   ☐ Deteriorated mortar : ☐ #1 ☐ #2
☐ Loose brick : ☐ #1 ☐ #2   ☐ Cracking at chimney cap: ☐ #1 ☐ #2
☐ Flue liner : ☐ #1 ☐ #2   ☐ Could not determine : ☐ #1 ☐ #2
☒ Chimney sweep needed : ☒ #1 ☐ #2   ☐ Repair/further inspection needed : ☐ #1 ☐ #2 *#3*
☒ Suggest further inspection / repair by licensed contractor

Utility Shut-offs: Water main shut off location: *FRONT*   Gas main shut off location: *REAR*

Electrical main shut off location: *REAR*   ☐ None (must turn off all breakers)

Remarks :
✱ CHIMNEY 3 - OK - SPARK ARRESTOR NEEDED
✱ CHIMNEY 4 - OK - SPARK ARRESTOR NEEDED
✱ CHIMNEY SWEEP NEED - #1 + #3

NOTE: See "Preface" and read paragraph "Page 2 of 11 - Exterior" further information, explanation and limitations.

STRUCTURAL / ROOF   PAGE 3

STRUCTURAL

A-Foundation :

Type : ☒ Poured concrete ☐ Block ☐ Brick ☐ Cripple walls ☐ Other _____

☒ Raised foundation ☐ Slab ☐ Partial Raised ☐ Partial slab

☒ Crawl space : ☒ Able to inspect fully ☐ Unable to inspect fully ☐ Not fully accessible

☐ Basement : ☐ Full ☐ Partial   Crawl or basement floor : ☒ Dirt ☐ Concrete

✗ ☒ Dry ☒ Clean ☐ Debris noted ☒ Moisture noted   Describe *SEE "REMARKS" BELOW*

✗ ☒ Foundation wall cracking noted : ☒ Minor ☐ Major   Location *WEST WALL MID WAY*
                         ─ HAIRLINE

☐ Settling : ☐ Appears minor ☐ Appears excessive   Possible cause _____

FOUNDATION BOLTING : ☒ Bolting observed ☐ No bolting observed ☐ See "Remarks"

Location of bolt observed *SUB AREA*   ☐ Retro-fit work performed

B-Floor System:

☒ Wood frame : ☒ Floor joists *2 x 10* ☒ Grade beam *4 x 6*

☒ Pier post support : ☒ Adequate ☐ Additional support suggested ☐ Pier posts leaning

☒ Concrete stem wall support : ☒ Appear solid/straight ☐ Leaning and cracking noted

☐ Slab : ☐ Feels/appears level ☐ Cracking noted ☐ Appears minor ☐ Appears major

         ☐ Slab covered and not visible ☐ Furniture and belongings prevent full evaluation

Remarks: ☐ Suggest further inspection by licensed foundation or structural contractor

✗ *MOISTURE AT CRAWL SPACE ENTRY DOOR - PROBABLY FROM SPRINKLERS*
MOISTURE ALONG MAIN DRAIN LINE - LIKELY FROM MAIN DRAIN LEAK
                                   ─ MOISTURE IS SIGNIFICANT ─

NOTE: See "Preface" and read paragraph "Page 3 of 11 - Structural / Roof" for further information, explanation and limitations.

ROOF

C-Type :

☒ Gabled ☐ Flat ☐ Hip

Material : ☒ Composition shingle ☐ Rolled composition ☐ Gravel/rock ☐ Wood shake

               ☐ Wood shingle ☐ Clay tile ☐ Concrete tile ☐ Slate ☐ Hot mop ☐ Metal

If sections vary in type, describe : _____

Approximate number of layers ___/___ ☐ Cannot determine

D-Condition :

✗ Age : ☐ Appears newer ☒ Appears older ☐ Appears mid-life

       ☐ Extended life expected ☐ Limited life expectancy

✗ Evidence of leak(s) : ☐ Yes ☒ No

☐ Leaks appear active ☐ Leaks do not appear active ☐ Cannot determine

Location of evidence of leak(s) _____

✗ ☒ Visible ultra-violet damage ☐ Split, warped, missing shingles ☐ Patching ☐ Bare spots

☐ Maintenance work needed ☒ Re-roof needed ☐ Roof certification needed

Remarks : ☒ Suggest further examination and/or repair by licensed roofing contractor

✗ HEAVY ULTRA-VIOLET DAMAGE ON SOUTH SIDE.

                                 IN NEAR FUTURE

NOTE: See "Preface" and read paragraph "Page 3 of 11 - Structural / Roof" for further information, explanation and limitations.

ELECTRICAL SYSTEM — PAGE 4

A-Service: ☒ Overhead ☐ Underground Line Condition: _OK_ Weatherhead condition: _OK_
Drip loop: ☒ Yes ☐ No Number of lines _3_ Volts _240_ ☒ Tree trim needed *

B-Panel(s): Main panel approximate capacity: _200_ amps ☐ Not labeled - unable to determine
Type: ☒ Breakers ☐ Fuses ☐ Futures
Main breaker: ☒ Present ☐ None Main breaker capacity: _200_ amps
Number of 110 volt circuits _2_ @ _0_ 15 amp and _2_ 20 amp breakers
Number of 220 volt circuits _2_ @ _0_ 30 amp _ 40 amp _2_ _50_ amp
Circuits labeled: ☒ Yes ☐ No ☐ Should be
Grounding: ☒ Yes ☐ No ☐ Could not determine   *_SUGGEST SUB PANEL LABELING_*
Number of sub-panels: _4_ Locations #1 _1 INSIDE EACH UNIT_ #2_____ #3_____

House main panel

SUB PANEL #4 (same)

Sub-panel #1 - _6_ 110 volt circuits _0_ 220 volt circuits Circuits labeled: ☐ Yes ☒ No
Sub-panel #2 - _6_ 110 volt circuits _0_ 220 volt circuits Circuits labeled: ☐ Yes ☒ No
Sub-panel #3 - _6_ 110 volt circuits _0_ 220 volt circuits Circuits labeled: ☐ Yes ☒ No

C-System: Wiring type: ☒ Conduit ☒ Romex ☐ Knob & tube ☐ Obstructed/Unable to determine
Receptacles: ☒ 3 prong ☐ 2 prong ☒ All receptacles hot ☒ Did not test all receptacles
Dead/ damaged receptacles at the following location(s): ☐ None _SEVERAL COVERS MISSING ON LIGHT SWITCHES & RECEPTACLES IN UNIT 2_

ADDITIONAL WIRING ADDED FOR FLOOD LIGHTS- SOME ROMEX IS LOOSE, INCLUDING A SPLICE IN ATTIC REPAIR NEEDED

Wire splice(s) located at he following location(s): ☒ None _1 IN ATTIC NEAR MIDDLE REAR_

Open junction box(es) located at the following location(s): ☐ None _NUMEROUS IN ATTIC_

Reverse polarity located at the following receptacle(s): ☒ None _____

Open ground located at the following receptacles(s): ☒ None _____

Switches: ☒ Appear functional ☐ Not functional ☐ Old and worn ☒ Did not test all switches
Ground Fault Interrupters(GFI): ☐ All tested operational ☐ Did not function properly
Describe: _NONE_
"GFI"s needed at: ☒ Kitchen ☒ Bathroom(s) ☐ Exterior ☐ Garage ☐ Laundry

Remarks: ☒ Licensed electrician needed to inspect, repair and certify system.
☒ SUGGEST FULL REPAIR
" LABELING ALL SUB PANEL CIRCUITS.

Note: See "Preface" and read paragraph "Page 4 of 11 - Electrical System" for further information, explanation and limitations.

PLUMBING SYSTEM — PAGE 5

A-Water Lines:

Main line: ☒ Copper ☐ Galvanized ☐ PVC ☐ Other_____ Size: 2"

Main valve: ☒ Appears dry & functional ☐ Leaking ☐ Corrosion visible

Location FRONT Pressure test: Time of day 9:40 PSI 50 LBS + OR -

Supply lines: ☒ Copper ☐ Galvanized ☐ Other_____

☒ Appear dry & functional ☐ Corrosion visible ☐ Active leak ☐ Evidence of previous leak

Exterior hose bibs: ☒ Copper ☐ Galvanized ☐ PVC ☐ Functional ☒ Not functional *EXTERIOR VALVE HANDLES REMOVED*

Volume test: ☒ Adequate ☐ Minor loss ☐ Significant loss

✱ ABS ADDED AT NUMEROUS DRAINS IN SUB-AREA →

B-Drain Lines:

✱ MOISTURE UNDER #2 TUB IN SUB-AREA →

Type: ☒ Cast iron ☒ ABS ☐ Galvanized ☐ Corrosion visible ☐ Other_____

☒ Drainage adequate ☒ Slow/stopped up Vent lines: ☒ Adequate ☐ Other_____

☐ Appear dry & functional ☒ Evidence of leakage Exterior Clean-out: ☒ Yes ☐ No

Water treatment system: ☐ Present ☒ None ☐ Hook-ups present

REMARKS: ☒ Licensed plumbing contractor needed to repair system

✱ SIGNIFICANT MOISTURE (WET SOIL) ALONG 75% OF MAIN DRAIN LINE IN SUB AREA. PIPE IS PARTIALLY SUBTERRANIAN - NO VISIBLE LEAK - SUSPECT SEEPAGE, POSSIBLE CRACKED OR BROKEN PIPE ✱ CAP MISSING ON WEST CLEAN OUT

NOTE: See "Preface" and read paragraph "Page 5 of 11 - Plumbing System" for further information, explanation and limitations.

PLUMBING NOTES PER ROOM

✱ ☒ Bathroom # 2 ☒ Kitchen # 2 ☐ Laundry Room # ___ ☐ Other _____ ☒ Repair Needed
Findings: UNIT #2 - TOILET LOOSE, UNIT #2 - DISPOSAL LEAKING

✱ ☒ Bathroom # 3 ☐ Kitchen # ___ ☐ Laundry Room # ___ ☐ Other _____ ☒ Repair Needed
Findings: NO SHOWER HEAD (UNIT #3)

✱ ☒ Bathroom # 4 ☐ Kitchen # ___ ☐ Laundry Room # ___ ☐ Other _____ ☒ Repair Needed
Findings: VERY SLOW SINK DRAIN, SHOWER HEAD DRIPS (UNIT #4)

☐ Bathroom # ___ ☐ Kitchen # ___ ☐ Laundry Room # ___ ☐ Other _____ ☐ Repair Needed
Findings: _____

☐ Bathroom # ___ ☐ Kitchen # ___ ☐ Laundry Room # ___ ☐ Other _____ ☐ Repair Needed
Findings: _____

☐ Bathroom # ___ ☐ Kitchen # ___ ☐ Laundry Room # ___ ☐ Other _____ ☐ Repair Needed
Findings: _____

☐ Bathroom # ___ ☐ Kitchen # ___ ☐ Laundry Room # ___ ☐ Other _____ ☐ Repair Needed
Findings: _____

WATER HEATERS - HEATING & AIR CONDITIONING PAGE 6

WATER HEATERS

Water heater #1 - Location _LAUNDRY ROOM_ .... Size: _100_ gallon Approximate age _11_ years

☒ Gas ☐ Electric Pressure relief valve: ☒ Present ☐ Not present ☐ Needed

Vent: ☒ Intact ☐ Not intact Earthquake strap: ☒ Yes ☐ No ☐ Improper — _BOTTOM STRAP LOOSE FROM WALL_

Water heater #2 - Location _____ Size: _____ gallon Approximate age _____ years

☐ Gas ☐ Electric Pressure relief valve: ☐ Present ☐ Not present ☐ Needed

Vent: ☐ Intact ☐ Not intact Earthquake strap: ☐ Yes ☐ No ☐ Improper

Water heater #3 - Location _____ Size: _____ gallon Approximate age _____ years

☐ Gas ☐ Electric Pressure relief valve: ☐ Present ☐ Not present ☐ Needed

Vent: ☐ Intact ☐ Not intact Earthquake strap: ☐ Yes ☐ No ☐ Improper

Water heater #4 - Location _____ Size: _____ gallon Approximate age _____ years

☐ Gas ☐ Electric Pressure relief valve: ☐ Present ☐ Not present ☐ Needed

Vent: ☐ Intact ☐ Not intact Earthquake strap: ☐ Yes ☐ No ☐ Improper

Remarks: ☒ Licensed contractor needed to perform service / repair and certify.
* HEAVY CORROSION ON CONNECTIONS, RUST ON EXTERIOR - HEAT SHIELD MISSING
  * VERY LIMITED REMAINING LIFE - CONSIDER REPLACEMENT

NOTE: See "Preface" and read paragraph "Page 6 of 11 - Water Heaters" for further instruction, explanation and limitations.

HEATING & AIR CONDITIONING SYSTEM

A-Heating System:

Number of units _1_ (Electric wall heaters not included)

Location: ☐ #___ Garage ☐ #___ Attic ☐ #___ Interior closet
☒ # _1_ Other _EACH WALL_

Type: ☐ #___ Floor Furnace ☒ # _1_ Wall Heater ☐ #___ Forced Air System
☐ #___ Radiant Heat ☐ #___ Gravity System ☐ #___ Other _____

Approximate BTU rating # _ALL 4 ARE 35000 BTU_ ☒ Gas ☐ Electric

Gas line: ☒ Flex ☐ Rigid Electrical connection: ☐ Conduit ☐ Wire

Thermostat: ☒ Functional ☐ Non-functional / ☐ Damaged ☐ Manual (on unit)
_#1-3-4_
☒ Unit responded ☒ Unit did not respond ☐ Reason unknown ☐ Gas off   _#2 PILOT OUT?_

Duct work: ☐ Appears intact ☐ Damaged ☐ Asbestos-like wrap on duct

* 1 CAP ON ROOF IS MISSING → Vents: ☒ Appear intact ☐ Limited access prevents full evaluation

☒ Gas Co. exam suggested ☐ Routine service call suggested ☐ Repair needed

B-Air Conditioning:

Type: ☐ Central ☐ Window mount ☒ Wall mount ☐ Roof mount Other _____

Number of units ___ Location: _____

☐ Tested ☐ Did not test ☐ Responded ☐ Did not respond ☐ Routine service/repair needed

Remarks: ☒ Licensed contractor needed to perform routine service/ repair and certify system.
* — ALL UNITS - PRIOR TO CLOSE OF ESCROW
* UNIT #2 - WALL HEATER COVER DENTED & DAMAGED
  " " - THERMOSTAT COVER MISSING.

NOTE: See "Preface" and read paragraph "Page 6 of 11 - Heating & Air Conditioning" for further instruction, explanation and limitations.

✱ ACOUSTIC CEILING PRESENT

Units GENERAL NOTES	PAGE 7

Unit # 1 — KITCHEN - OK. RIGHT REAR BURNER WOULD NOT LIGHT. DIRTY??

Living room _OK_

Bedroom #1 _OK_

Bedroom #2 _OK - SCREEN MISSING_

Bathroom #1 _OK - NO SINK STOPPER_
MINOR GROUT NEEDED AROUND TUB TILE.

~~Bathroom #2~~

Laundry Room _ALL APPEARS FUNCTIONAL_

~~Water Heater~~

Heater _WALL UNIT - RESPONDED_

UNIT - OVERALL CLEAN!

Unit # 2 — KITCHEN - OK - DISPOSAL LEAKS

Living room _OK - KNOB HOLE AT FRONT DOOR WALL._

Bedroom #1 _OK - KNOB HOLE IN WALL. 1 CRACKED WINDOW PANE._

Bedroom #2 _OK - CLOSET DOOR MISSING. 1 MISSING SCREEN._

Bathroom #1 _OK - TOILET VERY LOOSE. MOISTURE DAMAGE TO FLOOR AT TOILET._

~~Bathroom #2~~ TUB. GROUT NEEDED INSIDE AND OUTSIDE OF TUB. NO SINK OR TUB STOPPERS - NO SCREEN. UNIT - VERY DIRTY

Laundry room _APPEARS FUNCTIONAL_

~~Water heater~~

Heater _WALL UNIT. NO RESPONSE - NO COVER ON THERMOSTAT. UNIT COVER IS DAMAGED._

Unit # 3 — KITCHEN - OK - MISSING SCREEN

Living room _OK_

Bedroom #1 _OK_

Bedroom #2 _OK_

Bathroom #1 _OK - SHOWER HEAD MISSING_

~~Bathroom #2~~

Laundry room _APPEARS FUNCTIONAL_

~~Water heater~~

Heater _WALL UNIT - RESPONDED_

UNIT - VERY CLEAN

Unit # 4 — KITCHEN - OK

Living room _OK_

Bedroom #1 _OK - MISSING SCREEN_

Bedroom #2 _OK -_

Bathroom #1 _OK - FAN IS UNPLUGGED_

~~Bedroom #2~~
UNIT - VERY CLEAN

Laundry room _APPEARS FUNCTIONAL_

~~Water heater~~

Heater _WALL UNIT - RESPONDED_

NOTE: Read opposing page for further instruction, explanation and limitations

✱ SMOKE ALARMS INCOMPLETE!

GARAGE / ATTIC / GROUNDS   PAGE 8

GARAGE

A-Garage:

1 BROKEN SPRING ON #4 DOOR

Size: ☐ Single ☐ Double ☐ Triple ☒ 4 car ☐ Tandem ☐ Attached ☒ Detached

Floor: ☒ Intact ☒ Cracking noted ☒ Minor ☐ Other _____

Garage Door: ☒ Wood ☐ Aluminum ☒ Swing ☐ Roll-up ☐ Other _____
— *NONE* — ☒ Operational ☐ Non-operational ☐ Other _____

Garage door opener: ☐ Operational ☐ Non-operational ☐ Other _____
Safety reverse: ☐ Yes ☐ No

Firedoor: ☐ Solid ☐ Hollow **Self closer:** ☐ Functional ☐ Non-functional ☐ None

Exterior door: ☐ Solid ☐ Hollow ☐ Good condition ☐ Weathered/damaged

Window(s): ☐ Appear operational ☐ Non-operational ☐ Other _____

ATTIC

B-Attic:

Rafters: 2x6 **Joists:** 2x6   *★ BIRDS NESTS IN ATTIC — REPAIR EAVE VENT SCREEN*

Insulation type: ☒ Blown ☐ Rolled ☐ Rock wool ☐ Fiberglass ☒ Cellulose ☐ None

Attic access location: UNIT #3 - MASTER BED CEILING ☐ Limited access ☐ No Access

☒ Full view ☐ Limited view ☒ View obstructed By BLOWN INSULATION

GROUNDS

C-Flatwork:

☒ Driveway ☒ Walkways ☒ Steps ☐ Patio

Condition: ☒ Normal Cracking ☐ Heavy cracking ☐ Buckling ☐ Trippers present
☐ Root lift ☒ Settling *MINOR* **Describe:** _____

D-Fencing:

✗ **Type:** ☒ Wood ☐ Block ☐ Brick ☐ Stucco ☐ Chain link ☐ Other _____
Condition: ☒ Over-all good ☒ Leaning ☐ Cracking ☒ Post rotting *IN REAR AND ON WEST*
Gates: ☒ Operational ☐ Need work ☒ Over-all functional

E-Retaining Walls:

✗ **Type:** ☒ Concrete ☐ Block ☐ Rail tie ☐ Other _____
Condition: ☒ Over-all Normal ☒ Normal cracks ☐ Heavy cracks ☐ Bulging ☐ Leaning
☒ Stable at present ☐ Unstable ☐ Repair needed

F-Decks & Stairs:

✗ **Type:** ☒ Wood ☐ Metal ☐ Concrete/masonry ☒ Other _____
✗ **Condition:** ☐ Good seal ☒ Cracking noted ☒ Deterioration noted ☒ Seal work needed
Railings: ☐ Sturdy ☒ Loose ☐ Inadequate ☒ Repair needed *LOOSE ON WEST STAIRS-RIGHT RAILING*
Note: See termite report for condition of all wood

G-Sprinklers:

☒ Timers ☐ Anti-siphon ☐ Able to test ☒ Unable to test ☐ None present
☒ Timers on ☐ Visible broken heads ☐ Maintenance suggested

Remarks: HAVE SELLER DEMO SPRINKLERS & TIMER.